Russian Speakers in Post-Soviet Latvia

Russian Language and Society Series

Series Editor: Lara Ryazanova-Clarke, University of Edinburgh
This series of academic monographs and edited volumes consists of important scholarly accounts of interrelationships between Russian language and society, and aims to foster an opinion-shaping 'linguistic turn' in the international scholarly debate within Russian Studies, and to develop new sociolinguistic and linguo-cultural perspectives on Russian. The series embraces a broad scope of approaches including those advanced in sociolinguistics, rhetoric, critical linguistics, (critical) discourse analysis, linguistic anthropology, politics of language, language policy and related and interdisciplinary areas.

Series Editor
Dr Lara Ryazanova-Clarke is Senior Lecturer in Russian, and the Academic Director of the Princess Dashkova Russian Centre, at the University of Edinburgh.

Editorial Board
Professor David Andrews (Georgetown University)
Professor Lenore Grenoble (University of Chicago)
Professor John Joseph (University of Edinburgh)
Professor Vladimir Plungian (Institute of Russian Language/Institute of Linguistics, Russian Academy of Sciences)
Professor Patrick Seriot (Université de Lausanne)
Dr Alexei Yurchak (University of California, Berkeley)

Titles available in the series:
The Russian Language Outside the Nation, ed. Lara Ryazanova-Clarke
Discourses of Regulation and Resistance: Censoring Translation in the Stalin and Khrushchev Era Soviet Union, Samantha Sherry
French and Russian in Imperial Russia: Language Use among the Russian Elite, ed. Derek Offord, Lara Ryazanova-Clarke, Vladislav Rjéoutski and Gesine Argent
French and Russian in Imperial Russia: Language Attitudes and Identity, ed. Derek Offord, Lara Ryazanova-Clarke, Vladislav Rjéoutski and Gesine Argent
Russian Speakers in Post-Soviet Latvia, Ammon Cheskin

Visit the Russian Language and Society website at
http://www.euppublishing.com/series/rlas

Russian Speakers in Post-Soviet Latvia

Discursive Identity Strategies

Ammon Cheskin

EDINBURGH
University Press

© Ammon Cheskin, 2016

Edinburgh University Press Ltd
The Tun – Holyrood Road
12(2f) Jackson's Entry
Edinburgh EH8 8PJ

www.euppublishing.com

Typeset in 11/13 Monotype Ehrhardt by
Servis Filmsetting Ltd, Stockport, Cheshire,
and printed and bound in Great Britain by
CPI Group (UK) Ltd, Croydon CR0 4YY

A CIP record for this book is available from the British Library

ISBN 978 0 7486 9743 4 (hardback)
ISBN 978 0 7486 9744 1 (webready PDF)
ISBN 978 1 4744 0999 5 (epub)

The right of Ammon Cheskin to be identified as the author of this work
has been asserted in accordance with the Copyright, Designs and
Patents Act 1988, and the Copyright and Related Rights Regulations
2003 (SI No. 2498).

Contents

Preface

Tas ir Lāčplēs's, kas te cīkstas	It is Bearslayer struggling there
Vēl ar svešo naidnieku,	The Strangers to eradicate.-
Laimdota tur pili skatās,	But long Laimdota's watching stare
Gaida, kamēr uzvarēs.	Upon his triumph yet must wait.
Un ar reizi nāks tas brīdis,	But still, the day will come, is sure,
Kad viņš savu naidnieku,	When he the Black Knight will cast down:
Vienu pašu lejā grūdis,	In Staburags's raging maw,
Noslīcinās atvarā, –	His deadly foe alone will drown.
Tas zels tautai jauni laiki,	Then for the folk new times will dawn;
Tad būs viņa svabada!	At last their freedom will be born!
(Pumpurs 1887)	(Pumpurs 2006)

Any visitor to Latvia's capital city Riga cannot fail to notice *Brīvības piemineklis* (the Freedom Monument) which proudly stands forty-two metres tall in the centre of the city. For many Latvians this is one of the preeminent symbols of Latvian independence and national identity. The monument, erected in 1935, is engraved with numerous images from Latvian folklore and history. On one side of the monument sits a carving of Lāčplēsis (Bearslayer), the hero from Andrejs Pumpurs' epic, national poem. In the poem Lāčplēsis is awarded the name Bearslayer when, in order to save his adopted father, he rips apart the jaws of a grown bear.

Lāčplēsis is considered a (perhaps *the*) classic of Latvian literature. As with many epic works, Pumpurs' masterpiece speaks not only of a mythical past, but also of a nation's present and future. The struggle for Latvian freedom against foreign oppressors (in Lāčplēsis' case against the German crusaders) has great resonance with Latvia's more recent Soviet past, but also of the present. There is, however, a particular irony in the story of Lāčplēsis. The bear slayer is, in fact, half bear.

Looking up at the beautiful Freedom Monument, a Latvian friend once wryly commented that this story was symbolic of Latvia's ethnic situation today. 'Latvians, half-bear', he explained with a smile, 'are just slaying themselves.' In the final parts of the Lāčplēsis epic, Dietrich, the Black Knight, discovers that Bearslayer's strength comes from his bear ears, inherited from his mother. After cutting off Lāčplēsis' ears, Dietrich manages to pull the hero down the cliffs with him, killing them both.

Undoubtedly this sardonic comparison is a neat one. Anyone who has spent any considerable time in Latvia, however, will know that ethnic relations between Latvians and Russians are not always as strained as one might expect. Whenever in Russia, for example, I am quite taken back by the images people have of the Baltic states. The Russian media portrays a Russian community under siege and almost at war with the Baltic states. This is, thankfully, an image quite removed from my personal (and, of course, subjective) experiences in these countries.

This is not to say that there are no problems in the Baltic states. There are significant problems – not unlike most parts of the world in the twenty-first century. Tensions and resentments remain and can be evident in conversations with Latvia's inhabitants. Sometimes tensions can even be seen and heard on the country's streets. On the other hand Latvia is, and has long been, a diverse, multicultural country. I can recount numerous occasions when I have witnessed, and also participated in, bi- and tri-lingual conversations which move seamlessly between Latvian, Russian, and English. In a bar in Riga, for example, I can recall playing cards with four Rigans. Two of them were speaking solely in Russian, two entirely in Latvian, while I chose to speak only in English. In that small group, as in many small groups throughout Latvia, it appeared that we were oblivious to the country's language politics and ethnic tensions, themes so often highlighted in the media and by politicians.

It is thus with an understanding of the complexity of group relations in Latvia that this book has been written. I have had the privilege of visiting Latvia on numerous occasions and have spent a number of happy years there. I have met hundreds of people, each of whom has helped me gain further insights into the realities of life in Latvia.

This work would not have been possible without the help of a number of very important people. Firstly my thanks go to my wife, Amy, for her unwavering support and for spending many wonderful days with me on the beautiful white sands of Latvia's coastline, wondering the splendid streets of Saint Petersburg, visiting the gorgeous churches of Kyiv, and generally complaining that all I talk about is Latvian, Russian, and

Ukrainian politics. I am also very grateful to Professor Geoffrey Swain and Professor David Galbreath who provided me with expert scholarly advice. My mum and dad have also been instrumental in allowing me to follow an academic path. While they have often been bemused that it was possible to go so long without a 'proper job', I would not be here today were it not for their material and symbolic support.

REFERENCES

Pumpurs, A. (1887), *Lāčplēsis*. Full text available at <http://www.korpuss.lv/klasika/Senie/Pumpurs/6.dala.html> (accessed 22 June 2015).

Pumpurs, A. (2006), Bearslayer: A free translation from the unrhymed Latvian into heroic English verse. Translated by A. Cropley. Project Gutenberg eBook, available at <http://www.gutenberg.org/cache/epub/17445/pg17445.html> (accessed 22 June 2015).

Acknowledgements

An expanded version of sections from 'Russian-language media and identity formation' (Chapter 4) was published in A. Cheskin (2010) 'The discursive construction of "Russian-speakers": The Russian-language media and demarcated political identities in Latvia' in M. Golubeva and R. Gould (eds), *Shrinking citizenship: Discursive practices that limit democratic participation in Latvian politics*, Amsterdam: Rodopi. I am grateful for Rodopi for granting permission to use extensive parts of this chapter in this book.

Abbreviations

CPS	Constitutional Protection Bureau of Latvia
FF/LNNK	For Fatherland and for Freedom/LNNK (LNNK, in turn, stands for Latvia's National Independence Movement – *Latvijas Nacionālās neatkarības kustība*)
FHRUL	For Human Rights in a United Latvia
HC	Harmony Centre
ICC	International Coordinating Council of Russian Compatriots Living Abroad
LFP/LW	Latvia's First Party/Latvia's Way
LNIM	Latvia's National Independence Movement
MFA	Ministry of Foreign Affairs
PACE	Parliamentary Assembly of the Council of Europe
PFL	Popular Front of Latvia
RUL	Russian Union of Latvia (originally For Human Rights in a United Latvia)
Ruvek	Russian Century (*Russkii vek*)
SDPH	Social Democratic Party 'Harmony'

Glossary

Atmoda	(Latvian) Literally: the awakening. Refers to the period of National Awakening in the late Soviet era. Also the title of the Latvian Popular Front's newspaper
Chas	(Russian) Literally: the hour. Russian-language, daily newspaper
Demokratizatsiia	(Russian) Democratisation
Diena	(Latvian) Literally: the day. Latvian-language daily newspaper
Dom Moskvy	(Russian) Literally: The Moscow House: cultural centre largely funded by Moscow's municipal government promoting cultural and business links between Riga and Moscow
Interfront	(Russian) Abbreviated form of: *Internatsional'nyi front trudiashchikhsia Latviiskoi Sovetskoi sotsialisticheskoi respubliki* (International Front of the Workers of the Latvian Soviet Socialist Republic). Similar organisation to *Interdvizhenie* (Intermovement) in Estonia: a reactionary political movement which sought to maintain the Soviet status quo
Korenizatsiia	(Russian) Literally: 'nativisation'. The Soviet practice of using local cadres in the ranks of the Communist Party within the separate Soviet republics
Korennaia natsiia	(Russian) Literally: root nation
Krievvalodīgie	(Latvian) Russian-speakers
Latviisk/ii -aia	(Russian) Latvian: see *latyshsk/ii - aia*

Latyshsk/ii -aia	(Russian) Latvian: referring to people, places, or things which are ethnically or culturally Latvian, as distinct from *latviiskii* which refers to objects from Latvia regardless of ethnic considerations
Līgo svētki	(Latvian) Traditional pagan festival which marks the summer solstice and is widely celebrated in Latvia
Nācija	(Latvian) Nation: differs from *tauta* which generally signifies more of an ethno-cultural nation
Narod	(Russian) Nation: Russian equivalent to the Latvian *tauta*
Natsional'nost'	(Russian) Nationality, often translated into English as ethnicity
Pamatnācija	(Latvian) Core nation: derived from the Latvian *pamats* (foundation) and *nācija* (see *nācija*)
Pamattauta	(Latvian) Core nation: derived from the Latvian *pamats* (foundation) and *tauta* (see *tauta*)
Rossiiane	(Russian) Russians: implying civic connections to the Russian state, most commonly citizens of Russia. Distinct from *russkie* which usually refers to ethnic Russians
Rossiisification	(Anglicised Russian) Term used in this work to denote efforts to create political ties between Russian speakers and the Russian state. Used deliberately to distinguish from Russification, a term commonly used to describe cultural tendencies
Rossiisk/ii -aia	(Russian) Russian: see *russk/ii -aia*
Rossiiskaia diaspora	(Russian) Russian diaspora
Russk/ii -aia	(Russian) Russian: referring to people, places, or things which are ethnically or culturally 'Russian', as distinct from *rossiisk/ii -aia* which conventionally refers to objects from Russia regardless of ethnic considerations
Russkogovoriashye	(Russian) Russian-speakers: from *govorit'* (to speak)
Russkoiazychnye	(Russian) Russian-speakers: from *iazyk* (language)
Ruvek	(Russian) Abbreviated form of *Russkii vek* (Russian Century), an internet portal for Russian compatriots
Saeima	(Latvian) The Latvian Parliament
Satversme	(Latvian) The Constitution of the Republic of Latvia
Sootechestvenniki	(Russian) Compatriots: term used by the Russian

	Federation to refer to Russian-speakers outside Russia
Tautība	(Latvian) Nationality: derived from the Latvian *tauta*
Tauta	(Latvian) Nation: see *nācija*
Vesti Segodnia	(Russian) Literally: today's news. Russian-language daily tabloid

CHAPTER 1

Introduction

This society has acquired freedom. It has been freed politically and spiritually, and this is the most important achievement that we have yet fully come to grips with. And we haven't, because we haven't learned to use freedom yet. (Gorbachev 1991)

At the start of Mikhail Gorbachev's tenure as general secretary few could have predicted that, in the space of a few years, Baltic nationalism would emerge as a key centrifugal force in the disintegration of the Union of Soviet Socialist Republics (USSR). By the mid-1980s there had been small pockets of dissent across the three Baltic republics of Estonia, Latvia, and Lithuania. However, the feeling among the Soviet elite was that nationalism was largely (although perhaps not totally) under control. Things changed dramatically soon after Gorbachev came to power. Although never his aim, Gorbachev's ill-fated policies of restructuring (*perestroika*), openness (*glasnost'*), and democratisation provided the freedom, opportunities, and impetus needed for Baltic nationalism to thrive once more.

The National Awakening (*Atmoda*), as this period has come to be known in Latvia, developed at such speed that it took everyone by surprise. The Baltic Popular Fronts, initially backed by Gorbachev, soon spearheaded a nationalist revival that was able to generate a genuinely mass movement. The sheer degree of mass mobilisation was evident on 23 August 1989, when approximately two million Baltic inhabitants (out of a total population of around eight million) linked arms and formed the Baltic Way, an almost continuous human chain linking the republics' three capitals – Tallinn, Riga, and Vilnius – and spanning over 600 kilometres. For many people, the fervour of the time, which culminated in the successful (re)acquisition of independence, signified a rebirth of

Baltic national identities, freedom from Soviet occupation, and a long-awaited 'return to Europe'. It was in this period that the hitherto outlawed, national symbols of pre-Soviet independence were rehabilitated and consumed with gusto. In Latvia the maroon, white, maroon flag was proudly displayed throughout the country, underpinning a popular revitalisation of Latvian nationalism and national identity.

For some, however, the fall of the Soviet Union was far more problematic. What, for example, should the Baltic states' ethnic Russian populations make of these seismic societal and political changes? Could Russians be part of this extraordinary National Awakening or would their status be under threat from the new political order? If Russians in Russia experienced a post-Soviet identity crisis (Suny 2001), then Russians outside Russia 'might be said to have received a blow of the post-Soviet identity crisis twice over' (Kolstø 1999: 610). Not only did they have to contend with the loss of Soviet identity, but they also emerged as 'beached diasporas' (Laitin 1998). People who had one day been living in 'their' country – the Soviet Union – woke up the next in an independent country, unclear whether they had been transformed into foreigners overnight.

The status of these individuals was further complicated by the restrictive citizenship policies enacted by the Estonian and Latvian states. Unlike in Russia, where individuals were transformed from Soviet into Russian citizens, in Latvia a majority of Russian speakers were transformed from Soviet citizens into non-citizens. Officially these people were neither Russians nor Latvians. Instead they occupied a liminal space somewhere in between.

The purpose of this book is therefore to examine how 'Russians', living in post-Soviet Latvia, have (or have not) been able to deal with this dual identity crisis. With over twenty years now passed since the acquisition of Latvian independence, this study explores the trajectories that Russian-speaking identities have been following in Latvia. The central aim of this research is to determine how Russian speakers in Latvia frame their identities in relation to Latvia and Russia. To what extent do these individuals share Russian identities (however defined), and to what extent do they identify with Latvia?

It is argued that new forms of identity have been emerging in Latvia which are neither entirely 'Russian' nor entirely 'Latvian'. This assertion, in and of itself, is not necessarily new (see Laitin 1998). However, this monograph examines Russian-speaking identity (as it will be termed) from a discursive perspective, and examines a number of social, political, and journalistic sources in order to build up a complex picture of how Russian-speaking identities are developing in Latvia. This study does not view Russian speakers as a group that simply shares 'Russian' cultural and political identities. Instead, focus is placed on the interplay between competing national discourses and narratives that Russian speakers are forced to negotiate. At the centre of this analysis, therefore, is the acknowledgement that Russian-speaking identity is a precarious compromise between popularly articulated discourses of Russianness and Latvianness that are encountered in numerous spaces.

In order to trace discourses of Russian-speaking identity, great attention is paid to the state and nation-building practices of the Latvian nationalising project, as well as the discourses produced by the country's various political and cultural 'elites'. The historical discourses and narratives that have been presented and enforced by the Latvian state have, at times, been rather exclusionary towards non-Latvians. At the same time the Latvian space has much to offer Russian speakers, not least in terms of generally higher standards of living than in other areas of the former Soviet Union, but also the hugely important fact that Latvia, not Russia (or anywhere else), is home for these individuals. There are therefore contradictory pressures placed on Russian speakers resident in Latvia. On the one hand the policies and discourses associated with the Latvian state make it difficult for Russian speakers to associate and identify with Latvia. On the other hand Latvia is their home. For an increasing number of Russian speakers they have had no other home, not even the Soviet Union. There is therefore a natural desire to identify with Latvia on some level.

Another key area of concern for this study is the relationship between Russian speakers and Russia. As this research demonstrates, a great deal of political and media discourse in Latvia depicts Russian speakers in Latvia as inseparable from Russians in Russia. These discourses portray an explicit mistrust of Latvia's Russian speakers, highlight their lack of loyalty to Latvia, and stress the historical illegitimacy of their presence in the country. Nevertheless, detailed analysis of the relationships between Russia, Latvia, and Russian speakers demonstrates a much more complicated picture. Again, there are contradictory identity pressures associated with the contemporary Russian state. While there is some potential for Russian speakers to identity with Russia, it is also a foreign country which, in many respects, is far removed from the actual experiences of many Russian speakers in Latvia today. Conversely, as the study highlights, Russia has been increasingly strident in its efforts to forge institutional and discursive links between the Russian Federation and its so-called diaspora.

In this respect this book is a case study of how it is possible for the identities of a minority group, potentially backed by a powerful kin-state, to be integrated within the discourses of the dominant majority. The current literature would suggest that 'Latvian' and 'Russian' discourses in Latvia are diametrically opposed to one another (Zelče 2009; Kattago 2010: 383). However, this book argues that Russian-speaking discourse is notable for many remarkable successes in integrating into Latvian narratives and discourses. There is still a long way to go in order to overcome ethnic, historical, and political tensions, and we cannot be sure what the future may hold. Nevertheless, by tracking changes in Russian-speaking identity discourses this study demonstrates how and why the minority identity discourses of Russian speakers have been evolving over time.

This temporally grounded approach allows the researcher to stop focusing solely on the differences between Russian-speaking and Latvian identities, and instead to consider the process of relative convergence which, it is argued, has also been taking place since the collapse of the Soviet Union. It is not suggested, however, that Russian speakers are simply becoming 'Latvianised', or that they are slowly assimilating into Latvian culture. Instead, analysis of Russian-speaking discourse demonstrates how certain groups of Russian speakers are increasingly integrating into Latvian society while maintaining/developing, a heightened sense of group identity that is defined both in opposition to, and in synthesis with, Russian and Latvian identities. Conversely, it also points to the potential for further mobilisation among other sections of Latvia's Russophone population.

RUSSIAN SPEAKERS IN LATVIA AND THE BALTIC STATES

In the Soviet era, Latvia experienced a large movement of immigration from other areas of the USSR. Whereas in 1935, in pre-Soviet Latvia, ethnic Latvians comprised 77 per cent of country's total population, by 1989 this had fallen to 52 per cent. Conversely the combined proportion of Russians, Belarusians, and Ukrainians went from 10 per cent in 1935 to 42 per cent in 1989 (Jubulis 2001: 47). Following the collapse of the Soviet Union the proportion of Latvians started to rise again as many Soviet-era immigrants, especially those who had emigrated relatively recently, returned to Russia and other parts of the former Soviet Union. According to Latvia's 2011 census Latvians accounted for 62 per cent of the total population (1,285,136 out of 2,070,371), while Russians, Ukrainians, and Belarusians made up 32 per cent (671,119 out of 2,070,371) (Figure 1.1).

As detailed below, while the vast majority of ethnic Latvians were

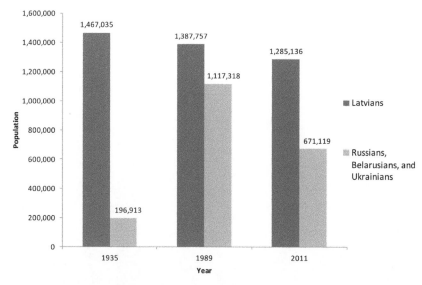

Figure 1.1 Absolute number of Latvians compared to Russians, Belarusians, and Ukrainians 1935, 1989, and 2011

Sources: Jubulis (2001: 47); Central Statistical Bureau of Latvia (2011)

granted citizenship following the acquisition of independence, a majority of non-Latvians (primarily Russian speakers),[1] were excluded from the main body of citizenry. As of 2010 only 59 per cent of Russians who were permanent residents of Latvia had citizenship. For Belarusians the figure was 39 per cent, while only 33 per cent of Ukrainians had Latvian citizenship. In contrast 99.79 per cent of Latvians enjoyed Latvian citizenship (see Figure 1.2).

As a result of these controversial and highly charged demographic and citizenship issues Russian speakers in the Baltic states, especially in Latvia and Estonia, have been the subject of a great deal of academic and political attention. This section therefore provides a brief overview of research which has been carried out on Russian-speaking identity in Latvia and the Baltic states. It should, of course, be noted that the situations in each of the three Baltic states are far from identical. Lithuania, for example, experienced far lower levels of immigration during the Soviet era and therefore felt confident enough to award citizenship to all of the country's permanent residents. However, irrespective of the many differences that exist between the Baltic states, a great deal of important research into Russian-speaking identities has been conducted across the three countries, with particular attention being paid to Latvia and Estonia. As such it is important to provide an overview of the literature from all three countries rather than focusing solely on Latvia.

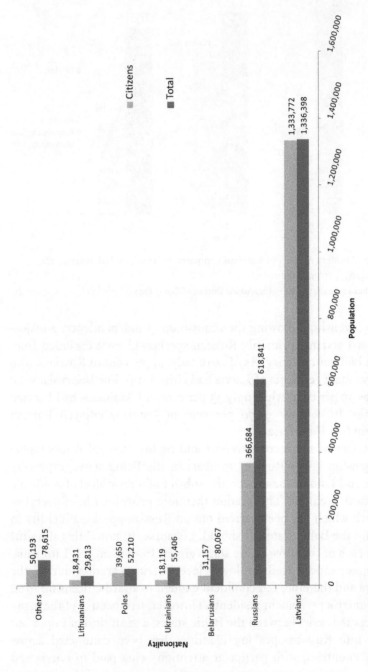

Figure 1.2 Citizens and non-citizens in Latvia by ethnicity (2010)

Source: Ministry of Foreign Affairs of the Republic of Latvia (2010)

Russian-speaking nationality?

A major question that has occupied researchers is whether or not Russian speakers have formed a specific group identity in the Baltic states. Earlier research on Russian-speaking identity in the region found that there was actually rather a weak sense of collective identity based on the idea of being a Russian or a Russian speaker (Aasland 1994; Melvin 1995: 24). The collapse of the Soviet Union left many people whom we now commonly refer to as 'Russian speakers' without a solid identity. Many of the early Baltic barometer surveys (Rose and Maley 1994: 51; Rose 1995:47; Rose 1997: 46), for example, showed that the majority of these people identified primarily with their city or locality rather than with Russia or their state of residence (see also Galbreath 2006b: 396–8). In the early 1990s, Aksel Kirch (1992: 207–8) highlighted the diffused nature of the 'Russian community', singling out three distinct identity orientations among Russians in the Baltic states: individuals who were orienting themselves towards the Russian Federation, those who saw their futures with the newly independent Baltic states, and those who looked back to the Soviet 'empire'. 'Russians' were therefore never a clearly defined or unified group.

Because the Russian/Russian-speaking community was so fragmented from the start of the post-Soviet era, it could be argued that any study into 'Russian-speaking identity' is potentially problematic from the outset. Indeed, Poppe and Hagendoorn (2001) note the various difficulties of categorising this disparate group, citing the inappropriateness of various terms (Russians, Russian settler community, Russian diaspora). For one thing this was not a community of 'Russians'. According to the rigid Soviet system of categorising ethnicity (*natsional'nost'*) a number of Russian speakers (that is, people whose first language was Russian) were actually Ukrainians, Belarusians, or even Poles. The contradictory nationality policies of the Soviet Union (see Brubaker 1996) meant that when the Union collapsed in the early 1990s, there was no single monolithic form of identity. While culturally Russian had been upheld as the trans-republic language of communication, commerce, and education, the 'titular'[2] languages of the republics were also given special, republic-wide status. Additionally, individuals were not at liberty to choose their nationality. It was, instead, inherited from their parents. A person resident in Ukraine, for example, could not officially be considered Ukrainian if both of their parents were officially Russian.

On top of this there was a conflation between Soviet and Russian forms of identity. Soviet nationality policy paradoxically encouraged republic-centred forms of identity to emerge among the so-called titular groups (Agarin 2010). The Latvian Socialist Soviet Republic, for example, had its own communist party, its own governmental structures, and its own educational and cultural programme. Although the scope of these organisations was limited by the ideological and political expediencies of the centre, it nonetheless ensured that Latvians continued to associate with Latvia rather than with the Soviet Union as a whole. In contrast, Russia lacked many of the institutional arrangements of the other republics. Instead Moscow was the federal centre of the Union and Russian was officially used throughout the USSR. Russians, and also Russian speakers who lived outside their 'national homeland', were therefore encouraged to associate with the entire Soviet space rather than specifically with the Russian Soviet Federative Socialist Republic. Interestingly, research from the early 1990s shows that Russian speakers initially felt relatively weak attachment to Russian or to any form of Russian-speaking identity (Boeck 1993: 78). In one survey from 1990 as few as 4.2 per cent of non-Latvians, for example, were able to answer that they felt primarily 'of Russia' (Linz and Stepan 1996: 411).

More recently, however, a number of authors have suggested that the identity of belonging to a linguistic community of Russian speakers has become one of the most important, emerging identifiers and markers of identity in the Baltic states (Laitin 1995; Khanov 2002; Kronenfeld 2005: 272; Cheskin 2010a). David Laitin (1998) goes as far as outlining the emergence of a specific 'Russian-speaking nationality', distinct from Russian identity. In many respects this identity is a result of the 'Balticisation' of Russian speakers (Melvin 1995). Put simply, life in the Baltic states is different from life in Russia which, it is asserted, has led to the divergence of Russian and Baltic Russian identities. Indeed, a number of studies support this thesis by showing that Russian speakers in the Baltic states increasingly consider themselves to be very different from Russians in Russia (Vihalemm and Masso 2003; Fein 2005; Zepa 2006).

In understanding the dynamics of this emerging group identity, Neil Melvin (1995: 55) pays specific attention to the shared experience of discrimination. He suggests that this has been a major factor leading to the relative consolidation of a form of group identity among Russian speakers in the Baltic states. The restrictive state policies on citizenship and language have led non-Latvians to feel more similar to one another because they feel equally discriminated against. As discussed in Chapter 3, the salience of language in post-Soviet Latvia has meant that the Latvian state has introduced a number of measures to increase the prestige of the Latvian language while simultaneously trying to limit the use of Russian in various public spheres. For this reason Tabuns (2010: 260–4) argues that the Russian language has emerged as a central form of identification for *Russian-speakers*.[3] This is evident from the increased use of the term Russian-speakers (in Latvian *krievvalodīgie*, in Russian *russkoiazychnye*) that is used in place of other terms such as Russians, Russian diaspora, Russian settler community and so on (Khanov 2002: 14). This trend is evident not only in media discourse but also in academic studies (this one being no exception).

Nevertheless, irrespective of any 'Balticisation' of Russian speakers, it remains true that popular discourses continue to depict Russian speakers as entirely different and separate from Latvians. For example, studies of media discourse in Latvia (Šulmane and Kruks 2001; Rožukalne 2010) have revealed a sharp division between the form and content of Latvian-language and Russian-language media. It is often argued that the stereotypes and intolerance of many of the country's media publications help to further demarcate, construct, and propagate divisions between the two constructed communities. For this reason it is asserted that these media practices have a very real impact on group identities. Indeed this is something that this current research investigates in some detail below.

In the field of Latvian politics, analysts have identified an equally visible and sharp division between 'Latvian' political parties and 'Russian' ones (Kažoka 2010; Golubeva and Kažoka 2010). Here, 'Latvian' parties are seen to represent the interests of the imagined community of 'Latvians' while 'Russian' parties largely draw their support from the imagined community of 'Russian-speakers', whose interests they claim to represent. In this respect Latvian politics is far more ethnicised than in Estonia where the majority of Russian speakers with Estonian citizenship tend not to vote for 'Russian' parties but instead most commonly vote for the Estonian Centre Party (*Eesti Keskerakond*). This leads Solska (2011: 1099) to the optimistic conclusion that 'In Estonia, ethnicity is not politicised any more, and economic issues, and recently accession to the Euro-zone, have dominated the public debate and rendered the Estonian political path an unprecedented success story among former Soviet republics'. Solska's optimism is almost certainly overstated. Nevertheless, the comparatively less ethnicised nature of Estonian politics has led some commentators to suggest the possibility for Estonia's Russian speakers to articulate an increasingly globalised, or Europeanised, identity based on economic well-being and prosperity (Vihalemm and Masso 2003; Laitin 2003). Perhaps tellingly, there has been an absence of any such predictions for Latvia's Russian speakers which in many ways is related back to the country's far more ethnicised political spectrum (see Chapter 7).

Collective memories

In terms of pinning down what differentiates the identities of Russian speakers from Latvians (within political and media discourses at least), the theme of historical interpretation has increasingly been seen as a crucial factor. In the analysis of international relations between Russia and Latvia there has been much discussion of the so-called 'memory war' (Mälksoo 2009) between the two sides. As argued above, memories and collective memories can be seen as essential elements in the formation of group identities. For this reason Nils Muižnieks (2011b: 9) argues that it is impossible to understand Latvian–Russian international relations without an understanding of the role identity and memory play in forming these relations.

According to Berg and Ehin (2009) the official, historical interpretations of the Latvian and Russian states towards the history of the twentieth century are wholly incompatible and antagonistic. From Russia's perspective the Red Army heroically liberated Europe from the grip of Nazism. Within the official Russian narrative, the Baltic states were not occupied, and the Soviet Union was able to bring many positive achievements to Estonia, Latvia, and Lithuania. On the other hand, the Latvian, historical narrative casts Stalinism in the same evil light as Nazism. The Soviet era is portrayed as brutal, and emphasis is placed on the Soviet Union's illegal occupation of a previously independent nation state.

While the issues of collective memory and historical interpretation have been effectively explored in studies of Latvian–Russian relations, the literature has so far been less successful in tackling these issues from the domestic perspective. This is evidenced in the focus of the extensive literature on the integration and acculturation strategies of Latvia's Russian speakers. To date scholars and policymakers working on integration have preferred to focus more on linguistic proficiency, perceived discrimination, a sense of geographical association with Latvia, and contemporary state policies, than on the issue of historical interpretation (Laitin 1998; Tabuns 1999; Priedīte 2005; Pisarenko 2006; Zepa et al. 2006, 2008b).

It has only been relatively recently that memories have been analysed seriously as aspects of social integration. In 2011, in recognition of the importance of historical interpretations on the integration process, the Latvian government introduced 'social memory' as a key element in its new integration programme. In the Latvian government's *Guidelines for national identity, civil society and integration politics*, 'the creation of collective social memory' (Culture Ministry of the Republic of Latvia 2011: 6) is therefore one of the key criteria for social integration.

Integration

Before the introduction of 'social memory' as a key component of Latvia's integration policy, focus was largely placed on linguistic integration – ensuring that Russian speakers could (and would) speak Latvian. David Laitin suggested in 1998 that Russian speakers in Latvia and Estonia would gradually choose to assimilate fully into Latvian and Estonian cultures at the expense of their own Russian cultures. Laitin's sophisticated rational choice model examined individual behaviour from a largely economic perspective. His 'tipping' perspective suggests that as soon as the economic and social benefits of learning Latvian are considered higher than maintaining monolingualism, Russian speakers will assimilate by learning and speaking Latvian and by adopting cultural norms associated with the Latvian state.

Recent research, however, has shown that Russian speakers have not always favoured assimilation strategies. Based on the terms commonly used in cross-cultural psychology (Sam and Berry 2010), the evidence suggests that Russian speakers generally favour integration (identifying with both Latvian culture and Russian culture) over assimilation (full integration into Latvian culture at the expense of Russian culture), marginalisation (retreat from both Latvian and Russian cultural life) or separation (maintenance of Russian culture with no integration into Latvian culture) (Kronenfeld 2005; Pisarenko 2006; Šūpule 2007). Thus, while approximately 95 per cent of Russians in Latvia believe that everyone in Latvia should be able to speak Latvian freely (Zepa et al. 2008b: 7), Russian speakers have nevertheless been adamant of their right to continue to use Russian in private and public spheres, and especially in public education (see Hogan-Brun 2006).

The fact that a majority of Russian speakers would prefer to maintain some form of Russian-speaking identity (even if it is not explicitly articulated), while concurrently integrating into Latvian society and culture is hugely significant. Policymakers in Estonia and Latvia initially expected that an increase in linguistic proficiency in the state languages (Estonian and Latvian respectively) would lead to wholesale increases in patterns of integration (Nimmerfeldt et al. 2011). While language knowledge of Latvian has been increasing (Ernstone and Mežs 2008: 195), especially within younger age cohorts (SKDS 2014: 27), this has not led to the realisation of the goals set out in the state's early integration programmes (Muižnieks 2010: 284). The clear divisions in Latvian politics and in the country's media space demonstrate that while many Russian speakers have been able to integrate linguistically, many of them have also maintained a form of separation.

This highlights a major deficiency in the current integration literature in Latvia. Just as there has been a lack of focus on history and memory, so has there been a general neglect towards the discourses and narratives associated with the Latvian state. Structural integration, which refers to the access to major political, economic, and social institutions, can be increased through linguistic measures to improve the knowledge of Latvian among Russian speakers. Such measures, however, may be less effective in increasing identificational integration.[4] The discursive stances of the Latvian state, on the other hand, are potentially key to understanding why some Russian speakers continue to preserve separate forms of group identities.

A number scholars working on Latvia have, however, examined Latvian state-building policies and discourses in their own right. In the late and post-Soviet eras political and cultural elites have gone to great lengths to articulate coherent narratives of Latvia's nationhood and statehood. The discourses identified by scholars include narratives of a spatial and temporal 'return to Europe' and 'return to normality' (Eglitis 2002), official historical interpretations of the past (Onken 2007), focus on particularly 'Latvian' conceptions of nature (Schwartz 2007), and the belief that 'Latvians' need to be the 'core' and dominant nation in a post-Soviet and independent Latvia (Smith 1999a: 82).

Brigita Zepa et al. relate how the development of these discourses has resulted in the emergence of popularised ideals of what it means to be a 'Latvian'. This individual, whom Zepa et al. ironically refer to as 'homo Latviensis' (Zepa et al. 2006: 74), must speak Latvian, maintain 'Latvian' cultural values and traits, and display loyalty to the Latvian state by not questioning the state's official narratives and historical interpretations. In many respects this category of citizen can be contrasted to the idealised Soviet individual 'homo Sovieticus' (Peschel 1998: 304) and the 'neo-Soviet' narratives which formed the basis of Interfront activities in the perestroika period (Smith et al. 1998: 10). It can also be contrasted to a person loyal to the ideals and official interpretations of the Russian Federation (homo Rossicus).

While these state discourses have been studied and identified very effectively, the literature has failed to examine in sufficient detail the status of Russian speakers in relation to these narratives and discourses. It may, in fact, be relatively easy to gain linguistic proficiency in Latvian, especially for younger generations who now learn Latvian from a young age in the state's schooling system. Being able to integrate into, and accept, discourses and narratives which are largely hostile to Russian speakers, on the other hand, is perhaps a much more problematic scenario.

One particularly visible result of Latvian state discourses and narratives can be seen in the country's much-discussed and controversial citizenship laws (Brubaker 1992; Chinn and Truex 1996; Aasland 2002). These citizenship laws initially conferred citizenship only to those people who could trace their ancestry to the pre-Soviet Latvia of 1940 (see Chapter 3). This newly (re)constructed citizenry therefore represented Latvia's 'core nation', and was part of the drive to return Latvia to its 'normal' and 'European' self. The vast majority of the group most commonly known today as 'Russian speakers' were ineligible for citizenship as it was thus initially defined. These were people who had mostly arrived in Latvia during the Soviet occupation and were therefore neither 'normal', 'European', nor part of the 'core nation'. As such they became non-citizens until, following pressures from the European Union (EU), Organization for Security and Co-operation in Europe (OSCE), and Council of Europe (Galbreath 2006a), Latvia partially relaxed its citizenship laws to allow for a process of naturalisation, based on linguistic proficiency in Latvian and a basic knowledge of Latvian history.

Because national identity and a sense of belonging is so closely linked with reciprocal relationships with the state (Croucher 2004), these narratives of Latvian statehood and history can be seen as especially problematic for Russian speakers resident in Latvia. Official state policies have discursively placed them outside the 'core nation'. A major theme of this research is that it is rather difficult for individuals to identify with a polity that portrays them as alien and unnatural. On the other hand, it is argued that the process of 'Balticisation' or 'Latvianisation' has led to the development of a particular Baltic, or Latvian, Russian identity. This has meant that Russian speakers in Latvia are also largely unable to align their identities fully with the Russian Federation.

The current literature therefore highlights a number of contradictory tendencies. On the one hand research has highlighted some tendencies for Russian speakers to feel increasingly loyal to Latvia and to Latvian symbols of nationhood (Rodins 2005; Zepa et al. 2005a). On the other hand scholars have established the presence of strong identification towards the Russian language and culture, and consequently towards emerging forms of Russian-speaking identity. As is evident from the media analysis in this research, these identifications are often construed as proof that Russian speakers are, in fact, neither loyal to Latvia nor to 'Latvian values'. At the same time many Russian speakers in Latvia have not displayed high levels of association with Russians in Russia or with the Russian Federation (see Chapter 5).

Brubaker's triadic nexus

It is evident that there is a complex interplay in the three-way relationships between Russian speakers, Latvia, and Russia. In order to encapsulate this relationship many scholars have employed Rogers Brubaker's triadic nexus model. Brubaker's much-cited work suggests that, in order to understand minority nationalism in post-communist Central and Eastern Europe, it is necessary to focus on three elements: 'national minorities, the newly nationalizing states in which they live, and the external "homelands" to which they belong' (1996: 4). This nexus has come to be the dominant framework with which to study Russian speakers in the Baltic states (see Cheskin 2015). The nexus allows Russian speakers to be situated not only as inhabitants of their 'nationalising state' (for the present case study – Latvia), but also as individuals within a less territorially bound Russian space. Additionally, a number of authors have seen fit to add a fourth node, that of international institutions (Smith 2002; Kelley 2004; Galbreath 2005). This node reflects the 'Europeanised' space that Latvia inhabits, especially from the time of EU accession negotiations onwards.

This approach has been very fruitful in attempting to determine the reciprocal influences of international organisations (the EU, OSCE, Council of Europe), external homelands (Russia), nationalising states (Latvia), and national minorities (Russian speakers). Again, however, analysis has not focused sufficiently on the discursive elements of this triadic/quadratic nexus. Brubaker was at pains to stress that the reciprocal relationships of the nexus were a result of both *stances* and *representations* (1996: 68–69; see also Cheskin 2015; Pettai 2006: 133). He was not interested in observing the objectively defined relationships between the three nodes per se. Instead he understood that each node produces different stances which can be manifested either as 'expressly articulated "positions"' (Brubaker 1996: 63), or in the form of representations by others. In other words, 'nationalising states' can produce stances through policies and rhetoric, but stances also develop as a result of interpretations by 'national minorities' or 'external homelands'. As a result of this, the question for Brubaker was not so much what the various forms of nationalism on the nexus are. Rather the model was introduced to examine the processes, or how these nationalisms, or stances, are enacted.

The nexus model therefore has great applicability to discursive approaches. An institutional study of Latvia's post-Soviet politics can reveal a great deal about the interactions between Russian speakers, the Latvian state, Russia, and the EU. If such an institutional study is detached from the study of representations and discourse, however, then it will be rendered less useful and more static. This study therefore builds upon Brubaker's nexus and emphasises the discursive elements that characterise relations between Russian speakers, Latvia, Russia, and the international context in which Russian speakers are located.

OVERVIEW OF THE BOOK

Chapter 2 of this book sets out the central theoretical frameworks that form the basis of this study. The concept of discourse is firstly enumerated with an explanation of why this concept is potentially so fruitful for a study of Russian-speaking identities in contemporary Latvia. Specific attention is paid to the question of how and why discourses change over time and the implications of these changes. This chapter also highlights the link between memory and national identity formation. Drawing on the work of a number of memory scholars, it is argued that memories can form an important link between the past and the present and that memories can possess power to create strong group identities.

Centrally important to this research is a discourse-historical approach to studying discourse. Consequently, this chapter provides a set of theoretical, conceptual, and methodological justifications for this approach. It is argued that contemporary discourses should not be studied in isolation. Instead they should be contextualised by analysis of how they evolve through time.

Chapter 3 examines Latvia's state and nation-building policies that have been pursued in the late Soviet and early independence periods. The main discourses that have been used in order to justify Latvia's new, post-Soviet order are examined and studied in relation to the status of non-Latvians – primarily Russians and Russian speakers. Memories and historical interpretations are singled out as especially significant in Latvia's nationalising project. As such the 'memory war' between the Baltic states and Russia is examined in detail.

It is demonstrated that discourses which revolve around memories and historical myths are of prime importance in the Baltic states and especially in Latvia. Gramsci's concept of organic crisis is employed to highlight the importance of the late Soviet and early independence periods in forming hegemonic identity blocs in Latvia. Based on this understanding, this chapter specifically analyses discourses which emerged in these periods of time. The practices of state and nation-building are examined which have attempted to (re)define the Latvian nation and the inhabitants thereof.

Chapter 4 provides a detailed analysis of media discourse in Latvia, with a specific focus on the country's Russian-language press. Firstly this chapter explores the means by which the media have attempted to construct a sub-national group of Russian-speakers in Latvia, and to what extent they have managed to imbue this imagined community with certain characteristics and traits. Secondly, a comprehensive discourse analysis of the Russian-language dailies *Chas* and *Vesti Segodnia* is conducted. Specific attention is paid to how journalistic elites respond to the various 'Latvian' discourses of statehood and nationalism which have been identified in earlier chapters. It is demonstrated that Russian-speaking discourses are not simply 'anti-Latvian'. Instead the analysis also reveals the emergence of a more positive Russian-speaking identity which is increasingly premised upon the acceptance of various Latvian narratives and discourses.

Chapter 5 moves away from an analysis of so-called elite discourse and instead analyses discourses and understandings of Russian speakers at the ground level. This chapter is based on focus group interviews with groups of Russian speakers in Riga. As part of this analysis, focus group participants were asked to respond to various quotations that were picked out from the previously conducted media analysis (Chapter 4). Their responses are analysed and comparisons are made between elite production of discourse and its ground-level consumption. The influence of discourses which emanate from Russia and from Latvia is also analysed as part of an attempt to understand how Russian speakers are negotiating their sense of identity in Latvia.

Chapter 6 returns to the theme of memory which was explored in Chapter 3. This time, however, the focus is on ground-level perceptions of history and collective memory-myths. Data is analysed from a survey of Russian speakers in Latvia, conducted at the site of the 2011 Victory Day celebrations. In this chapter special emphasis is attached to generational changes which are potentially occurring among Latvia's Russian speakers. It is argued that, by focusing on generational change, it is possible to understand how young Russian speakers are negotiating bottom-up and top-down identity pressures. The data suggest that young Russian speakers have been greatly influenced by Latvian memory discourses. As such, younger cohorts of Russian speakers are displaying identity and memory positions which increasingly differ from those of their parents' and grandparents' generations.

Chapter 7 offers an examination of political discourses and the composition of Latvian politics. It is argued that the realm of politics is largely responsible for artificially inflating ethnic tensions and reinforcing group boundaries in Latvia. Data is examined from interviews with Latvian politicians alongside analysis of political initiatives that have mobilised ethnically demarcated groups. The analysis traces the peculiarities of Latvia's ethnic (rather than ideological or policy-based) party political spectrum. This spectrum, it is argued, often encourages political entrepreneurs to pursue discursive strategies that strengthen internal (ethnic) group identities.

Chapter 8 examines the role of the Russian Federation in sponsoring and facilitating discursive identity strategies for Latvia's Russian speakers. The chapter traces contemporary developments in Russia's compatriot discourses and policies, and outlines how Russia has recently stepped up its efforts to politicise and mobilise 'Russian compatriots'.

Following an analysis of Russian discursive strategies, attention is turned to Latvia's two main 'Russian' parties and how they have responded to these developments, especially in light of the Ukraine crises of 2014. Analysis of the political discourses of these parties shows how contemporary Russian-speaking discourse in Latvia continues to represent a synthesised position between Latvian and Russian discourses.

NOTES

1. That is, people whose first language was Russian.
2. Within the federal system of the Soviet Union titular ethnicity (*titul'naia natsional'nost'*) referred to the ethnic groups which the union republics, autonomous republics, autonomous oblasts, and autonomous okrugs were named after; their so-called 'root nation' (*Korennaia natsiia*). So, in the Latvian Soviet Socialist Republic – 'Latvians'; in the Chechen–Ingush Autonomous Soviet Socialist Republic – 'Chechens' and 'Ingushians'. The word 'titular', notwithstanding its Soviet usage, is still widely used in the literature on post-Soviet minority politics today.
3. In this study a distinction is made between Russian speakers (without a hyphen) and Russian-speakers (with a hyphen). 'Russian speakers' is used as a more neutral term to describe people whose first language is Russian. 'Russian-speakers' is used to refer to an imagined community of Russian speakers. See also Chapter 4 for further discussion of this distinction. When used in adjectival form the hyphen is retained, for example 'Russian-speaking discourse'.
4. Drawing on John Berry's (1997) theories of acculturation, the literature commonly distinguishes between structural, cultural, social, and identity integration. Structural integration relates to access to a society's institutions, cultural integration is the level of cognitive change when two cultures come into contact with each other, social integration is a measure of the levels of social interaction between groups, and identity integration refers to levels of personal and group identifications.

Discourse, Memory, and Identity

The structured totality resulting from the articulatory practice, we will call *discourse*. (Laclau and Mouffe 1985: 105)

In the beginning was the Word, and the Word was with God, and the Word was God. (John 1:1)

DISCOURSE

This research is grounded on a discursive theoretical approach. That is to say that it is interested in how discourses become a central element of personal and group identities. A variety of Russian-speaking discourses from Latvia have been selected for analysis from a wide range of sources including newspaper articles, focus-group discussions, survey data, news articles from political parties, and interviews with Latvian politicians. This analysis traces how various discourses are socially constructed, altered, and challenged over time, and how they relate to personal and group identities.

Narrowly defined the term 'discourse' can be understood in purely linguistic terms. By this definition discourses are instances of language use, either verbally or in written form, or even as gestures. Without question these verbal, written, and gestural 'texts' constitute central elements of discourse. Discourse, however, encapsulates more than just language. Fairclough (2003: 3), for example, distinguishes between lexical units and discourse in general. 'Discourse in general' is used to acknowledge that language is only ever meaningful within a social context. When, for example, one reads the words 'man', 'woman', 'Russian' and so on, these particular lexical units are only meaningful because the reader has had social experience of these concepts. The reader has a subjective idea of what 'men', 'women', and 'Russians' are, how they act, and even what they look like.

For this reason many theorists of discourse refer to lexical units as 'signifiers'. The individual letters that are put together to create a word do not provide any meaning. Instead signifiers are given meaning by the social context that surrounds them. In this respect words do not simply create social realities, but are also constructed by them. For Saussure (1966) a clear distinction is therefore drawn between the signifier and the signified. While the signifier is the linguistic construct which is used to document a concept (R-u-s-s-i-a, for example), the signified refers to the meanings that individuals give to this signifier (the images that are produced by the human mind in response to seeing/hearing the signifier). Nevertheless, it is also possible to see how, in turn, the social world is not only reflected, but also constructed, in the production of language. Social contexts are used to endow words with meaning, but once these words have meaning, they can help to give meanings to other words. In essence words and meanings become part of our social context, and it is hard to imagine how the social world would function without them.

A concise definition of discourse is therefore one which acknowledges both the linguistic and social aspects of the concept. Discourses are both linguistic units *and* the meanings that are attached to these units. Russian-speaking discourse, for its part, refers to any discourse which can be related to the position of Russian-speakers. Europeanness, for example, is a concept which crops up on numerous occasions within this research. The various discourses of 'Europe' form part of Russian-speaking discourse because they are used (in numerous, often contradictory, ways) to give meaning to Russian speakers in Latvia. If Russian speakers are, or are not, considered 'European' then this affects the discourse associated with this group of individuals.

Significantly, discourse theorists assume that discourses have the potential to be powerful determinants of human behaviour and identities. For example, if a person considers themselves to be a 'British' 'man', and if they have a subjective idea of what these two words mean, then they may well be inclined to act like 'British men' should. Alternatively, if they have an inclination towards behaviour that does not fit within dominant discourses, they may find pressure to conform to 'normal' modes of behaviour, for example to 'man up', or to respect 'British values'.

This has led to the emergence of critical discourse analysis (CDA) as a prominent methodological approach in academic research. Van Dijk (2001: 352) defines CDA as, 'a type of discourse analytical research that primarily studies the way social power abuse, dominance, and inequality are enacted, reproduced, and resisted by text and talk in the social and political context'. CDA places a significant emphasis on the way in which language usage and power relations are interwoven. CDA is therefore less interested in which particular words are used, but rather *how* these words are used, and how meanings, and consequently power, are produced within discourse.

This approach is key to this study. CDA allows the researcher to focus on particular concepts and words and to see how they are used to create stable meanings and stable patterns of expected behaviour. Foucault (2002b: 133) refers to these stable meanings as 'regimes of truth'. Within these structures 'true' meanings are sustained by complex social relations. At the same time these 'truths' are then endowed with their own power to be socially constructive and form an integral aspect of the social world. There is therefore a circular relationship between truth (meaning) and power.

Discourse and change

While there is a circular relationship between discourse and power, it is also the case that meanings and discourses can, and do, change with time. 'Homosexuality', for example, has been treated very differently in different locations and times. In all instances it refers to a similar phenomenon – same-sex attraction – and yet the surrounding, associated discourses vary greatly, ranging from psychological illness and sin, to tolerance and progressiveness. Indeed, this ability for discourses to change is evident in this research. Identities are not static and Russian identities, just like Russian-speaking identities, can, and do, evolve and develop through time.

Nevertheless, it is not a case of agents simply choosing which meanings should be attached to specific discourses. For example, if an individual wishes to convince the world that 'men' should be associated with homemaking, dresses, lipstick, and the colour pink then their task will be rather difficult. This is not because men cannot, or should not, be associated with these various other concepts, but because of the social history of 'men'. Historically, men have been associated with numerous discourses which make association with these ideas rather problematic. Likewise, if a person wishes to convince a Latvian audience that 'Russians' should be associated with Europeanness, civilisation, and a lack of chauvinism, then the historical and social experience of Latvia may well go against them. Indeed this is explored in some detail in this study.

Consequently, this book does not set out simply to examine and identify contemporary forms of Russian-speaking identity in Latvia.

Latvia's Russian-speaking discourse, it is argued, does not emerge out of a vacuum. Instead it has to be placed within the historical context of over twenty years of post-Soviet independence and approximately fifty years of Soviet rule. If contemporary discourses are historically and socially constituted, then it is not possible to ignore these contexts.

Additionally, Russian-speaking discourses need to be examined in relation to the particularly visible and stringently defined narratives and discourses of the Latvian political order. Following the collapse of the USSR, Russians in Latvia were transformed from the majority group to a minority. They were suddenly faced with a set of well-articulated discourses that overtly challenged previously dominant Soviet discourses. As independence became more and more of a reality, for example, the relatively inclusive rhetoric of the popular fronts became increasingly nationalistic and less accommodating to non-Latvians. Exclusionary discourses of Latvianness are therefore treated in some detail in this account. As is argued throughout this work, contemporary forms of Russian-speaking discourse can only be understood when examined alongside the majority discourses associated with Latvia's political space.

Within a historical approach to discourse it is therefore understood that meanings can change, but also that meanings have a form of stability which is historically determined. In order to theorise this phenomenon Laclau and Mouffe (1985) put forward the idea of *nodal points*. Nodal points are 'partial fixations' of meaning (1985: 112), that is, meanings which have historically become embedded with a relatively stable meaning. These nodal points, in turn, facilitate a certain amount of stability which is required to allow other meanings to emerge.

Foucault uses the term *episteme* to describe a similar concept. For him the validity and meaning of a discourse is founded on its historical *a priori*, that is the historical conditions that underpin any given social concept (2002a: 143–4). Foucault does not mean by this that there is an eternally existing, absolute, and fixed *a priori* that produces discursive meaning. Instead it refers to the fact that each discourse has its own particular history. The *a priori*, therefore, 'has to take account of the fact that discourse has not only a meaning or a truth, but a history, and a specific history that does not refer it back to the laws of an alien development' (2002a: 211).

A major difference between Foucault's *episteme* and Laclau and Mouffe's nodal points is that, for Foucault, *epistemes* do not refer to individual discursive units. Instead Foucault sees the *episteme* like a 'worldview' and defines it as 'the total set of relations that unite, at a given period, the discursive practices that give rise to epistemological figures, sciences, and possible formalized systems' (2002a: 211). Nodal points, on the other hand, can refer to single, discursively meaningful units rather than the totalised system of prevailing discourses. For this reason the concept of nodal points are far more conducive to empirical investigation than the relatively abstract and generalised notion of an *episteme*.

Hegemony and hegemonic blocs

Another important concept, when considering the social power of discourse to create identities and shape behaviour patterns, is that of hegemony. In the work of Antonio Gramsci there is a distinction between political and cultural hegemony (see also Anderson 1976). Political hegemony relates to the material power of the ruling elite who are able to maintain control through the use of coercive measures. Cultural hegemony, on the other hand, is a much subtler form or control which rests not on material force, but instead can be formed in the realm of ideology. While Gramsci uses the term ideology in a particularly Marxist, and therefore materialistic, way (Purvis and Hunt 1993), there is a great deal of overlap with ideology and the concept of discourse, as it has been defined in this study. One of Gramsci's lasting contributions has therefore been his insight that hegemonic relations of power can be formed first in the field of ideology (discourse). For Gramsci, ideologies, values, and culture can form a central element of the reigning political order:

> Previously germinated ideologies become 'party', come into conflict and confrontation, until only one of them . . . tends to prevail, gaining the upper hand and propagating itself throughout society. It thereby achieves not only a unison of economic and political aims, but also intellectual and moral unity . . . It thus creates the hegemony of a fundamental social group over a series of subordinate groups. (Gramsci 1971: 181–2)

Therefore, although Gramsci understood that hegemony can be exercised through 'domination' he also conceives of power as resting upon successfully articulated discourses and ideologies – or as he terms it 'intellectual and moral leadership' (1971: 57). This is important because, according to Gramsci, cultural and political hegemonies establish power relations over the people they govern. In essence hegemonic orders are able to control societies by articulating and consolidating an established set of acceptable norms and values. For this reason Gramsci believes in the primacy of politics and in the necessity of understanding the political in order to understand the social:

Critical understanding of self takes place therefore through a struggle of political 'hegemonies' and of opposing directions, first in the ethical field and then in that of politics proper, in order to arrive at the working out at a higher level of one's own conception of reality. Consciousness of being part of a particular hegemonic force (that is to say political consciousness) is the first stage towards a further progressive self-consciousness in which theory and practice will finally be one. (Gramsci 1971: 333)

Hegemonic blocs can therefore be understood as groups of individuals who have consolidated their leading positions through the use of a mixture of coercive and non-coercive measures. When these blocs possess cultural hegemony in tandem with political hegemony, their position is widely considered legitimate or unquestionable. Such hegemonic blocs will have great latitude to ensure that their associated discourses are able to penetrate deep into society.

For the case of Latvia this is highly significant because of the new political and cultural hegemony that has emerged in the post-Soviet era. As the following chapters (especially Chapter 3) argue, a particularly 'Latvian' hegemony has emerged that is based both on political power and discursive articulations. In order to understand the identity strategies of Latvia's Russian speakers it is therefore vital firstly to understand the basis of this hegemony and its implications for group identities.

MEMORY

In recent years there has been a steady rise in academic interest in theories of memory and remembering, and of their relevance for group formations and identities. In the Baltic context this trend has also been evidenced with an increasing number of articles appearing on the theme of memory, and especially conflicting memory (for example, Onken 2007, 2010; Hackmann and Lehti 2008; Mälksoo 2009). As stated above, this book does not represent a singular attempt to isolate and study contemporary discourses. Instead this research focuses on how discourses change with time, and especially how they are utilised by minority groups (in this case Russian speakers in Latvia), who are already faced with a set of well-defined majority discourses. As a result 'memory' is of vital conceptual importance.

Within the emerging discipline of memory studies, memories are treated as political, social, and cultural practices that are grounded in the past, but which are used to relate to contemporary concerns. For example, an individual need not experience an historical event first hand for the historical interpretation, or 'memory', of that event to play a major role in their sense of personal and group identification. Memories can therefore be conceptualised as discursively created understandings that are embedded in the past, but which are very much contemporary phenomena.

As such, memories can operate as important sources of personal and group identification. National identities, for example, are commonly defined by a specifically articulated history (Hobsbawm 1992), allowing individuals to make sense of their present with recourse to a particular version of the past. 'A history of Latvia', for example, only makes sense if observed from the present, with the understanding that all the historical events leading up to this point have led to the emergence of the Latvian nation and state as currently constituted.

This has led memory theorists to talk of 'collective memories' as important distinguishers of group identities. Maurice Halbwachs, who published his seminal 'Social frameworks of memory' in 1952 (1992), distinguishes between autobiographical memory and historical memory and also between history and collective memory (see also Olick and Robbins 1998: 111). Autobiographical memory is personally experienced and personally generated memory. Historical memory, on the other hand, is memory which is transmitted to individuals via various media including written and oral accounts, images, monuments and so on, to which those people have no direct experience. Collective memory differs from history insomuch as collective memory refers to a past which plays an integral role in the formation of our identities in the present, while history refers to a past which does not.

James Wertsch provides a succinct overview of what separates 'collective memory' from 'formal history' which is detailed in Table 2.1. While Wertsch admits that this is necessarily an overly simplified dichotomy, it is nonetheless very useful methodologically. Formal history corresponds very closely to the idea of a 'democratisation of memory' (Brüggemann and Kasekamp 2008: 441), whereby individuals are able to reflect critically on historical events rather than rely on simplified myths and cultural axioms linked with a particular group. Within this 'democratisation' there is acknowledgement by all sides that history is complicated and ambiguous, and alternative views of history are tolerated or accepted. In the Baltic context, Brüggemann and Kasekamp argue that this democratisation of memory is the only way to resolve the current tensions between opposing memory-orientated groups in the Baltic states – issues which are examined in Chapter 6.

Chapter 3, for example, documents how collective memories have

Table 2.1 Collective memory and formal history

Collective memory	Formal history
'subjective'	'objective'
Single committed perspective	Distanced from a particular perspective
Reflects a particular group's social framework	Reflects no particular social framework
Not self-conscious	Critical reflective stance
Impatient with ambigiuities about motives and the interpretation of events	Recognises ambiguity
Denies 'pastness' of events	Focuses on historicity
Links the past with the present	Differentiates past from present
Ahistorical, antihistorical	Views past events as 'then and not now'

Source: Wertsch (2008: 150)

been utilised by the Latvian state to create cohesive and legitimate identities in the present. Certain historical narratives have been explicitly selected and emphasised by the Latvian state while others have been deliberately left out of official accounts. In this respect collective memories overlap markedly with national myths. Duncan Bell (2003: 75), for example, understands a nationalist myth as 'a story that simplifies, dramatizes and selectively narrates the story of a nation's past and its place in the world, its historical eschatology: a story that elucidates its contemporary meaning through (re)constructing its past'. In this respect myths also serve a vital function of ensuring and anchoring one's self-identity within national identities, allowing the self to be placed within wider frameworks of meaning and belonging. As Bell acknowledges though, myths do not occur and reproduce in a vacuum. Instead he refers to the terrain where myths and memories interact as a mythscape. The 'national mythscape' therefore is 'the discursive realm, constituted by and through temporal and spatial dimensions, in which the myths of the nation are forged, transmitted, reconstructed and negotiated constantly' (2003: 75).

In light of Bell's understanding of the constantly evolving nature of memories and myths, he is critical of much of the literature which examines nationalism as a phenomenon with specific temporal origins. Instead he argues that national identities emerge in specific instances and then are 'translated over time' (2003: 69). In other words, myths are organic entities, constantly being translated and, at times transmuted, through their everyday usage. Memories do not simply emerge as a result of the linear development of specific historical events. Just as with any discourse, memories are concepts which are constituted within a social setting. Memories are therefore also signifiers whose meaning is always liable to change as social contexts also change.

As has already been stressed, this study does not focus solely on contemporary forms of discourse but instead examines changes in discursive meanings that occur over time. Memories, which represent very significant forms of discourse, are of central importance in this respect. As Bell observes, memories and myths emerge within specific mythscapes. It is therefore important to understand the technologies that can facilitate changes in memory perceptions within these mythscapes.

Top-down and bottom-up memories

Aleida Assmann's (2004) 'four formats of memory' typology provides a clearly defined, conceptual approach that can help to understand such technologies. Assmann differentiates between individual, social, political, and cultural memory. Individual and social memory can be understood as bottom-up memory, that is, memories which are transmitted by and between individuals or groups of individuals. Political and cultural memory, on the other hand, can be best understood as top-down memory, created and transmitted by political and cultural 'elites' (see also Onken 2010 for a discussion of these processes in the Baltic states). In this light collective memories, which can form central elements of group identity, are a mixture of top-down and bottom-up processes (Assmann 1995). Individual memories are augmented, mediated, and framed by the top-down process of political and cultural discursive construction. Without any form of top-down mediation, individual memories would remain fragmented and would not be able to form collective memories. National narratives that emerge through the manipulated use of, among other things, archives, museums, libraries, and public monuments (Brown and Davis-Brown 1998), can therefore be seen as mechanisms which allow the individual to feel a meaningful connection to 'their' particular nation, and 'their' particular in-group.

Nevertheless, the national myths of a particular group have to be able to find a way to be compatible with individual and social memories. Therefore, for top-down memory-myths to be effective, and to be accepted by large numbers of people, they cannot ignore bottom-up pressures, perceptions, memories, and discourses. Importantly, however, bottom-up memories are very susceptible to change, especially when they are transmitted from one individual to another. This is all the more apparent when the person to whom the message is being transmitted was not present at, or not even alive during, the event in question. For this reason a number of authors have noted the impact of 'generational effects' on collective memories (Schuman and Scott 1989; Diuk 2012; see also the ten case-studies in Volkmer 2006). Schuman and Scott (1989:

361), for example, note that although the 'surface memory' of an event is often similar for different age cohorts, the meaning is often different when it is transmitted across generations.

A person who personally experienced and lived through the Second World War may transmit their autobiographical memories of the war to their children. That child, however, will then pass on *historical* memories to their children in a form which has been mutated and framed by that person's own social experiences. Thus, while it may be true that there can be a relatively stable memory of the war, it nonetheless must necessarily change with time generationally. This is a theme which is returned to in Chapter 6, where Russian-speaking attitudes to history are analysed by age group and where the theme of generational changes is explored in some detail.

According to Halbwach's definitions this transmission of memory moves from autobiographical to historical in form. This does not necessarily mean, however, that there is a shift from history to collective memory, or vice versa. Both the veteran of the Second World War, and their child who was born after the war, may well maintain different views of the war according to their personally experienced social contexts. In both instances, however, these memories may well also function as collective memories rather than as history. For the child, the memories may have been altered to fit their own realities. Nevertheless, these memories may still serve to anchor their own personal and group identities.

IDENTITY AND DISCOURSE

The word identity has been used repeatedly up to this point and is clearly a concept which is of central importance to this research. A very straightforward way to understand identity is to see it simply as a process of identification. The Oxford Dictionary (2013), for example, defines the verb and preposition 'to identify with' as, 'associate someone or something closely with; regard as having strong links with'. An identity is therefore an association of one object or concept with another. To take one example, if an individual identifies themselves with being working class he or she is, in effect, saying that the concept of being working class is something that characterises them personally.

Some theorists have seen fit to distinguish between social identity and personal identity (see Laitin 1998: 16). For David Laitin, whose very thorough book set much of the subsequent research agenda into Russian speakers outside Russia, 'identities are inalienable, at least when we are talking about personal identities. Identities are also constructed, when we are talking about social membership' (1998: 15). Laitin is happy to accept a largely primordialist interpretation of personal identities which rests primarily on genetics and specific histories. As a result of this, personal identities are seen as 'real' (1998: 16). Social identities, on the other hand, he defines as 'constructed' and liable to manipulation by external agents.

While Laitin's work is very sophisticated in a number of respects, his division between personal and social identities (that is, between primordial and constructed identities) is an artificial one. It is true, as Laitin asserts, that an individual's personal identity is often codified through legal means. Almost every individual reading this book, for example, will have had their name officially registered in their country of residence or birth. Likewise individuals' nationalities will be recorded in passports that are required for most international travel, for the opening of bank accounts, and as proof that we are who we claim to be. These practices, however, are not genetically preconfigured, or 'real' as Laitin suggests. Instead they are discursive practices that have been determined by the state or other authoritative bodies. As discussed above, the Soviet Union had a rigid system of categorising nationality. The signifier 'nationality' (*natsional'nost'*) was defined with reference to supposedly inherited paternal and maternal genetics. It could quite conceivably have been defined geographically or even ideationally (I think I am an Armenian therefore I am an Armenian), but it was not.

Identities are thus explicitly tied to discursive practices. It is true that there can be extra-discursive limitations placed on our ability to identify with anything. (Our personal identity as superheroes is, alas, hindered by the lack of superpowers such as X-ray vision or the ability to fly.) Just like the nature versus nurture debate, the material versus discourse debate will almost certainly continue to rumble on indefinitely.[1] This book, however, follows Laclau and Mouffe in viewing all objects as discursively constructed. That is not to say that there are no material or primordial elements to discourse. As Laclau and Mouffe are happy to concede, it is only because of the material existence of an object that it can be brought into the discursive realm (1987: 85). Without discourse, however, it is impossible to access the material world. How would it be possible to understand what a mountain is without some humanly imposed form of discursive categorisation? For this reason, on ontological grounds, it is possible to reject the distinction between 'real' and 'constructed' forms of identity.

A clear and workable definition of social identity (which can be treated as coterminous with identity generally) is proposed by Richard Jenkins. According to Jenkins (1996: 5) social identity is 'our understanding of who we are and of who other people are, and, reciprocally, other people's understanding of themselves and of others (which includes us)'. Identity is therefore about associating ourselves with others – people with whom we can identify common attributes, tastes, appearances and so on, either subjectively or objectively. There is, of course, a vast literature on the subject of identity. In its simplest form, however, identity refers to how individuals position themselves in relation to other individuals and to other social positions. In an extremely complicated world, which is impossible to understand fully, identities serve as a simplifying principle that enables us to categorise ourselves and others relatively quickly (Mole 2007: 5). It is therefore possible to see someone who is wearing the shirt of a particular sports team, someone who enjoys a specific genre of music, someone who speaks with a similar accent and so on, and to instantly identify with, or discriminate against, that person.

It goes without saying that the foundations for social identities are numerous, interdependent, and complex. As individuals we are able to choose between, and construct, various overlapping identities that may refer to (among other things) specific or general aspects of our political, economic, and social preferences, our geographical location, our ethnic and racial background, our family and national histories, our gender, and the country name printed in our passports. Nevertheless, each of these areas of identity is liable to be affected by others (Craib 1998). The political preferences of a black woman, or a white man, for example, may be motivated by both her/his gender and her/his race (Gay and Tate 1998; Conlin Casilla and Fowler 2005). Likewise, a homosexual person's (and, equally a heterosexual person's) sexual identity may lead them to adopt additional identities and patterns of behaviour which, on the face of it, have no direct correlation with sexual orientation (Epstein 1992).

From the outset then it is admittedly problematic to attempt to isolate national or ethnic identities from other forms of social identities. Indeed, even within the category of 'national identities', there may exist several layers of national, sub-national, and supra-national identification. A person living in the Highlands of Scotland, for example, may or may not identify themselves with Highland culture, Scottish culture, British culture, or European culture (however they define such things).

THE DISCOURSE-HISTORICAL APPROACH

While it may be difficult to isolate and identify specific forms of identity, in the realms of the media and politics, there often exist well-defined and concrete discourses of nationality and ethnicity. Cultural, media, and political 'elites' are commonly held up as individuals in privileged discursive positions. Unlike the average person who lacks the resources and means for their words and discourses to reach large audiences, these elites are potentially able to make their discourses widely known. It is for this reason that so-called 'elite discourses' are often analysed in order to map out discursive constructions of nations and nationalisms (see, for example, Blackledge 2002). Indeed, the ability for elites to produce such widely disseminated discourses leads de Cilia et al. (1999) to outline the process by which these elites can discursively construct national identities.

The approach taken by de Cilia et al. fits well with the ontological assumptions of this research. The authors do not treat elite discourse as a phenomenon which creates national identities *ex nihilo*. Instead they outline their discourse-historical approach which explains how elites maintain or change existing discourses. This approach is based on an 'intertextual' CDA which does not simply examine discourses in their contemporary form. For de Cilia and his colleagues it is important to also examine previously existing discourses. Therefore they provide four categories of macro-strategies which are employed to change or maintain the content and form of national identities: '(1) constructive strategies; (2) perpetuation and justification strategies; (3) transformation strategies; and (4) dismantling or destructive strategies' (1999: 160).

These macro-strategies are ones which allow an agent to engage with previously articulated discourses in order to ensure that their contemporary articulations enjoy enough congruence with the nodal points of the past. Based largely upon the categories for macro-strategies which have been enumerated by de Cilia et al., this research employs three generalised categories for the potential form of discursive engagement which are explained in more detail below. The three categories proposed for this research are: anti-discourse, integrational discourse, and constructive discourse.

Anti-discourse represents an attempt to delegitimise the preceding discursive relations of an object in order to establish new nodal points, effectively freeing or disentangling a discursive unit from its preceding points of reference. For example, if a monarch holds that their power derives from the God-given 'divine right of kings', and an individual wishes to delegitimise this position, they may well direct their discourse against God, religious belief, the church, or any discursive aspects associated with the legitimacy of the monarch's position. If enough people can be convinced that God does not exist, or that God is not the same deity that the king has portrayed, then this nodal point (although there may well be other important nodal points) is effectively delegitimised.

This allows an agent to alter the discourse of one concept by detaching it from associated concepts.

Integrational discourse, on the other hand, seeks to work within existent discursive relations in order to give legitimacy to another object. A state's decision to go to war, for example, will most likely be framed within the already established and generally accepted prisms of discursive 'reality' that the public can easily understand ('democracy-building', 'holy war', 'security' and so on). In other words, a particular discourse gains its legitimacy by being able to slot into, and become associated with, pre-established nodal points.

Constructive discourse differs from anti-discourse and integrational discourse insomuch as it does not directly address (either positively or negatively) the pre-established nodal points which anchor a given discourse. Instead it indirectly engages with them by seeking to create a whole new nodal point, or series of nodal points, for the object. Naturally, there has to be a certain amount of overlap between this and the other two forms of discursive engagement. The new relations introduced between the object and a new nodal point may well contradict and weaken the previous nodal points but they may also serve to strengthen them.

The categories of anti-discourse and constructive discourse correspond almost exactly with the categories of dismantling and destructive strategies and constructive strategies proposed by de Cilia et al. The authors' categories of transformation strategies and perpetuation and justification strategies, however, have been combined to form the single category of integrational discourse. For de Cilia et al., perpetuation strategies aim to maintain the meanings of given discourses for their continued use in the present. Transformation strategies, on the other hand, attempt to instil new meanings into already established signifiers.

The grounds for amalgamating these two categories are that all discourse is necessarily transformed when reproduced in the present. As previously discussed, discourse needs to be understood as the relations one object has with all the other objects that are discursively connected to it, and which are located in a social setting. This means that when the linguistic signifier 'king' is used today, the discursive relations of this sign are different from what they were a thousand years ago, and even twenty years ago. Therefore, perpetuation and justification strategies are simultaneously transformation strategies. Social contexts change with time and so, therefore, do discourses. Explicit attempts to transform discursive meanings can also be captured within the categories of integrational and anti-discourse. This is because attempts to transform the meaning of a particular signifier are achieved by changing the relations of that signifier with other, associated discourses.

Othering

In the literature on identity formation the process of othering has assumed an increasingly prominent position. According to Laclau and Mouffe (1985: 111), the formation of a meaningful group identity is almost impossible without some reference to an external group, or an 'other'. This is because there are innumerable differences that exist without any given group. For example, any two 'Latvians' will actually be distinct along thousands of identity and behavioural axes. Although they may well consider themselves to be part of the same group they almost certainly will have different interests, different tastes, different modes of thinking, come from different socio-economic backgrounds, and can be separated by an infinite number of differences.

In order to further elaborate on this point Laclau and Mouffe (1985) introduce the concept of *the logic of equivalence*. The logic of equivalence refers to a process whereby diverse individuals are discursively portrayed as similar to one another, not because of actual similarities, but because they are equally different from an external group. For example an individual can say that he or she is 'British' (whatever that might mean) because he/she is not French. For Howarth and Stavrakakis the logic of equivalence establishes 'equivalential identities that express a pure negation of a discursive system' (Howarth and Stavrakakis 2000: 11); every Frenchman is equally different from 'us' *because* he is French. Rather than a positive identification this is a negative one which relies upon the othering of a specific out-group.

According to Laclau (1995) the most effective way of constructing this system of equivalential identities is to suggest an externality that is not simply representative of another difference, but a real existential threat to (and therefore a negation of) one's own internal identity. The logic of equivalence therefore seeks to place people neatly on either side of a discursively created divide that then creates contingent frontiers separating group identities. It is for this reason that it can be very difficult to integrate certain group identities. As the following chapter demonstrates, Latvian identity discourses are largely premised on the depiction of Russians and Russian speakers as a real threat to Latvian identity.

Naturally, in order to create an image of an external threat it is necessary to create an overly simplified depiction of the 'other'. In the case of Latvians who wish to portray Russia and Russians as an inherent threat to their own identity, there is the problem that members of the out-group are also extremely diverse. Just as no two Latvians are actually the same, so too are no two Russian speakers entirely similar. For this reason Laclau notes how the diversity of the out-group is simplified into a 'particular' (1995: 147–50). In other words a specific representation of Russians/Russian-speakers is produced and discursively constructed which is used to signify *all* Russians/Russian-speakers.

In order to understand contemporary Russian-speaking discourse it is vital, therefore, to take stock of the importance that particularised representations of Russian-speakers play in the identity formation of 'Latvians'. It is argued, through the course of this book, that it is very difficult for Russian speakers to find a legitimate place within Latvian discourses because the process of othering is central to the formation of Latvian identity in the first instance.

MEMORY, DISCOURSE, AND RUSSIAN SPEAKERS

As has already been established, this book pays a great deal of attention, not only to Russian-speaking discourses, but also to Latvian and to Russian (*rossiiskii*)[2] discourses. Each node of Brubaker's triadic nexus (nationalising states, national minorities, and external homelands) may be said to represent specific, although overlapping, mythscapes. Top-down articulations of political memory are markedly different in Latvia compared to Russia (as demonstrated most clearly in Chapters 3, 6, and 8). Top-down projections of cultural memory, as manifested in the popular media, also vary greatly in the respective Latvian and Russian mythscapes. However, Russian speakers can be said to inhabit both mythscapes in some measure. As shown in subsequent chapters, Latvia's Russian speakers often consume Russian (*rossiiskii*) TV and media products. Russian speakers are therefore exposed to the top-down cultural and political memory articulations which are produced in the Russian Federation. As permanent residents of Latvia, however, they are also exposed to the Latvian mythscape.

These mythscapes, it is important to note, are not confined to the realms of media production. There are also a number of other important sites which are potentially important spaces for discursive construction. Brown and Davis-Brown (1998: 22), for example, note that archives, libraries, and museums also comprise an important part of cultivating a shared sense of collective memory. Such institutions are highly political because of their reliance on external funding, but also because of the subtle and mostly latent practices that allow any given archive to function. The role of the state in determining these practices can affect, sometimes rather expressly, who is allowed access to specific materials, how the archives are organised and labelled, which materials are collected and which are not.

In Latvia specific academic attention has therefore been paid to the politicised role of museums (Velmet 2011; Ķencis and Kuutma 2011) and monuments (Kruk 2009; Muižnieks and Zelče 2012) as sites of memory creation. While monuments have not been as politicised in Latvia as in Estonia (see Burch and Smith 2007; Smith 2008; Brüggemann and Kasekamp 2008; Ehala 2009), they nonetheless serve as important markers of identity. In the independence era Soviet monuments were quickly removed from public locations, and new statues were erected which fitted in with the officially articulated historical narratives of the time. A statue to Kārlis Ulmanis, Latvia's pre-war 'benign' dictator, which was erected in 2003 in the centre of Riga, is one good example of this process. While the funding for the Ulmanis statue came largely from private donations, permission to erect the monument was still required from Riga's municipal government (Arklina 2001). The monument was therefore only permitted because it was congruent with the memory narratives of the Latvian state.

These mnemonic and discursive practices surrounding museums, monuments, and archives constitute a significant element of the Latvian mythscape. Significantly it is a mythscape that Latvia's Russian speakers are also part of. Education policies and officially sponsored programmes of historical instruction are also key elements of this memory landscape. Educational instruction is often viewed as a centrally important method of creating collective memories and inculcating official discourses into popular consciousness (Karahassan and Zembylas 2006: 701; Crawford and Foster 2007: 8). In Latvia, as is shown in later chapters, education policy has proven to be a contentious issue. Again, it has meant that Russian speakers, or at least the younger generations of Russian speakers, have direct experience of officially proscribed historical narratives of Latvia's past, which they must learn in order to meet the requirements of the scholastic curriculum.

In the subsequent chapters, therefore, much attention is paid to an analysis of various discourses and also to a range of mnemonic and discursive practices. A number of methods have been employed in order to examine a wide range of discursive sites, and to take account of both top-down and bottom-up process of discursive change. Russian-language media discourses are examined in some detail in Chapter 4. Additionally, focus group interviews, survey data, and 'elite' interviews with Latvian politicians are all employed within a triangulated framework to explore the discursive elements of contemporary Russian-speaking identity in Latvia. The influence of the Latvian hegemonic order on Russian-speaking identities is also extensively examined, as well as the influence of the Russian (*rossiiskii*) hegemonic order.

In light of the historical approach, outlined above, this research starts by examining the emergence of Latvia's current hegemonic order in the late and post-Soviet periods. The discourses that helped to delegitimise Soviet rule will be examined as well as their subsequent impact on the discursive construction of Latvian identities. This will then be examined from the perspective of Russian-speaking identities.

NOTES

1. See, for example, the exchange between Geras (1987) and Laclau and Mouffe (1987).
2. The Russian word *rossiiskii* is used here and throughout this research to indicate that a concept is tied not culturally and ethnically to Russia, but rather politically and territorially. In Russian *rossiiskii* is an adjective which is commonly used to refer to nouns associated with the Russian Federation. *Russkii*, on the other hand, indicates a cultural or ethnic connection with Russia (see also Glossary). This point is of crucial importance in Chapter 8 where the 'Rossiisification' (as opposed to 'Russification') of Russian compatriots is discussed.

Latvian State and Nation-Building

Mīli tēvu, mīli māti,	Love your father, love your mother,
Vairāk mīli savu tautu!	Love your nation more!
Nomirs tēvs, nomirs māte,	Father will die, mother will die,
Paliks tauta paglābēja	The nation, our saviour, will remain
	(Rainis, *Daugava*)

'ORGANIC CRISIS' AND THE COLLAPSE OF THE SOVIET UNION

In certain periods of time discursive meanings appear to be particularly stable. That is not to say that discursive change does not occur. Rather, when it does occur it proceeds gradually and largely imperceptibly. In other periods of time, however, meanings undergo seismic changes. In order to understand why certain eras are more conducive to discursive change than others this research employs Gramsci's notion of 'organic crisis'. According to Gramsci, in periods when the political power of the ruling classes is in decline, there is an opportunity for another hegemonic bloc to emerge:

> A crisis occurs, sometimes lasting for decades. This exceptional duration means that incurable structural contradictions have revealed themselves (reached maturity) and that, despite this, the political forces which are struggling to conserve and defend the existing structure itself are making every effort to cure them, within certain limits, and to overcome them. These incessant and persistent efforts . . . form the terrain of the 'conjunctural' and it is upon this terrain that the forces of opposition organise. (1971: 178)

As discussed above, the work of Gramsci has been key in developing our understanding of how ruling orders are sustained by a mixture of political and cultural hegemony. As Althusser (2008) explains, ruling elites wield power not only through the use of 'repressive state apparatuses' (the police, the army and so on), but also by employing 'ideological state apparatuses' (religion, education, media, families and so on). In essence, most ruling orders will need to secure ideological, or discursive, legitimisation in order to sustain their rule.

This means that once a set of 'incurable structural conditions' starts to diminish the power of the ruling hegemony there are also extraordinary opportunities to create new discursive meanings. The ruling hegemony's grip over education, media and other ideological state apparatuses is weakened. Space is therefore opened up for alternative hegemonic blocs to use the conditions of this organic crisis for their own benefit, and to create alternative discourses and meanings to the ones that have been kept stable by the existing political order.

This description of organic crisis seems to fit almost perfectly the demise of the Soviet hegemony from the mid/late 1980s up to its dramatic collapse in 1991. There has been much debate as to the reasons for the collapse of the Soviet Union, with arguments being based on, among other things, economic decline (Wallander 2003), nationalism (Fowkes 1997), the key agency of Gorbachev (Brown 1996), and external pressures from international actors and countries (Wohlforth 1994). Much time has therefore been devoted to an analysis of both the structural and agential conditions leading to the organic crisis of the USSR.

Whatever the reasons for the regime's collapse, it is clear that this period of time was extraordinary for the political, social, and economic changes that occurred with such rapidity. Significantly, the demise of the Soviet regime left room for a new hegemony to emerge. Essentially this meant that many of the nodal points securing the legitimacy and power of the ruling classes were eroded. By the mid-late 1980s, discourses of 'world revolution', 'communism', 'anti-capitalism', 'internationalism', and the many other legitimising nodal points of the Soviet order were becoming less able to provide legitimacy to the ruling polity. There was therefore a space for new, or reconfigured, ideologies and discourses to be articulated by the groups who wished to create their own hegemonic bloc, and who wished to assume power.

Within the historical context of the perestroika period, the decisions made at this time will have had a lasting impact on subsequent discursive formations in post-Soviet, independent Latvia. Of course, many discourses will have survived this organic crisis, and will have continued with relatively little disruption or change. Many will have had their genesis long before the Soviet era. Nevertheless, in order to understand contemporary discourses and identity politics in Latvia, the late Soviet era must be seen as a key period of concern. It was during this time that the Soviet regime dramatically started to lose its discursive legitimacy. In contradistinction, it was in this period of time that the now-prevailing hegemony of the Latvian state started to gain its discursive legitimacy. It was therefore an era wherein rapid discursive change was made possible as a result of the declining fortunes of one hegemonic bloc, and the rising fortunes of another. As this chapter goes on to explain, in the perestroika period, political and cultural elites were able to articulate specific programmes and to outline new forms of Latvian identity. Because the discourses of this time were essential in forming a new hegemony, new nodal points were therefore created.

From the perspective of contemporary, Russian-speaking discourse the importance of this period is clear. As outlined above, discursive agents, if they wish to engage with discursive meanings, will have to do so through the use of either anti-, integrational, or constructive discursive strategies. For Russian speakers (indeed for any individual or group of individuals) who are now resident within a relatively new hegemonic order, it is difficult to ignore the discursive constructions that have been propagated by this self-same order. As demonstrated in this chapter, the topics of Russian-speakers, Russia, (de)Russification, and (de)Sovietisation have often been at the centre of contemporary Latvian identity discourses, and at the centre of a number of significant Latvian state policies. In order for Russian speakers in contemporary Latvia to create meaningful identities for themselves, these discursive relations of the recent past are vitally important as a reference, as a support, and as a target to destroy. This chapter therefore pays specific attention to the forms of discourse that emerged in the late Soviet period, and how the Latvian hegemonic order was established. In later chapters focus is placed on how Latvia's Russian speakers currently relate to these various discourses, and how they have affected the course of contemporary Russian-speaking identities.

The emergence of Latvia's new political order

In many ways it was Mikhail Gorbachev's *perestroika* (restructuring) programme that opened up the political field for alternative and oppositional voices to emerge. While Gorbachev did not seek fundamentally to overhaul the Soviet system, he was nevertheless aware of the need for change, famously noting in 1985 that 'we can't go on living like this' (Till 2011). Arguably one of the most significant policies adopted by Gorbachev was that of *glasnost'* (openness). Being a committed socialist, Gorbachev thought that the Soviet system could be reinvigorated through the introduction of a limited degree of democratisation (*demokratizatsiia*), and through the relative easing of censorship.

Before the introduction of perestroika, Soviet hegemony had been maintained through recourse to a mixture of coercive and discursive practices. Discursively the regime went to great lengths to limit and censor popular discourse (see Hopkins 1970). At the same time, the state exerted coercive control by employing a vast network of security and police personnel whose actions were closely intertwined with the bureaucratic structures of the Soviet system. Tight ideological and coercive controls have led a number of commentators to see the Soviet Union as totalitarian (Arendt 1951; Friedrich and Brzezinski 1966; Karklins 1994b). Of course, the Brezhnev years can hardly be categorised as totalitarian in the same way that the years of Stalin's reign can. In reality the coercive force officially sanctioned within the Soviet Union had been diminishing from the time of its horrific apex during Stalin's Great Terror. Nevertheless, as Vladimir Shlapentokh notes, the subsequent Soviet elites under Khrushchev, Brezhnev, and even Gorbachev shared many of the coercive controls practised under Stalin (2001: 12). As a result they were still able to control most of the popularly disseminated discourses through rigid control of the media and through the threat of punitive penalties (although not as appallingly as under Stalin's reign).[1]

In formulating his theories of hegemony, Gramsci (1971: 57) noted that 'The supremacy of a social group manifests itself in two ways, as "domination" and as "intellectual and moral leadership".' It was Gorbachev's aim to increase the *moral* legitimacy of the Soviet regime which prompted him to introduce *glasnost'*. Essentially Gorbachev thought that it would be possible to reduce the coercive domination of Soviet rule and in its place increase the regime's moral leadership.

This policy of openness, however, had a number of unintended consequences for Gorbachev and his fellow reformers. Karklins (1994b), for example, notes how the policy of *glasnost'* redefined official Soviet ideology 'in a way that undermined its claim on a monopoly of truth'. This meant that people were made aware of their ability to utilise and produce language publicly in a much more open way than had previously been possible under a more authoritarian system of rule. Consequently, the authority of the Communist Party was undermined as people began to question and debate, among other things, the history of Stalinism, the nationalities question, and even the activities of the party (Tolz 1995: 94), all of which turned out to be important nodal points for the regime. For Karklins, totalitarian regimes (she argues that it is still appropriate to label the Soviet regime totalitarian at the time when Gorbachev became general secretary), rely not only on the use of harsh punitive measures, but also on the control over ideological production.

In hindsight it is perhaps not surprising that the policy of *glasnost'* would lead to huge shifts in political discourse and participation. Throughout the immense expanse of the Soviet Union, the perestroika period soon witnessed the formation of numerous political and social movements. These included organisations professing a desire to 'democratise' the Soviet Union, notably the 'popular' movements in the Baltic states led by *Sajūdis* (the Movement) in Lithuania,[2] *Latvijas Tautas Fronte* (the Popular Front of Latvia) in Latvia, and *Rahvarinne* (the Popular Front) in Estonia.

If full national independence for the Baltic countries was the long-term goal for these organisations then they had the sense to realise that the structural conditions were not, at the beginning of Gorbachev's reforms, conducive to such demands. While the introduction of *glasnost'* brought with it new political opportunities, it did not mean that all discursive limitations were lifted. The popular fronts understood very well that they still needed to work within a number of extant discursive frameworks. In line with Gorbachev's perestroika programme, 'democratisation' (*demokratizatsiia*), as well as environmental, historical, and cultural campaigning, were the main platforms initially available for the emerging hegemonic demands of the popular front movements. This, however, soon led to new opportunities as the organic crisis of the Soviet Union revealed itself with much more rapidity than the vast majority of people expected.

As Soviet control started to unravel, outright nationalism (that is, the demands for national self-determination based on particular constructed concepts of the nation) emerged as a unifying theme for the popular fronts (Karklins 1994a; Jubulis 2001; Tuminez 2003). Democratisation had revealed itself to be a relatively unifying hegemonic pole of attraction. Indeed, it was able to unite and coordinate the actions of thousands of individuals against the existing political order. Nevertheless, nationalism proved a far more mobilising and powerful tool. This is perhaps because, as Jubulis (2001: 198) states, 'nationalism serves the *collective* interests of the nation, while liberal democracy is concerned with *individual* rights and interests'. Nationalism is, by definition, a movement or ideology that seeks to create a cohesive group out of disparate individuals. In order to create a hegemonic bloc, nationalism was therefore essential as it allowed individuals to see themselves as *collectively* opposed to the Soviet order. It therefore allowed 'Latvians' to be framed as equivalently different from Soviets, and, by extension, from Russians.

The structural reasons for nationalism's ability to become such a consolidating factor in the emergence of new hegemonic orders can also be traced to many of the historical discourses and practices of the Soviet Union. Soviet practices, including the policy of *korenizatsiia* (the use of local cadres in the ranks of the Communist Party), and the Soviet federal system of union republics, maintained clear distinctions between the officially recognised Soviet nations and therefore nationalities (see Agarin 2010). For this reason it is reasonable to challenge Hiden and Salmon's claim that 'In the years between 1945 and 1985 the Soviet Union came closer than any past rulers to extinguishing the national identities of the Estonian, Latvian and Lithuanian peoples' (1994: 126). Instead, as Tuminez notes, Soviet policies were able to consolidate nationalist and ethnic identities, particularly at the level of the separate republics of the USSR. For Tuminez (2003: 96) it was these Soviet republics that 'evolved into building blocks for the possible – but certainly not inevitable – attainment of separate states in the future'.

From this discussion it should be clear that the perestroika period was a crucial time in terms of the emergence of new hegemonic orders. In Latvia this period, from the mid-to-late 1980s up to the early 1990s, is most commonly referred to as *Atmoda*: the Awakening.[3] It is referred to as an awakening in the primordial sense that 'the nation' is perceived as a real and historically persistent entity which was simply sleeping or repressed. While this research rejects many of the assumptions of primordialism, from a constructivist point of view this period is no less significant.

As enumerated above, this research analyses discourse from a historical perspective. That is to say that it does not examine discourses as wholly contemporary constructions. Instead discursive meanings have complex histories which change through time. As a consequence, if agents wish to create new identities and new discourses in the present they will have to engage with the previously articulated meanings of the past. The perestroika period must be seen as a crucial historical time in this respect. Discourses were able to change much more significantly than in other periods of relative political and social stability. For this reason the remainder of this chapter examines a number of relevant discursive tropes that emerged during and immediately after the perestroika reform period.

This historical analysis then forms the basis of the contemporary analysis of Russian-speaking discourse which is developed in later chapters. By mapping out how Latvia's post-Soviet nation and state building have progressed it is also possible to evaluate the relationships between the discourses of the *Atmoda* period and more contemporaneous discourses.

Focusing on national identities, this chapter pays attention to how the Latvian state became conceptualised and institutionalised during the period of *Atmoda*. It also examines how the Latvian nation was imagined and who was included or excluded from this construct. This examination is based on previously conducted research into Latvia's post-Soviet nation-building, as well as discourse analysis of the Popular Front of Latvia's (PFL) official publication *Atmoda*.

THE POPULAR FRONT OF LATVIA: SETTING THE AGENDA FOR LATVIAN NATION-BUILDING?

It has often been noted that the initial rhetoric of the Popular Front of Latvia was far more conciliatory and inclusionary in relation to the country's non-Latvian inhabitants than in the years after independence had been regained (Antane and Tsilevich 1999: 83). Mara Lazda (2009: 519), for example, writes of the PFL: 'rather than an exclusively "ethno-nationalist" force, the Latvian movement of 1989 was equally, perhaps even more importantly, a transethnic and transnational movement that informed the reestablishment of democratic institutions after 1989'. As the above discussion of organic crisis suggests, the relatively inclusive discourses of the PFL would make sense when contextualised within the structural realities of the time. Had the Popular Front initially outlined a citizenship policy based on the principles of legal continuity or Soviet occupation then it is unlikely that either the Communist Party organs, or Gorbachev himself, would have tolerated the activities of the PFL, thereby reducing their power to operate in the public space. Instead, the Popular Front was forced to adhere to certain discursive positions (at least publically) in order to maintain a relatively high degree of conformity with the reigning hegemonic order. It was only when it was becoming clear that the Soviet Union's hegemonic position was in irreversible decline that more overtly nationalistic discourses were able to be created and publicly articulated.

There has, however, actually been very little concrete analysis of evolving PFL discourses relating to non-Latvians, especially Russians and Russian speakers. This deficiency is all the more striking when consideration is given to the importance of creating new nodal points in times of organic crisis such as those seen towards the end of the Soviet era. The declining fortunes of the Soviet regime meant that new discourses could increasingly take centre stage, and that these discourses would form the core of new hegemonic orders, and therefore national identities, within Latvia. Moreover, because it was in this period of time that new hegemonies were being created, the legitimacy of these new hegemonies would be tied to the nodal points of this time for many years to come. Thus, with the emergence of any hegemonic order there are certain logics inherent within their position which become central to their subsequent legitimacy and therefore power. If we wish to understand contemporary, minority discourses of Russian-speakers it is therefore essential first to understand how majority discourses have evolved, and it is especially important to examine how they evolved during a time of organic crisis.

For this reason editions of the PFL's official newspaper *Atmoda* were analysed for two six-month periods running from January 1989 to June 1989 and then from January 1990 to June 1990. Included in this analysis were also two editions of *Atmoda* from December 1989 – the first two editions of the publication. The analysis of two separate six-month time periods, first in 1989, and then in 1990, was chosen to facilitate an analysis of the changing position of the various discourses employed by the Popular Front. As the analysis shows, the structural conditions of 1989 turned out to be quite different from 1990 as the Popular Front was becoming increasingly assertive and increasingly able to push aside previously sacrosanct Soviet discourses (nodal points).

One of the central goals of this analysis was to facilitate comparison with more contemporary discourse. Specifically it was important to see the extent by which the discourses of the PFL were in fact more inclusive than in the subsequent years of Latvian independence. Was it simply a case that the rhetoric of key Latvian politicians changed as the structural conditions opened up for them, or were many of the nation and state-building discourses, outlined above, evident in some form even at this early stage? Both the Latvian and Russian-language versions of *Atmoda* were examined. Any differences in their content were noted, and particular attention was paid to any articles which discussed issues relating to national identity, the Latvian state, and the role of non-Latvians in the political vision of the PFL. Contrary to expectation, even in this pre-independence period, relatively exclusionary discourses were being produced and propagated by the Popular Front. Discursive strategies often privileged ethnic Latvians as the core nation and legitimate bearers of statehood. As the latter part of this chapter documents, these discourses would be of central importance to Latvian state and nation-building in the post-Soviet era.

The nation

One of the most striking features of the *Atmoda* articles was how nationality was treated. In Latvian there are two words which can be translated into the English 'nation': *tauta* and *nācija*. Very often (although not always) *nācija* corresponds to the meaning of nation which is political, civic, economic, or geographical. Therefore, the Latvian *nācija* would most commonly refer to the geographical territory of Latvia and to all of the people resident therein. *Tauta*, on the other hand, has more of a cultural, or ethnic, connotation and corresponds more closely with the Russian *narod*. As such, the Latvian *tauta* generally refers to a construct which signifies people of Latvian ethnic origin.

In *Atmoda*, *tauta* was used almost exclusively to refer to ethnic Latvians. In fact a number of articles in *Atmoda* were at pains to point out the distinctness of the Latvian and Russian *tautas*. Interestingly this was most apparent in articles which dealt with the topic of Russians and their role in the political struggles of the time. One article entitled 'To the Russian community on the problems of Russians', which did not appear in the Latvian language edition, states:

> Our nation (*narod*) in this land is a guest and our interventions can only be to help the Latvian nation (*narod*) in its process of self-determination. Moreover, this help can only be offered when the Latvians agree to accept it. We have no moral right to intrude, we can only offer help. Whether they accept or decline this is up to the Latvian nation (*narod*) itself and its leaders. (Russian-language version of *Atmoda* 19 May 1989)

It is clear that the Latvian *tauta/narod* is conceived as a purely 'Latvian' construct with which members of the constructed 'Russian *narod*' have no inherent right to interfere. In fact, there were a number of articles which also appeared exclusively in the Russian-language version of *Atmoda* that echoed similar sentiments. Generally the content of the Latvian-language and Russian-language versions of *Atmoda* was almost identical with accurate translations of the Latvian articles being reproduced in the Russian-language edition. In the rare cases when articles were published solely in the Russian-language edition they were almost exclusively directed towards the roles that Russian speakers, or representatives of the Russian *narod*, were expected to fulfil. One such article that was not published in Latvian, goes to great lengths to explain that the duty of Russians in Latvia was to represent 'our' *narod*, that is, the Russian nation: 'We need to take into consideration the views and perspectives of Russians in Russia, in Asia, and in the Baltic. Then when we combine these things we can understand . . . our mission as representatives of our nation (*narod*).' (Russian-language version of *Atmoda* 20 February 1989)

In another article, which again appeared exclusively in the Russian-language edition, an Old Believer discusses the upcoming celebrations for the religious holiday *Paskha* (the Old Believer and Russian Orthodox Easter):

> For me, the Latvian, the Russian, the Jew – he who knows his history and culture, and who knows and respects his traditions, prepares himself to respect other cultures, especially if we are talking about the culture and traditions of the titular nation (*titul'nyi narod*).
>
> Today people are more or less starting to understand that there are not 'good' and 'bad' nations. *However, all nations (narody) are different.* The differences may be more or less significant, but they are always there – in mentality, understanding, temperament etc. Only non-scientific pedagogical ideas could lead to an attempt to organise under one roof the teaching of two psychologically dissimilar groups of pupils. (Russian-language version of *Atmoda* 24 April 1989, emphasis added)

It is evident, therefore, that within the discourses of *Atmoda*, Russians in Latvia were not perceived as an integral part of the Latvian nation, but rather as an appendage to it; perhaps tolerated and respected, but certainly distinct. 'Russians' had a duty to make sure that 'Latvians' had ample opportunity to preserve 'their' culture without interfering in any way.

In fairness to the Popular Front, it is important to point out that there was also a general desire to respect Russian, and other non-Latvian, cultures and groups. In one article outlining their programme for the elections to the Latvian Supreme Soviet in 1990, the Popular Front declares that:

> The Supreme Soviet must pass laws that would guarantee all national groups
> • The rights and opportunities to receive education in their native language.
> • Full participation in the forming of national opinion, by ensuring the rights of national groups and their representatives the right to participate in the parliamentary commission and in the work of the committees. (*Atmoda* 13 February 1990)

Indeed, there was a great deal of attention paid to quelling excessive xenophobia or anti-Russian sentiment: 'Dear parents! Do not sow hate among your children for those boys and girls who in the playground speak a different language than you choose to speak at home' (*Atmoda* 6

March 1989). Moreover, the PFL often called for unity among different ethnic groups for the united aims of achieving, initially, an autonomous Latvia within a Soviet federal framework, and then later, an independent Latvia:

> We categorically condemn efforts to stoke up the 'refuge syndrome' in our society and invite all people of all nationalities (*tautība*) who support the idea of an independent Latvia to join forces for the realisation of this goal.
> The PFL is against the use of any national criteria with which to determine property rights, income distribution, and the right to be accepted for leading positions in various spheres. (*Atmoda* 6 March 1990)

Nevertheless, while *Atmoda* often called upon Russians and other non-Latvians for support, and even talked of ensuring that their national and human rights were protected, it was still apparent that the Latvian *tauta* was to assume the leading position in the newly emerging hierarchy that was being envisaged. Among the most significant signifiers of this hierarchy were the words *pamatnācija* and *pamattauta* – the core nation,[4] which were employed time and time again.

> Ethnic relations often complicate the democratic order in post-colonial states. However, the future will require the reversal of colonially instigated unfairness, in order for the core nation (*pamattauta*) to regain its fair and leading position in Latvia. This equality can be gained through so-called POSITIVE DISCRIMINATION. (*Atmoda* 9 January 1990)

This is a significant discursive strategy that seeks to create a well-defined hegemonic group that can be contrasted to peripheral nations such as Russians and other non-Latvians. The discursive use of the concept of the 'core nation', therefore, has the inevitable effect of differentiating between 'us' (the Latvians) and 'them' (the non-Latvians, especially Russians). On the other hand, however, there is also a call for a measure of inter-ethnic political cooperation between the different ethnic groups. For example, the author goes on to say:

> Ideally of course there would be large, interethnic parties [in an independent Latvia]. If, however, there are minority parties then it is better to create them along geographical or religious lines. This would be similar to the status of minority politics in independent

Latvia where there was observed a high degree of loyalty towards the state among Russian minorities.

Therefore, while there are signs of the more inclusionary strategy of attempting to co-opt the Russian-speaking minority into Latvian political life, it is nevertheless clear that there is a distinct division between the different communities in Latvia, and that the 'core nation' should be comprised of 'the Latvians'. In fact, as time progressed, the creation and/or maintenance of distinct cultural boundaries between ethnic groups emerged as a central strategy of the Popular Front. In 1990 this was increasingly evidenced in *Atmoda*'s discussions of a future citizenship law for Latvia. As detailed below, the citizenship laws which were passed following the country's reacquisition of independence divided the country's inhabitants between citizens and non-citizens, largely signifying a general division between Latvians and non-Latvians. Even in *Atmoda*, however, the necessity of creating cultural boundaries is explicitly set out:

> We must pass a citizenship law which accords with preserving the interests of the Latvian nation (*latviešu nācija*). Nationalism is not intended to discriminate against other people, but rather as a cultural principle – an external boundary to protect you from others, and an internal boundary to protect others from you. Without boundaries it is not at all possible to have (separate!) interaction of national cultures. (*Atmoda* 12 June 1990)

For Castles and Davidson, rigidly defined and exclusive identities of the type seen above are essential if a culturally defined nation is to find congruence within a political entity. As the authors state: 'porous boundaries and multiple identities undermine ideas of cultural belonging as a necessary accompaniment to political membership' (2000: viii). It would seem that even within the PFL this need for concrete boundaries was understood, even when the organisation wanted simultaneously to engage with and attract the support of non-Latvians.

Learning to work with, or against, Soviet discourses

When analysing the discourses of the perestroika period it is vitally important to consider the influence of the Soviet structures and discourses that informed PFL strategies and understandings of the time. For example, the word *pamattauta* itself can be rendered into Russian as *korennaia natsiia* (Literally: root nation) and can be seen as analogous with the term 'titular nation'. This was a commonly employed term in the Soviet Union used to refer to the ethnic groups after which the union republics, autonomous republics, autonomous *oblasti*, and autonomous *okruga* were named. For example, in the Latvian Soviet Socialist Republic, 'Latvians' were the titular (or root) nation: in the Chechen–Ingush Autonomous Soviet Socialist Republic – 'Chechens' and 'Ingushians' and so on.

This Soviet practice of rigidly defining nationality (*natsional'nost'*), and of insisting that each territory was inhabited by a core nation, has led a number of commentators to see the Soviet Union as more of a nation-builder than a nation-killer (see for example Kaiser 1997; Agarin 2010: 45–52). In this context the repeated use of the linguistic signifier *pamattauta/pamatnācija* makes historical sense, as it is a plea to justify a new order on the basis of understandings from the (then) current one.

Indeed, in the earlier editions of *Atmoda* that were analysed, a number of the arguments for greater Latvian autonomy were contextualised within existing Soviet norms and discursive practices. Lenin was often cited in these earlier editions in order to justify and legitimise the PFL position. Likewise the Soviet Union's nationality policies were often referred to in order to bolster the legitimacy of the Popular Front's claims to greater freedom and autonomy for the Latvian nation:

> According to the constitution of the USSR and according to the 1922 Union Agreement, and by juridical practice, the Latvian SSR is a national state. What does that mean? What is the role of the Latvian nation (*nācija*) in this state? Is this role simply that Latvians have 'given their name' to the republic?
>
> In truth the role of the Latvian nation (*nācija*) in Latvia's statehood is as the bearer or subject of statehood. It was no accident that Lenin viewed the genesis of the nation (*nācija*) in connection with the process of forming national statehood. The nation (*nācija*) is the sovereign ethnos, in other words the ethnos is the bearer of statehood. (*Atmoda* 20 March 1989)

One article even created a fictional 'interview with V. I. Lenin' in order to show that Lenin would have supported the goals of the Popular Front over those of Interfront – the pro-Soviet, reactionary communist movement which opposed the activities of the PFL (*Atmoda* 24 April 1989).

Earlier three main categories for macro-level discursive engagement were enumerated: *anti-discourse, integrational discourse, and constructive discourse*. In these earlier *Atmoda* articles it would appear that integrational discourse was the most commonly utilised discursive strategy.

In order for the Baltic popular front movements to be able to wield any effective power they understood the necessity of initially fitting their demands within Mikhail Gorbachev's ambitious and newly emerging programmes of *perestroika* and *demokratizatsiia* (see above). Hence the PFL initially argued 'for the Latvian SSR's development only within the USSR' (*Atmoda* 16 January 1989).

With these structural conditions in mind it is possible to understand how the linguistic units *pamattauta* and *pamatnācija* emerged as essential nodal points which allowed PFL discourse to be integrated and find legitimacy within the Soviet hegemony of the period.

Because of the Soviet Union's contradictory nationalities policies (see Martin 2001; Agarin 2010), it was possible to use these concepts and integrate them within Soviet discursive practice. At the same time, Gorbachev's call for greater democratisation facilitated a concurrent emphasis on respecting all peoples/nations and individuals. This emphasis on democratisation therefore also led to the PFL strategy of discursively attempting to separate 'Russian-speakers' from entanglement with the discursive understandings of Communism, the Communist Party, and the Interfront movements:

> A number of anxious and indignant Latvians ask themselves and us: are the views and goals of our fellow Russian citizens truly expressed openly in [the Interfront] congress? It is sad that Latvia's ethnic Russian inhabitants have become victims of this event. *Our duty today is to fight for the honour of the many thousands of people for whom members of this small group arbitrarily spoke. These people represent only their own selfish interests.* (*Atmoda* 23 January 1989, emphasis added)

This discursive strategy can be seen as a positive one in that it allows space for more positive depictions of Russians and other non-Latvians in Latvia. The call to 'not let our prejudices oversimplify all of these diverse people into one generalised "enemy image"' (*Atmoda* 16 December 1988), for example, can be seen as a positive attempt to refrain from constructing an external 'other' with which to cement an internally unified 'us'. On the other hand, there is also a political expediency which lies beneath the surface of this strategy. It can also be viewed, for example, as part of an attempt to break up, and therefore lessen the power of, the externalised hegemonic grouping of Russian-speakers: 'We are witnesses to the bankruptcy of the chauvinistic term "Russian-speaking inhabitants" which levels, and moreover, humiliates all the nations (*tautas*) who live in Latvia and who do not speak Latvian' (*Atmoda* 6 January 1989).

In Chapter 4 focus is placed on how various representatives of the so-called Russian-speaking community have attempted, with some success, to unite various (constructed) ethnic groups into a unified community of 'Russian-speakers'. However, for the PFL such unification could have had a number of adverse effects on their attempts to form a political and cultural hegemony. It is not difficult to see the potential problem of facing a well-defined group comprised of almost 50 per cent of the total population, as opposed to a number of smaller groups. Just as Gramsci understood, in order to gain power it is necessary to enjoy some form of hegemony. The threat of a well-defined, non-porous hegemonic bloc comprised of 'Russian-speakers' was evidently a serious concern for the Popular Front. Divide and rule tactics were therefore far more preferable as the Popular Front attempted to ensure that 'Russian-speakers' were subdivided into smaller, national groups.

For this reason throughout 1990 *Atmoda* published a series of features, each focusing on a separate 'national minority in Latvia': Jews, Estonians, Crimean Tatars, Ukrainians, Lithuanians, and Armenians were all covered in the periods of analysis. Clearly the goal of the PFL was to highlight the distinct presence of a number of nations (*tautas*) that were separate from the Russian nation. In this regard the Popular Front discourse was aided by the ambiguities and paradoxes of Soviet nationalities policies. The PFL were able to seize upon the doctrines of Lenin on nationalities which upheld the ideas of separate nations and nationalities, for example his belief in 'the Right of Nations to Self-Determination' (Lenin 1972). This was a highly effective integrational discursive strategy which was used to contextualise contemporary discourse within the existing nodal points of the extant Soviet hegemony. At the same time, however, the Popular Front also selectively employed anti-discursive strategies. Soviet discourses of internationalism, for example, were targeted by *Atmoda*:

> Latvians have become a minority in their own country . . . a result of the systematic realisation of Stalin and Brezhnev's national policy, which aimed to create a Soviet nation (*tauta*) with one language – Russian. In other words the spirit of Russification has been cultivated and cannily hidden behind the words 'Soviet' 'Internationalism' and 'friendship of the nations'. (*Atmoda* 19 May 1989)

What is so interesting about this dual integrational and anti-discursive strategy is that in both instances the PFL relied on discourses which had been articulated by the Soviet hegemonic order. Stalin's and

Brezhnev's national policies are portrayed as illegitimate because they do not correspond to those of Vladimir Il'ich Lenin. An anti-discourse strategy is greatly aided, it would seem, by the ability to 'dig down' and uncover historical discourses which actually seem to support one's current articulations. By (selectively) appealing to Lenin's formulations on the national question, the PFL managed to pursue a sophisticated strategy that combined aspects of anti-, integrational, and constructive discourses. A simplistic attempt to rubbish Soviet discourses in their entirety without reference to historical nodal points would have been rendered less powerful. The PFL strategy aimed to demonstrate that certain Soviet discourses were invalid because they did not, in fact, correspond to previously articulated Soviet discourses. This therefore allows anti-discursive strategies to be employed under the guise of integrational discourse.

Interestingly, there was a noticeable change in the style and content of PFL discourse in the two periods of analysis. In the earlier period, there was a desire to integrate Popular Front discourses within selected Soviet discourses and realities. However, in 1990, the PFL had become more confident and secure in its social and political position. As the foundations of Soviet rule were being steadily undermined, it became increasingly clear that there was no longer any need to rely on these Soviet discourses. Lenin was no longer referenced as a legitimate source of support for the Popular Front. Calls were made for outright independence rather than autonomy within a federal Soviet Union.

This change in perspectives was summed up well in an interview with Anatolijs Gorbunovs, the chairperson of the Latvian Supreme Soviet. In the interview Gorbunovs was asked how he could be talking about full independence from the Soviet Union when, two and a half years previously, he had said that anyone who laid flowers at the Freedom Monument would be acting against the Latvian *tauta*. In reply Gorbunovs stated:

> In answer to your concrete question I can say that, of course, I am also changing, because the things I am telling you today I was not even sure about three months ago . . . so events have been before me and I have acted accordingly. (*Atmoda* 3 April 1990)

The structural conditions of 1989 had gone through seismic changes by 1990 and this was evident in Gorbunovs' response. No longer were the PFL and its supporters forced to work solely within the discursive frameworks of Marxism–Leninism, or to justify their positions within Soviet discourses. The strategies of the late 1980s had successfully engineered new nodal points with which to create new truths, and ultimately new political structures. Notwithstanding the fact that new nodal points had been created, that is not to say that the old nodal points had been entirely dismantled. Nevertheless, significant changes had occurred in the Soviet space so that discursive opportunities had opened up.

Certain nodal points, such as those surrounding nationality, were selectively retained. It is clear from this analysis, for example, that the nation (*tauta*) was a sacred entity deserving of special privileges for the Popular Front. This was as true in 1988 as it was in 1990. Moreover, the Latvian *tauta* was to be the core nation, whether this was to be within the confines of the Latvian SSR or within an independent Latvia. Representatives of other nations were not expected to represent Latvian culture or language. Instead they were representatives of their own ethnos, be it Russian, Ukrainian, Belarusian and so on. These people should help the Latvian nation, champion democratisation, and should support Latvian independence but they were not representatives of the core nation, and it was not envisaged that they would ever be so.

In many respects, these were therefore not entirely new nodal points. Certainly, as a Latvian hegemonic order started to emerge, meanings were necessarily transformed. Nevertheless, the emerging nodal points were not plucked out of thin air. Instead they were the result of a complex historical and social experience. They would, however, have a profound effect on the course of Latvia's post-Soviet state-building project.

Latvia's post-Soviet state-building: discourses, myths, and narratives

In the immediate years following the collapse of the Soviet Union and the Baltic states' successful reacquisition of independence, the issue of citizenship, that is, who constituted the legitimate body of citizenry, had to be resolved adequately in order to construct a workable and stable domestic polity. Both Estonia and Latvia opted for restrictive citizenship laws, defining their country's legitimate citizenry on the basis of their pre-Soviet citizenry. In Latvia, as in Estonia, the groundwork for these restrictive citizenship laws was laid in the late Soviet period by the so-called Citizens' Committees. In Latvia the Committee was established in 1989 by the more radical section of the Popular Front, under the direction of Latvia's National Independence Movement (LNIM). The Committee was intended to form a 'legitimate' alternative to the Supreme Soviet. Although Gorbachev introduced partially free democratic elections to the republics' national legislatures for 1989, the radicals insisted that the Supreme Soviet was not legitimate on the grounds that Latvia was still an occupied country. Following this logic, 'occupiers' (that is, Soviet instead of Latvian citizens) were being allowed to vote, rendering the Supreme Soviets illegitimate. The Citizens Committee was therefore comprised only of people who could prove a direct or ancestral link to the interwar republic.

In the post-Soviet era the question of citizenship became very contentious (see Morris 2003). Following a number of heated debates and much public scrutiny, a new citizenship law was only fully approved as late as 1995. To this day the amended Latvian citizenship law is explicit in setting out the policy of legal continuity: 'Latvian citizens are: 1) persons who were Latvian citizens on 17 June 1940, and their descendants' (Latvian Citizenship Law 1998). Although the law also allows for other categories of citizenship, including naturalisation, it is significant that this is the first category of citizenship, and that this was the sole category for the country's first post-Soviet elections.

The justification for invoking such a restrictive policy was that Latvia had been illegally occupied by Soviet forces. Therefore it was only the pre-Soviet order which had any legal legitimacy and authority. In other words the legal Latvian state ceased to exist in 1940 at the time of the incursion of Soviet troops and was only finally restored in 1991 when Latvia was able to declare full independence from the Soviet Union. As such, in 1993, the first elected parliament in the newly independent Latvia was referred to as the *fifth Saeima* (parliament) of the Latvian Republic (the fourth *Saeima* was elected in 1931).[5] Additionally, the 1922 constitution (*Satversme*) was restored and used as the legal basis for the country's renewed independence.

Along with this narrative of restoration there has also been a clear narrative of 'Europeanisation', or a 'return to Europe' (Smith et al. 1998; Eglitis 2002; Mikkel and Pridham 2005). Daina Eglitis (2002) outlines the two main Latvian narratives which, for her, have driven and framed the country's post-Soviet transition: spatial normality and temporal normality. Eglitis notes how in the narrative of spatial normality Latvia's 'place in space' was used as the core element of the country's transformation. From this perspective Latvia was conceived as being a natural member of the European family of nations, or more broadly 'the West'. In this context normality is defined not only spatially but also in terms of the perceived characteristics of Western European countries such as economic prosperity and democracy.

Temporal normality, as the name suggests, focuses on 'place in time'. Instead of looking towards the West, this narrative centres on Latvia's interwar republic which lasted from 1918 to 1940, until the time the country was incorporated into the Soviet Union, then invaded by Nazi

Germany before again being reincorporated back into the Soviet Union. For many Latvians this romanticised era represents a time of great prosperity. Therefore it was perhaps inevitable that calls were made for the full restoration of the political institutions of the interwar republic, along with a return to a traditional 'Latvian' way of life that had, in the words of Latvia's increasingly assertive Supreme Soviet, 'been brutally violated' throughout the Soviet period (Latvian SSR Supreme Soviet 1989: 133).

Graham Smith identifies similar discursive narratives in Baltic discourses of statehood. For him a central element in understanding these discourses is to be found in what he terms the 'core nation discourse'. According to Smith (1999a: 82), the core nation discourse links the legitimacy of the nation-state to the principles of 'one nation, one language, one political community'. It is thus a discursive strategy that is used in order to create a hegemonic 'core nation'. In their study of Baltic post-Soviet nation-building Smith et al. offer five Baltic narratives which have been used to create and cement this core nation discourse: titular nation status, de-Sovietisation, the standardising state, protection of the historic homeland's culture, and the return to Europe (1998: 99–109).

There is a great deal of overlap between these five narratives and the two used by Eglitis. It is, however, worth expanding on two particular points that Smith et al. highlight. In terms of ensuring *titular nation status* the authors note that, especially in the years after successfully regaining independence, the political elites in Latvia (and also Estonia) were almost entirely comprised of ethnic Latvians (and in the case of Estonia – Estonians) (1998: 99). This, they argue, was a strategy that allowed the 'legitimate' core nation (that is, Estonians and Latvians) to have full political representation at the expense of those groups which fell outside the core nation discourse. These political developments therefore appear to build upon many of the discursive strategies outlined in the discourses of the Popular Front, as analysed above.

The authors also note how the symbolic efforts to *de-Sovietise*, or de-colonise, the Baltic states can be evidenced in the relabelling of hundreds of thousands of Soviet-era immigrants as 'aliens' (Smith et al. 1998: 103). If the post-Soviet Latvian state was to be based on the principle of legal continuity from the interwar republic, then it is crucial to accept that Latvia was occupied by the Soviet Union. If this occupation could not be accepted unwaveringly then much of the rationale and momentum behind Latvia's state-building project would be invalidated. If the 'fact' of occupation is accepted, however, then, by extension, the civilians who relocated from other parts of the Soviet Union must also be seen as a consequence of this occupation.

Irrespective of one's stance on the occupation question, it is clear that the discourse of occupation has had significant consequences for Latvian state-building, and for the reconceptualisation of Soviet-era immigrants and their families. In any evaluation of contemporary discourses it is important to bear these narratives and discourses in mind. If Russian speakers wish to find discursive acceptance in contemporary Latvia, then it is important to recognise the importance of 'occupation' as a nodal point that anchors official Latvian identities and discourses. Contemporary discursive strategies will therefore have to engage with this nodal point either through anti-, integrational, or constructive approaches.

MEMORY POLITICS, 'MEMORY WARS', AND RUSSIAN SPEAKERS

As discussed above, the creation of national collective myths can form an integral part of national identity formation. In Latvia, as the previous section demonstrates, the notion of strong historical links to the past has been used to good effect in symbolically pulling Latvia away from the Soviet sphere towards its symbolically and politically reconfigured post-Soviet, 'Western' sphere. The attempts to construct collective state and national narratives have, however, not been without opposition. One of the problems encountered along Latvia's path of national myth-making has been a conflict of historical interpretation, often where people's individual and collective memories do not correspond to the official myths of the Latvian state. At the political level this conflict is especially visible in Latvia's relations with the Russian Federation, whose own officially proscribed memory narratives are in direct opposition to those of the Latvian state.

Siobhan Kattago (2010: 383) therefore argues that for the Baltic states 'two narratives of the recent past perennially conflict with one another'. For Kattago (2010: 383), whereas Baltic narratives highlight the victimhood of Soviet and Nazi occupations, the 'Soviet-Russian narrative emphasizes the USSR as the liberator of Europe from fascism and the willing annexation of the Baltic states to the USSR'. Berg and Ehin (2009: 1) argue that these competing narratives are not only incompatible, but antagonistic, adding that the competing tensions between the two sides have increased over time.

Certainly one of the most antagonistic aspects of these conflicting narratives can be found within the competing interpretations of the events and consequences of the Second World War. The Soviet Union's victory over fascist Germany in the Second World War is arguably one of the most important state narratives that the Russian state has at its disposal in order to create its own collective memories. In the Soviet period this victory was not only a source of immense pride, but it also served as a legitimating factor in Soviet policies (Tumarkin 1987; Weiner 1996). For Tumarkin (1987), the idealisation of victory in the so-called Great Patriotic War (alongside the embellishment of the cult of Lenin) held a central place in the legitimisation of the Soviet regime. Soviet leaders were quick to propagate simplified narratives of this victory in order to 'sustain, and sometimes inspire, popular solidarity with their policies' (Tumarkin 1987: 69).

In the post-Soviet era much time and money has also been invested in keeping the popular narrative of this victory alive. Consider, for example, the efforts and monies invested into Moscow's Victory Park in order to construct a vast architectural memorial to the war which includes a memorial chapel, mosque, synagogue, over 1,418 fountains (one for each day of the war), a museum of the Great Patriotic War, and a Tsereteli-commissioned statue of Nike, the God of Victory (see Schleifman 2001). Consider also the great pomp devoted to the annually celebrated Victory Day on 9 May – a national holiday of great importance in Russia.

This reverence for the Soviet victory in the Second World War, however, clearly clashes with the official position taken by all three Baltic states: that their countries were illegally and mercilessly occupied by the Soviet Union. Instead of the incursion of Soviet troops being seen as *liberation* from Nazi Germany, the Baltic states prefer to concentrate on the ensuing *occupation* by Soviet troops. Thus the Occupation Museum in Riga and the Museum of the Occupations in Tallinn stand testament to official myths[6] and receive financial assistance from the respective states of Latvia and Estonia. Indeed, for Aro Velmet (2011), one of the main functions of the significantly state-funded occupation museums in Estonia and Latvia is to reinforce coherent state narratives and myths. Velmet (2011: 192) relates how the Occupation Museum in Riga, 'according to its chief administrators, tries to subvert deliberate or accidental misinformation that dominates nationalist Russian discourses about the Latvian occupations'.[7]

In 2013 and 2014 the Latvian Parliament felt the need to further codify this 'Latvian' position by proposing and passing a number of legislative initiatives. In 2013, for example, the use of Soviet and Nazi symbols was banned from public events, while in 2014 the *Saeima* passed a bill introducing criminal charges (up to three years' imprisonment) to individuals who deny or trivialise Nazi and Soviet occupations of Latvia. In 2014 the parliament also accepted a new preamble to the Latvian constitution that states

The people of Latvia (*Latvijas tauta*)[8] did not recognise the occupation regimes, resisted them and regained their freedom by restoring
national independence on 4 May 1990 on the basis of continuity of
the State. They . . . condemn the Communist and Nazi totalitarian
regimes and their crimes. (Latvijas Republikas Saeima 2014)

Clearly both Latvia and Russia have been at pains to stress their particular interpretation of the Second World War, and have used it as a
basis for nation and state building projects. For Maria Mälksoo (2009)
this clash of historical interpretation has led to a series of 'memory wars'
between the Baltic states and Russia. The most notable and physical
expression of this largely symbolic 'war' was evidenced in Tallinn in
2007 during the so-called 'Bronze Nights'. In April 2007 the Estonian
authorities decided to relocate the 'Bronze Soldier' memorial from
central Tallinn to a military cemetery on the outskirts of the city.[9] The
memorial, initially called 'the Monument to the Liberators of Tallinn',
was located on the site of a small grave, where the remains of a number of
Soviet soldiers were buried who died in 1944, when Soviet troops retook
the city of Tallinn. The statue itself had served as a venue for unofficial
celebrations of Victory Day on 9 May and was therefore seen by many as
a site of symbolic antagonism against Estonian myths of statehood and
history.

It was perhaps unsurprising, taking into account the sacredness of this
statue and its important symbolism for a large percentage of the population, that the decision to relocate the monument to a military cemetery
on the outskirts of Tallinn was met with fierce opposition. This opposition culminated in extensive rioting by mostly Russian-speaking youths,
pickets against the Estonian embassy in Moscow, and a series of targeted
cyber-attacks on Estonian banks (Berg and Ehin 2009: 5). Russia's
foreign minister Sergei Lavrov was especially critical of the Estonian
authorities' actions, claiming in a letter to EU member states, that 'by
equalling the heroism of soldier-liberators and the crimes of Nazis and
their henchmen, Estonian authorities were attempting to rewrite history
and reinterpret the role of the anti-Hitler coalition in the victory over
fascism in World War Two' (as cited in Haukkala 2009: 206).

Thankfully both Lithuania and Latvia have not witnessed such heightened and explicit scenes of ethnic tension. In Latvia, however, 9 May is
also a politically divisive date for many. Each year, in the capital city
of Riga, tens of thousands of (mostly Russian-speaking) people gather
in Victory Park by the Monument to the Liberators from the German
fascist invaders in order to celebrate their 'Great Victory'. Likewise, 16
March is also a date with particular symbolic resonance which is able

to stoke passion and controversy. Each year on this date veterans from the Second World War and their supporters stage a march from Dome Square in Riga's Old Town to the Freedom Monument. The central controversy here, however, is that these veterans served within the ranks of the Latvian Legion of the Waffen SS.[10]

These two dates are therefore often symbolically pitched as polarised opposites in Latvia's memory politics (Denis 2008; Cheskin 2010a). To celebrate the Soviet victory in the Second World War is often portrayed as tantamount to celebrating the occupation of the Baltic states, while paying respects to those who fought in the ranks of the Waffen SS is similarly linked to a glorification of Nazism. In many respects this reveals the seeming incompatibility of the two competing historical interpretations proffered by the Russian Federation on the one hand, and the Baltic states on the other. Because 9 May is so widely celebrated *within* Latvia by a large number of the country's inhabitants, including an increasing number of Latvian citizens, the issue of historical interpretations and national memory-myths takes on a more complicated aspect.

The Russian Federation has spent a great deal of time and money symbolically and financially supporting Second World War veterans resident in Latvia and providing financial support for Victory Day celebrations in Latvia and in other post-Soviet countries (Lerhis et al. 2007: 45). Moreover, Russia has attempted to intervene in a number of cases at the European Court of Human Rights relating to Russian speakers in the Baltic states and the legacy of the Baltic states' Soviet past. Nils Muižnieks (2011a) refers to these interventions as 'memory battles' where Russia's interpretation of the past again comes into conflict with the historical interpretations of the Baltic states.

One of the most important and significant of these cases has been that of *Kononov* v. *Latvia* in which, in 2010, the European Court of Human Rights finally came down on the side of Latvia, repealing the previous 2008 judgement which had gone against Latvia. Kononov was appealing against the Latvian courts' decision to convict him for his involvement in a war crime in 1944. The crime in question was the murder of nine people, including a pregnant woman, carried out during Nazi Germany's occupation of Latvia by a group of Soviet partisans dressed in Wehrmacht uniforms (for an overview of this case see Mälksoo 2011). Russia was able to intervene in this case as a third party because Kononov gave up his Latvian citizenship (he had been a Latvian citizen of pre-Soviet Latvia and was therefore immediately eligible for post-Soviet citizenship) and, in 2000, took up President Putin's offer of Russian citizenship which was granted through special presidential decree.

It is clear from the attention paid to this case within Russia and Latvia that it was about more than just the actions of one Vasilii Kononov. As Mälksoo (2011: 107) argues:

> The *Kononov* case is a mirror image of the Baltic-Russian debate on the history of World War II . . . In Moscow's opinion, Kononov's actions were justified for essentially the same reason that Moscow continues to argue that the Soviet takeover of the Baltic states in 1940 was not an illegal occupation.

Although the court declined to pass any explicit judgement over whether the Soviet Union's incursion into Latvia in 1940 could be legally referred to as an occupation, it was clear that this was an important issue both legally and symbolically within the case (Mälksoo 2011: 106–7; Muižnieks 2011a: 222–4). Following the verdict the Russian Foreign Ministry released a statement which called the ruling 'a very dangerous precedent' noting also that: 'the ECHR Grand Chamber has actually agreed today with those who seek to revise the outcome of World War II and whitewash the Nazis and their accomplices . . .' (Ministry of Foreign Affairs of the Russian Federation 2010b).

In Russia the media also devoted much time and space to the Kononov case, most commonly (in the mainstream media it can be said *exclusively*) in support of Kononov and speaking out against the 'rewriting of history' and the emergence of 'neo-Nazism' in Latvia (Petrenko 2008; Denis 2008). This 'rewriting of history' again brings us inevitably back to the issue of Soviet occupation versus Soviet liberation. The reason the Russian Federation was willing to spend an estimated five million roubles on Kononov's defence (Mälksoo 2011: 104), and conversely why Latvia was so keen to convict a seventy-five year-old man for crimes committed over fifty years ago, is that the issue of Soviet occupation/ liberation is so central to both countries' meta-narratives.

One of the consequences of this memory war between Russia and Latvia has been a distrust of the Russian-speaking population of Latvia by state officials. As Øyvind Jaeger (2000) has noted, Latvia (along with Estonia and Lithuania) has often 'securitised' its non-Latvian population as a latent threat. This was seen most obviously in the early to mid-1990s. For example, the Latvian National Security Concept (1995: 1) states, 'because Latvia's external threat can be connected with foreign efforts to destabilise Latvia's internal situation, it is impossible to simply separate external threats from internal ones'.

Although Russia is not directly named here, it is clear that the 'foreign efforts to destabilise Latvia's internal situation' must be in reference to the Russian Federation. It is more than significant that the Latvian state saw fit to draw a direct correlation between the actions of Russia and those of Latvia's Russian-speaking population. Admittedly, in subsequent National Security Concepts the rhetoric was softened. In the 2008 document, for example, the focus was moved towards social integration. Nevertheless, an important aspect of this integration is identified as education, specifically educating people about Latvia's history: 'Social integration is one of the factors which stabilises the state's internal, political situation . . . Education has a special role to play – the teaching of language and Latvian history as well as its explanation' (Latvian National Security Concept 2008).

In this context the competing interpretations of history are again seen as a threat to Latvia's security, not simply at the international level but, in this case, at the level of domestic politics. For this reason education reform has been one of the most charged issues in Latvian domestic politics over recent years. The education reforms were initially passed in 1998 and originally envisaged all state-funded schools moving to 100 per cent of instruction being conducted in Latvian by 2004. However, following strong opposition from within and without Latvia, a compromise was reached whereby 60 per cent of instruction in state secondary schools would be conducted in Latvian with the other 40 per cent being free to be conducted in the language of the minority group (most commonly Russian) (see Galbreath and Galvin 2005; Hogan-Brun 2006). More recently, the governing coalition of the eleventh *Saeima* outlined their plans to abolish the use of foreign languages in all publically funded schools in Latvia (with the exception of language classes) by September 2018 (Cabinet of Ministers of the Republic of Latvia 2013).

Although the educational reform has ostensibly been about ensuring the status of the Latvian language, Galbreath and Galvin (2005: 450) note that 'policies are being reformed to suit a political project rather than simply a practical, educational logic'. For them the reform policies are indicative of a 'Soviet legacy of show politics . . . meant to express domination more than to influence daily practice' (2005: 455). In light of the discussion of Latvia's historical 'memory wars', memory politics can be added as another important factor in the country's education reforms. For example, Karklins has observed that in 1996 the majority of textbooks in Latvia's Russian schools were either imported from Russia or were published in the Soviet Union (as cited in Galbreath and Galvin 2005: 458). In terms of fostering collective memories which support Latvia's post-Soviet nation-building project it is possible to see how these textbooks could be a threat to Latvian security, as defined by the country's own National Security Concepts.

The school has to be one of the most effective institutions within the national mythscape which can be used to establish a coherent set of national, collective memories. The mere presence of schools that use materials that have not been published in post-Soviet Latvia is therefore a matter of potential concern, especially when the history taught in those textbooks does not correspond to the official state history and memory-myths that the state wishes to perpetuate. The Latvian government's *Guidelines for national identity, civil society and integration politics*, approved in 2011, state that one of the criteria for social integration is 'the creation of collective social memory' (Culture Ministry of the Republic of Latvia 2011: 6). While there is much that is positive in these guidelines, such as the desire to 'respect multifarious opinions' of history (2011: 21), the document nevertheless makes it clear that one of the country's central, social problems 'is conflicting social memory which is based on Soviet ideological interpretations of Latvia's occupation, Latvia's fate in World War II and life in the Soviet regime' (2011: 9). The document reaffirms Latvia's official position on this history (2011: 11, footnote 62) and calls for measures to teach 'true historical facts' to national minorities (2011: 37). The issue of 'false' teaching of history has thus been a central concern for the Latvian authorities.

For Maria Golubeva (2011), the simple division of Latvian (and Estonian) schools along ethno-linguistic lines is problematic for a state that wants to foster a commonly accepted, official, national narrative. To this degree, Golubeva (2011: 316) observes how

> The schools for Russian-speaking students, even when offering bilingual instruction, as in the Latvian case, are sometimes viewed as a locus of transmission of another country's historical narratives; and they are pressured to shift towards a more 'unified' model of national narrative to produce 'loyal citizens'.

Indeed, in Golubeva's research it was revealed that a large proportion of teachers in Latvia's so-called Russian schools (that is, schools where the language of instruction is Russian) often supplement the official curriculum with extra materials in order to provide, what they consider to be, a more balanced view of history – often explaining to the students that their textbooks were not always accurate (2011: 324). Because of this, teachers are able to uphold historical interpretations which do not necessarily correspond to the official narratives set out in the Latvian national curriculum.

This was further evidenced in a 2008 survey which compared historical knowledge and interpretations of school children in 'Russian' and 'Latvian' schools (Makarov and Boldāne 2008). The survey found

Table 3.1 School children's attitude to 9 May and 16 March by school's language of instruction

School's language of instruction	Positive	Mostly positive	Mostly negative	Negative	Difficult to say	Total
Latvian (n=207)	12.1	30.6	24.3	20.9	12.1	100
Russian (n=193)	82.3	12.5	2.6	1.6	1	100
Total	46	21.9	13.8	11.6	6.8	100
School's language of instruction	Positive	Mostly positive	Mostly negative	Negative	Difficult to say	Total
Latvian (n=207)	19.9	47.6	19.4	2.9	10.2	100
Russian (n=193)	3.2	7.4	13.7	65.3	10.5	100
Total	11.9	28.3	16.7	32.8	10.4	100

Source: Makarov and Boldāne (2008: 11)

that while there was little difference between the 'factual knowledge' displayed by the students of the different schools, it was in the interpretation of events where opinions were much more divergent. As such, students displayed a similar knowledge of key figures and dates in Latvian history. On the other hand, their interpretation of the two key dates of 9 May and 16 March varied considerably (see Table 3.1): whereas 82.3 per cent of students from Russian schools reported a 'positive' attitude to 9 May celebrations in Riga, only 12.1 per cent of children from Latvian schools shared this assessment. Conversely, whereas 67.5 per cent of pupils from Latvian schools had a 'positive' or 'mostly positive' attitude towards the 16 March procession, the figure for students from Russian schools was only 10.6 per cent.

In summary then, memory wars in Latvia have become an increasingly researched and salient topic. Much of the conflict comes from a competing interpretation of history which seems to centre on two main conflicting poles: the Russian Federation on the one hand and Latvia (along with the other two Baltic states) on the other. Later in this study focus is turned to a fuller quantitative and qualitative examination of the extent by which people's historical memory-myths diverge from these rigidly outlined 'official' histories.

CONCLUSIONS

Following on from the theoretical discussion of discourse and the enumeration of a discourse-historical approach, this chapter explored the ideas of history and memory from both a theoretical and empirical perspective. In the Latvian context it was argued that conceptions of Latvia's past have formed an integral part of the country's post-Soviet state-building project. The main post-Soviet narratives and state discourses which have served to legitimise official Latvian policy were explored in some detail. Relying upon a historical approach to the study of discourse, the earlier Soviet period was examined as a potential source for the articulation of discourses at the time of perestroika.

The work of Gramsci was important in understanding that periods of organic crisis (such as the collapse of the Soviet order) are fundamentally significant. It is in such periods of time that many of the nodal points which anchor given discourses are effectively delegitimised, leading to the possibility (and expediency) for actors to create new discursive relations and meanings. From this it was posited that the discursive constructions of the *Atmoda* period would be extremely significant in determining discourses and identities in Latvia today.

Gramsci's insights help to explain the emergence of political formations which are competing to create new hegemonic orders. In the case of Latvia, history and memory were clearly utilised as discursive tools that could help to construct a 'core' group of 'Latvians'. This core, and hegemonic, group was further unified through contrast to the external 'other' – 'the Russians'. The 'memory war' that has been witnessed between the three Baltic states and Russia was therefore examined in some detail and shown to be a continuing issue of great importance in Latvia's domestic and international affairs.

In order to understand the process of hegemonic formation more thoroughly the Popular Front of Latvia's official newspaper publication was analysed for two six-month periods. The analysis highlighted the emergence of many discourses which proved to be central to the Latvian hegemonising project. It was argued that the emerging discourses were constructed around a complex set of integrational, anti-, and constructive discursive strategies. What is striking about the analysis is that these emerging discourses were not entirely anti-Soviet. Instead many Soviet-era discourses were utilised in order to give legitimacy to the discursive constructions of the *Atmoda* period. In fact the Popular Front often sought to delegitimse Soviet hegemony through the paradoxical and selective use of Soviet discourses, arguing that existent Soviet practice did not always match up with previously articulated Soviet discourses.

The treatment of Russians and Russian speakers within PFL discourse was also examined. In the early years of *Atmoda* the external 'other' was, in many respects, the Soviet Union, or at least the then-current federal composition of the Union. As the power and influence of the Soviet Union waned, a need developed for a different external 'other'. There is therefore a paradoxical treatment of Russian speakers found within *Atmoda*. On the one hand the leaders of the PFL wanted to co-opt this community for their own political ends as a means to secure Latvian autonomy and independence. Indeed, the structural and demographic conditions in Latvia were such that this was a necessary step. On the other hand, there was the need to maintain strict boundaries between Latvia's imagined communities. Therefore, even when there were relatively inclusionary calls for Russians and Russian speakers to form an integral part of their hegemonising project, there were simultaneously discourses which explicitly delineated Russians and other nationalities as separate from the Latvian *tauta*.

The findings from this chapter are used to inform discussion of *contemporary* discourses and identities in Latvia, to help understand the discursive strategies that are being outlined and articulated today. As has been argued, the period of organic crisis is an essential one in determining the emergence of new hegemonic orders. The legitimacy of Latvia's post-Soviet order was forged in the *Atmoda* period and therefore the discourses of this time are likely to have a strong influence on contemporary identities and identity discourses. The discussion of post-Soviet state and nation-building practices and controversies highlighted the link between the discourses of the *Atmoda* period and their subsequent codification and institutionalisation.

This chapter largely focused on 'Latvian' rather than 'Russian/Russian-speaking' discourses. This was because of the need to document the emergence of Latvia's new hegemonic order. As argued above, this new hegemony was largely based on conceptions of a clearly defined, core Latvian nation. The role of non-Latvians, especially Russians, in Latvia's post-Soviet existence was seen as peripheral. The discourses of Russian speakers were, of course, important during this time. Nevertheless, it was the 'Latvian' discourses associated with first the Popular Front, and later the new political order of the Latvian state, which formed the basis of an emerging hegemony. While many Russian speakers were politically active during the late Soviet period, the voices of those who supported Latvian independence were largely indistinguishable from the main 'Latvian' discourses of the time (Lapsa et al. 2007: 171). At the same time, we must assume that a relatively large number of Russian speakers supported pro-Soviet discourses, especially those associated with the reactionary Interfront. However, survey data from 1990 and 1991 suggest that, among Russians, support for the Interfront was relatively low (27 per cent and 22 per cent respectively), and was actually lower than support for the Popular Front (42 per cent and 47 per cent over the same periods) (Karklins 1994a: 82).[11] In this period, Russian-speaking discourses were therefore mostly submerged within those of the dynamic ('Latvian') independence movement, or else were articulated by a vocal minority with a strong institutional (Soviet) platform (utilising the remaining Soviet and communist party structures), but hampered by any real lack of popular support.

Once it became apparent, however, that the Interfront and other reactionary forces were unable to prevent the emergence of a new Latvian hegemony, the discursive position of Russian speakers became correspondingly less clear. With the consolidation of a well-articulated hegemonic order that prioritised the 'Latvian nation', it was not immediately obvious how Russian speakers would be able to find a discursive place within this new order. In order to explore the discursive strategies used by a number of Russian-speaking 'elites', the following chapter analyses contemporary media discourses in Latvia.

NOTES

1. Shlapentokh (2001) describes the post-Stalin Soviet order as a 'normal totalitarian society', combining elements of coercive control with ideological (discursive) practices.
2. The original name of *Sajūdis* was the Reform Movement of Lithuania (*Lietuvos Persitvarkymo Sajūdis*). *Persitvarkymo* was used as the Lithuanian translation of perestroika. A more apt translation into English would therefore be the Perestroika Movement of Lithuania.
3. It is also known as *Trešā Atmoda* (the Third Awakening). The First and Second Awakenings refer to two previous periods of notable Latvian nationalist endeavours, firstly in the mid-to-late nineteenth century, and later leading up to the proclamation of Latvian independence in 1918.
4. Both these words derive from the Latvian *pamats* – foundation/base/principle and the two previously discussed words for 'nation' – *nācija* and *tauta*.
5. This principle of 'legal continuity', it seems, is in no way hampered by the fact that in 1934 the fourth *Saeima* was dissolved by Kārlis Ulmanis and replaced by an authoritarian system of rule which lasted right up until Soviet troops entered Latvia in 1940. Strictly speaking, the principle of legal continuity should therefore have led to the restoration of an authoritarian dictatorship.
6. It should be emphasised that 'myth' is not used in this research to indicate falsity or deception. Instead it refers to simplification and the creation of cohesive narratives out of complex historical events.
7. In fairness to the Museum of Occupation in Riga it should also be noted that, in Velmet's view, the museum (in contrast to the Museum of the Occupations in Tallinn) does also acknowledge its problematic role as an identity constructor.
8. There was much debate (and tension) during the legislative process of amending the *Satversme* and adding a preamble. Nationalist politicians from the National Alliance campaigned for the use of the term *valstnācija* (nation-state), a term they defined in

strictly ethnic terms to mean ethnic Latvians (see National Alliance 2014). They also pressed for the use of 'the ethnic Latvian nation' (*latviešu tauta*) but had to settle for the more neutral 'people of Latvia' (*Latvijas tauta*), except for two instances where *latviešu nācija* (the ethnic Latvian nation, but with slightly less ethnic connotations than *latviešu tauta*) was used. See Chapter 7 for more discussion of this issue.

9. For a more in-depth explanation of the reasoning behind the decision to relocate the statue see Burch and Smith (2007).

10. The formation and activities of the Latvian Legion are highly contested and controversial. It is difficult to find a measured and unbiased account of the proceedings. The 'Latvian' argument claims that those who volunteered or were conscripted to the Waffen SS were fighting against Soviet occupation, and for the freedom of Latvia but not for fascist ideology (see Rislakki 2009: 127–42). The 'Russian' argument, on the other hand, places the Latvian Legion on equal terms with the other legions of the SS proper, and therefore sees the organisation (and all of its members) as criminal and fascist (see Chernov and Shlyakhtunov 2004). For a good overview of the activities of the Latvian Legions see Felder (2009).

11. This data comes from the Social Research Centre for Latvia. While support for the Popular Front amongst Russians stood at 43 per cent in June 1991, it fell sharply to 24 per cent in September. However, there is no comparable data for support for the Interfront in September 1991.

Russian-Language Media and Identity Formation

– Нет документа, нет и человека, – удовлетворенно говорил Коровьев (Bulgakov, 2004a)

'Remove the document and you remove the man,' said Koroviev with satisfaction (Bulgakov, 2004b)

The mass media of communication are often singled out as an important locus of identity and hegemonic construction. This is especially true for studies that employ a discursively centred approach. Teun van Dijk, a leading scholar of CDA, for example notes that, while most elite discourse is restricted to small circles, 'Mass circulation and sharing among the ingroup of ethnic prejudices and ideologies presuppose mass communication, that is, expression or (re)production in the mass media' (1989: 203). Certainly the mass media must be seen one of the most prominent sources of discursive articulation in modern societies. Quite simply, the mass media possess enormous coverage and outreach and media messages can reach millions of people almost instantly. This effectively means that the words, images, and depictions ('texts') of the mass media are potentially integral to the formation of any collective social identities that may be accepted by the public at large. It was for this reason that Benedict Anderson cites the emergence of the printing press and the subsequent proliferation of what he terms 'print capitalism' as one of the most important factors leading to the formation of the modern nation state, and the formation of collective identities on a national scale (2006: 44).

This research is premised on an understanding that in modern societies media have a potentially important role in constructing and propagating collective identities. George Gerbner (1985), for example, argues that mass communication has the macrosociological function of creating its own publics and providing a sense of common identity. For Gerbner understanding culture, which he defines as 'a system of messages that regulates social relationships' (1985: 14), is essential for an understanding of media influence. Culture regulates social relationships, he suggests, by providing a framework of possible actions:

> The communications of a culture not only inform common images; they not only entertain but create publics; they not only reflect but shape attitudes, tastes preferences. They provide the boundary conditions and overall patterns within which the processes of personal and group-mediated selection, interpretation, and interaction go on. (1985: 14)

It would be almost impossible for particular discourses to function at a collective level without the intercession of media dissemination. This research largely rejects biological and primordial explanations for the emergence of large-scale, collective identities. For this reason it is assumed that identities can only be 'imagined' if there is a relatively standardised and uniform production of discourse.

While 'media effects' are highly contested (see, for example, Sparks 2013: 50–70), it is clear that the formation of collective identities and shared discursive understandings on a national scale could not occur without technologies that can articulate and disseminate discourses on such large scales. The mass media therefore potentially play a vital role of making available standardised discourses across huge spaces. It is therefore important to examine the discourses that are contained within media messages, and to determine who is responsible for their content. It is, however, important to be wary of 'hypodermic' models of media effects, which claim that media discourses can, and are, simply accepted and internalised by their audiences. The media analysis of this chapter is therefore treated with at least some caution. Later chapters, for example, investigate the receptive discursive strategies of Russian speakers. This facilitates a more comprehensive analysis of how media discourses are 'decoded' (Hall 1980) by their audiences. The joint focus on productive and (in later chapters) receptive functions of discourse helps to build up a more nuanced picture of how discourses operate in contemporary Latvia.

METHODOLOGY

This chapter examines Russian-speaking media discourse in Latvia. The main source for this analysis is *Chas* (the *Hour*), which, at the time this data was collected, was a leading Russian-language daily in Latvia. *Chas* can best be described as a tabloid publication. In comparison to its nearest Russian-language competitor of the time, *Vesti Segodnia* (*Today's News*), *Chas* presented a more liberal stance on Latvian politics. Nonetheless, it was still a far more opinionated and provocative publication than the other main Russian-language daily *Telegraf* which positioned itself as a professional and impartial source of information (for a brief overview of Latvia's main newspaper publications in 2010 see Rožukalne 2010: 73). In December 2012, following the collection of the data for this analysis, *Chas* was merged with *Vesti Segodnia* and the publication was continued under the *Vesti Segodnia* brand.

Chas was extensively examined for two six-month periods separated by a gap of twelve months. The first monitoring period covered 15 November 2008 to 15 May 2009. The second period ran from 15 May 2010 to 15 November 2010. During these two monitoring periods every article that appeared in the electronic version of the newspaper was analysed. Initially the individual articles were scanned to see if there was any content which could be related to the themes of national identity: broadly speaking – portrayals of Russians, Latvians or Russian speakers, articles on history which could be related back to identity formation, views on education reforms and language practice in Latvia generally, reports on events and developments in Russia, coverage of European politics which were somehow related back to Latvia, articles which attempted to defend the rights of Russian-speakers, views which were directed towards the Latvian state, and anything else that was it was felt warranted a more comprehensive reading. The articles for which a scan indicated the possibility of relevant content were subsequently read in their entirety. Initially notes were taken on each relevant article on an individual basis. It was only once the monitoring periods in question had been completed, and the individual articles had all been read, that they were compared and categorised according to their thematic content.

The choice of focusing primarily on one newspaper, and not all three of the national Russian-language dailies, was perhaps a difficult one. During the periods in which *Chas* was examined, however, limited attention was also paid to the online version of *Vesti Segodnia*.[1] This entailed a daily examination of the newspaper's contents. This was, however, limited to a brief survey of the day's main headlines. In instances when the headline indicated that the article was of direct relevance to this research then the article was analysed in more detail. As a result, far less time was devoted to the examination of *Vesti Segodnia* articles than for those of *Chas*. In the case of *Vesti Segodnia*, the text was often skim read unless it was of particular interest. If the content of a specific article was felt to be particularly relevant only then was it read comprehensively.

The time frame which was adopted for this research made it possible to cover all the official and non-official cultural and commemorative events that occur annually in Latvia and which inevitably generate a number of specific articles. Examples of important events are 9 May, Victory Day, and 16 March, Remembrance Day of the Latvian legion-naires. In light of the previous discussion of the role of memories in the formation of national identities, the interpretation and framing of these commemorative events is an area of crucial importance to this study. Therefore it was considered important to be able to cover every calendar day. By factoring in a twelve-month gap between the two monitoring periods, it was also possible to compare the two periods to see if there had been any generally observable trends or evolution in the discourses employed within the newspapers in question. Such a comparison was deemed essential in order to map out the current evolution of media discourse in Latvia. Also, in accordance with the discourse-historical approach outlined above, it was hoped that this would highlight how discursive nodal points were being created and deconstructed over time. Importantly this would thereby facilitate an in-depth observation of the possible trajectories of Russian-speaking discourse in Latvia.

THE DISCURSIVE CONSTRUCTION OF 'RUSSIAN-SPEAKERS'[2]

While this is a study of 'Russian-speaking discourse', the use of the term 'Russian-speakers', does not come without its problems. Following the collapse of the Soviet Union, many people were unsure of how accurately to describe the groups of Soviet-era migrants that found themselves living in newly independent states and outside their 'natural homelands'. Although 'ethnic Russians' were the largest of these groups, the terms *Russians, Russian settlers, Russian diaspora*, and *Russian community* all came replete with their own inaccurate assumptions (see Poppe and Hagendoorn 2001: 57–71). In Latvia, for example, Poles, Ukrainians, Belarusians, and other former Soviet nationalities were also broadly included in these groups. While many of these nationalities, especially those living outside their 'titular homeland', had been exposed to cul-tural and linguistic Russification within the USSR the word *Russian* was still therefore somewhat of a misnomer. For Aidarov and Drechsler (2013: 106), the broad use of the term Russians in the post-Soviet context simply 'perpetuates the result of their Tsarist or Soviet colonization'.

Added to this, the evidence (see Introduction) suggests that 'Russian-speaking' and/or 'Russian' ethnic identities were rather weak when Latvia first gained independence (Melvin 1995: 27). Additionally, many Russians actively supported Latvian independence and saw their futures in an independent Latvia as opposed to Russia or the Soviet Union.[3]

These considerations notwithstanding, the political and commercial value of binding these people together with a single identity, distinct from Latvian identity, has long been apparent to political and journalistic elites. It is in the commercial and political interests of newspapers and politicians to convince the public that there exists a definite, identifiable community, whose interests the papers and parties can then claim to defend. As Friedhelm Neidhardt (1993: 341) notes, 'mass media create mass audiences, and they exist if they are successful at doing this. They become successful by creating a widespread demand for themselves.' In other words, the resonance of political representation is greatly enhanced if the represented group can be depicted as a holistic and unproblematic entity, rather than be acknowledged as diffuse and diverse. In large part because of these commercial and political requirements, the linguistic categorisation 'Russian-speakers' has become the most useful and broad term that can be applied to this disparate group of individuals.

In many ways language marks a social identity, which according to David Laitin (1998: 22), 'often has a near mystical quality conferring membership in a category of similarly endowed people'. 'Russian-speakers' has therefore come into popular parlance as the most ostensibly applicable way of describing what is essentially an imagined community. Moreover, Poles, Ukrainians, Jews, Belarusians, and numerous other Soviet nationalities can suddenly be united under the broad banner of Russian-speakers. The Latvian education reforms of 2004 helped to add momentum to this tendency for people to use the Russian language to demarcate ethnicised identity. Legislation demanded that Russian-language schools conduct at least 60 per cent of their teaching in Latvian. This enabled pupils and parents from Russian-language schools to unite meaningfully as a group that was perceived to be experiencing similar discrimination by the Latvian state against the use of their native language. Interestingly, as early as the mid-1990s, Melvin (1995: 55) noted that Russian-speaking identity was often based more on the issues of human rights than it was on a strong attachment to Russia or a genuine collective group consciousness.

For this reason, the linguistic categorisation and referential strategy of referring to a Russian-speaking community must be seen as centrally important not only in articulating a coherent, ethnicised Russian-speaking identity in Latvia, but also in leading to a clear discursive demarcation between Latvians and Russian-speakers. Such has become the axiomatic strength and resonance of the term that, within popular discourse, there is rarely any space for any other groups; either you are a Russian-speaker or you are a Latvian, but nothing in-between. Thus, for Denis Khanov (2002),

> The term Russian-speaker is a good illustration of how greatly schematised [Latvian] society treats definitions of cultural identity by creating two levels of identity – either Russian, or Latvian [which] is most clearly revealed in lexical analysis of the press, television, surveys, and official documents.

It should be noted that this term is also of great importance to many *Latvian* nationalistic forces, who have perceived non-Latvians as a threat to the country's post-Soviet nation-building project. The Popular Front programme often attempted to limit the influence of a potentially powerful and unified community of Russian-speakers by separating them into smaller national groups (see Chapter 3). However, in the post-Soviet period, with the establishment of a 'Latvian' hegemony, the term Russian-speaker helps to differentiate a whole section of the population away from the core nation discourse discussed above. It is therefore clear that the categorisation of Russian-speakers, although seemingly innocent, is in fact highly charged. The mere fact that these people are primarily identifiable as Russian-speakers often serves to exclude them from the ideology of a Latvian state which proclaims the need for only one language and one political community. If the public can be convinced of the reality of a concrete and unproblematic Russian-speaking community, then it is easier subsequently to exclude them on the basis that this community is a real threat to the core (and equally unproblematic) community of Latvians. It is a strategy that fits very much within the hegemonising project of the Latvian state.

As such, the term 'Russian-speakers' (*russkoiazychnye* or *russkogovoriashie* in Russian and *krievvalodīgie* or *krieviski runājoši* in Latvian), must be understood in its wider political and social context. The Russian-language press often employs this as a purposeful dichotomy that aims to differentiate Russian speakers from Latvians. This is most commonly manifested in articles devoted to the government's perceived harsh treatment of Russian speakers: 'Yesterday the Committee of the Ministerial Cabinet reviewed planned changes to the labour law, which have been called upon to further complicate the lives of Russian-speakers' (*Vesti Segodnia* 17 February 2009).

It is clear that the term Russian-speaker represents more than a reference to people's linguistic proficiency of Russian. Rather, Russian-speakers are discursively portrayed as an oppressed political group. This idea is propagated time and time again in the pages of the country's Russian-language print media. Moreover, this ethnically defined, and politically oppressed group, is commonly referenced in relation to discrimination from the ruling class (read ethnic Latvians): 'An integrating society is a society of numerous opportunities, and not solely political. However, we see a huge discrepancy in the civil rights of Latvians and Russian-speakers, which also relates to all national minorities' (*Chas* 10 March 2009).

In order to emphasise that the discursive position of Russian-speakers is in strict opposition to that of the Latvians, the media adopt what Laclau and Mouffe (1985) refer to as *the logic of equivalence*. According to this logic, *all* Russian-speakers are portrayed as equal to one another irrespective of their real social, cultural, educational, and political differences because they are all equally different from the discursive 'other' – the Latvians. This is not an identity based on any perceived, positive characteristics of Russian-speakers. Instead it is a negative identity, solely premised on the fact that Russian-speakers are not Latvians.

Insofar as Latvia's media are so obviously and sharply divided between Latvian and Russian-language materials, the linguistic divisions can therefore be self-perpetuating. There is an implicit understanding that Russian-language print media is intended for a Russian-speaking audience (that is, Russian-speakers and not simply speakers of Russian), while Latvian print media is likewise intended for dissemination among a 'Latvian' audience. Thus, when *Chas* confidently states that '*We* have always been here' under the heading '*Our* inheritance' (*Chas* 3 January 2009, emphasis added), 'we' is clearly not addressed to the wider audience of persons proficient in Russian. Instead this reflects the separateness of Latvia's two media spaces, and of the discursive distinctness of the country's two main ethnic groups. It is understood that 'we' refers to Russian-speakers as a social group with shared values, experiences, and motives.

For this reason, the simple act of reading a Russian-language newspaper is linked to an understanding that the reader is a definite, identifiable member of the Russian-speaking community, and that this community is somehow distinct from the Latvian community. The act of reading a newspaper is thus a performative act, linking the individual with a whole series of sedimented understandings that underpin the newspaper's discourses. If the reader of a Russian-language newspaper is automatically linked to membership of the Russian-speaking community, then it must be anticipated that this newspaper also has power to articulate the very features of this community.

Politically this is manifested in the overt support given to certain political parties; parties that are deemed also to represent the interests of Russian speakers. In Latvia the discursive division of Latvian and Russian-speaking communities is even apparent in the political spectrum used to describe political parties. In Latvia it is not common to use the customary left/right-wing dichotomy which separates political parties by ideological beliefs. As a general rule, in Latvia 'left wing' refers simply to 'Russian-speaking' parties (often referred to as 'pro-Russian' parties) while 'right wing' is most commonly used in reference to 'Latvian' parties (see Kažoka 2010). In Latvia's Russian-language media 'left-wing' parties are given unwavering support while 'right-wing' parties are most commonly depicted as discriminatory and hostile to the needs and interests of Russian speakers. This can be seen in the number of articles where so-called 'left' and 'right-wing parties' are mentioned in both the Latvian and Russian-language media. Unsurprisingly Russian-language newspapers give column space to left-wing parties more frequently than to the right – although the reverse tendency is far more obvious in the Latvian-language press, where left-wing parties are frequently ignored (Čigāne 2007: 13).

Previous pre-election analysis of Latvian newspapers has revealed a clear tendency for the country's two main Russian-language dailies, *Chas* and *Vesti Segodnia*, to lend direct support to left-wing parties (Kruks and Šulmane 2002). As such For Human Rights in a United Latvia (FHRUL) was a constant favourite for the Russian-language press (since 2014, the Russian Union of Latvia). The Russian media have often seen this party as a representative of the Russian-speaking community in much the same way that they attempt to portray their own role as defenders of Russian-speaking rights. Thus, *Chas* and *Vesti Segodnia*, in all of their editorials and informative news articles constantly refused to question FHRUL policy, or to submit their politicians to rigorous and unbiased scrutiny. Even in interviews, questions are constantly framed so as to facilitate an unhindered regurgitation of political sound bites and are devoid of critical analysis or questioning (Society for Openness 'Delna' 2002).

Harmony Centre (HC), currently the most popular of Latvia's 'left-wing' parties (since 2014, operating as the Social-Democratic Party 'Harmony'), also enjoys similar patronage in the Russian-language print media. For example, in one *Chas* article attention is drawn to HC's application to the Constitutional Court to acknowledge the unlawful use of the Administrative Violations Code to convict people for the non-use of Latvian. The main body of the article is 344 words long and yet a full 271 words are given over to an unabridged quotation from HC representative Valērijs Agešins,[4] who is also pictured (*Chas* 9 March 2009). In a *Chas* interview with HC politician Jānis Urbanovičs, under the headline 'We are the only alternative', the *Saeima* deputy has ample opportunity to outline his party's programme for the then upcoming European elections as well as the 2009 mayoral elections in the country's capital Riga:

> Journalist: What is the largest opposition party going to be doing in the near future?
> Urbanovičs: Getting ready for the elections. We will put forward a very good programme for the elections to the Rigan local government which will envisage turning Riga into an industrial centre of the Baltic Sea Region.
>   A strong team will be making a start in the European elections. I think that Harmony Centre will have two MEP [Member of the European Parliament] representatives in the European Parliament. And I would like to emphasise that they will not be isolated soloists; they will be working in one of the largest MEP blocs in the European Parliament – the socialist party, with whom we are already working successfully. And so this will be an effective mechanism to resolve many pressing issues for Latvia. We have a lot of work to do. (*Chas* 5 March 2009)

Not at any stage are party policies subject to debate or question and Urbanovičs is given free rein to reply using fragments of his party's programme. For this reason a number of analysts have pointed to the undeniable presence of hidden political advertising in the Russian-language print media (Society for Openness 'Delna' 2002; PROVIDUS 2007a). For example, pre-election media analysis of the Russian-language press before the eighth *Saeima* elections revealed that FHRUL was mentioned in a positive light on 73 per cent of occasions, while negatively only 4 per cent of the time (Society for Openness 'Delna' 2002: 38).

In the 2006 *Saeima* elections, similar accounts of hidden advertising were uncovered in the main two Russian-language dailies. Not only did *Chas* and *Vesti Segodnia* provide an unquestioning and pliable media canvas for their favoured parties, but they also afforded political actors extra media space through pseudo news reporting – creating news stories out of trivial events in order to give further publicity to certain politicians (PROVIDUS 2007b). In order to sustain such high levels of publicity for politicians and political parties, the Russian-language press is forced to employ a number of tactics that essentially facilitate hidden electioneering. For example, HC and FHRUL representatives are often called upon as trusted social commentators and experts. Thus, on any given topic, be it education reform, language, Latvia's status within the EU, or any other topic, a 'trusted' politician is always at hand to posit their opinions and share their 'expertise'. In a *Chas* article on the European elections and the possibility of obtaining pre-election materials in Russian, the paper turns to both Tatjana Ždanoka (MEP and FHRUL member) and Boriss Cilevičs (*Saeima* deputy and HC member). Instead of the author directly providing the reader with the information himself, the additional publicity is given to Boriss Cilevičs: 'Boriss Cilevičs, chairperson of the PACE subcommittee on the Election of Judges to the European Courts of human Rights and *Saeima* deputy (HC), explained that in the European Union there are no general language rules for information and campaigning' (*Chas* 9 March 2009).

Among the numerous examples in *Vesti Segodnia* is an article on Latvia's budgetary deficit and the country's need to cut back spending by 700 million lats:

> Vice-chairman of the *Saeima* FHRUL fraction Juris Sokolovskijs told *Vesti Segodnia* that, 'At the meeting with our fraction Dombrovskijs and D. Zaķis, head of the New Era fraction who accompanied him, also warned of the necessity to raise taxes. According to them the IMF [International Monetary Fund] is demanding this. Moreover, without raising taxes and cutting the budget we will not be able to maintain our budget deficit at 4.7% of GDP, but this is precisely what the Godmanis government promised the IMF.' (*Vesti Segodnia* 3 March 2009)

In the example above it is unclear why it is necessary to turn to a FHRUL politician in order to tell the readers the opinions of the Latvian government, rather than directly asking the government themselves. It would seem that the Russian-language press prefer to use Russian-speaking 'representatives' not only to represent the Russian-speaking community, but also to represent Latvian political parties and the Latvian community. Members of 'Latvian' parties therefore appear to be denied a legitimate voice in the pages of the Russian-speaking press. Events, policies, and announcements that come from the 'other' community are instead framed through a process of mediation by Russian-speaking representatives and are therefore presented from the perspective of these social gatekeepers. The Russian-language press therefore reinforces the notion that Russian-speakers must be represented by Russian-speakers, and that Latvians, in turn, will be represented by 'their own'. It is therefore a mechanism that reinforces the non-porous boundaries between Latvia's two communities.

Added to this, numerous politicians from 'Russian' parties have held journalistic positions in both *Chas* and *Vesti Segodnia*. The Soros Foundation Latvia and the Society for Openness 'Delna' (2002: 30) uncovered such problematic practices of the Russian-language press, whereby, 'Russian newspapers were staffed by journalists who were simultaneously deputy candidates or municipal deputies'. As a result of this, the political and media spheres in Latvia are closely intertwined, at least for the case of Russian-language media. The aims of both the media and politicians have often been similar: to create a unified bloc of voters and consumers who are expected to act in certain ways and to take on certain values. In what follows, attention is given to the precise nature of these 'Russian-speaking values' that are proscribed by the Russian-language media.

ANALYSING RUSSIAN–SPEAKING MEDIA DISCOURSE[5]

Drawing on the discursive-historical approach espoused primarily by Ruth Wodak and her colleagues, three main categories were earlier proposed for discursive engagement with past discursive meanings: anti-discourse, integrational discourse, and constructive discourse (see Chapter 2). In the course of this media analysis all three engagement strategies were clearly identifiable. In the section that follows Russian-speaking media discourses are examined through the prism of each of these three categories. Below is a brief overview of some of the main characteristics and manifestations of each strategy within the texts that were studied. The specifics of each of these strategies are subsequently discussed in much greater detail.

1. Anti-discourse (negative identity construction): a strategy wherein 'Russian' parties and journalists attempt to shore up their own identity by dismantling and deriding Latvian narratives, arguing that their incorrect and morally suspect implementation has been the major reason for Latvia's political and economic instability.
2. Integrational discourse (integrational identity construction): this is perhaps the most interesting and increasingly utilised of the three discursive strategies. Instead of simply deconstructing the main narratives of Latvian statehood, Russian-speaking elites argue that they are also committed to the ideals of *Atmoda*, that Russian speakers are loyal to the Latvian state, respect Latvian values and culture (including the Latvian language), and support Latvia's post-Soviet 'normalisation'. However, they also argue that Latvian narratives of

statehood and nationalistic discourses have become distorted in the years following independence.

3. Constructive discourse (positive identity construction): a stage of discursive posturing characterised by attempts to construct new narratives for contemporary Latvia which include and embrace the presence of the country's Russian speakers. This element is a logical progression from the earlier stages of anti- and integrational discourse. By attempting to destroy certain nodal points while simultaneously integrating within others, an analysis of Russian-speaking discourse reveals that Russian-speaking elites are becoming increasingly able to forge a unique discursive position for Russian speakers in Latvia, as a bridge between Russia and Europe.

ANTI-DISCOURSE

There is much space devoted in Latvia's Russian-language media to the debunking of Latvian discourses of normality. In many ways this is a predictable, discursive counter-reaction to the core nation discourse which has played a major role in the post-Soviet hegemonising project. This core nation discourse, although a central feature of Latvian state-building in the immediate post-Soviet period, has been evidenced to various degrees in more contemporary Latvian media and parliamentary discourses (PROVIDUS 2008), and has both a constructive and a destructive macro-function (Reisigl and Wodak 2001: 40). Constructively this discourse sets out the legitimising foundations for a stable model of Latvian statehood and governance in the post-Soviet era. Destructively it marginalises the efforts of those people found outside the core nation discourse to find representation and recognition within this system.

Exclusionary discourses can be found in the Latvian-language media and Latvian public space which depict Russians, Russian-speakers, and non-citizens as alien, occupiers, and as separate from the main body of Latvia's 'normal' citizenry (see Kruks and Šulmane 2002; PROVIDUS 2008; Rožukalne 2010). It is important to note at this point, that while such discourses are visible, it does not necessarily follow that these views represent a majority view, or that more liberal, tolerant discourses are not also existent in Latvia's public media space. However, from the perspective of elites who are positioning themselves as the leaders of the 'Russian-speaking community', objective reflection on diverse opinions is not as important as manipulating discourses which are advantageous to their political and commercial interests.

For this reason, discourses which are perceived to be discriminatory and harmful to Russian speakers are seized upon as a negative way in which to shore up Russian-speaking identity. By creating a totalised perception of discrimination against all non-Latvians, Russian-speakers are linked in a chain of negative equivalence in opposition to 'the Latvians'. On the other hand, the dismantling of these discourses and the narratives that underpin them can also potentially provide Russian speakers with the chance to create a positive pole of identity by creating a legitimate and meaningful place within contemporary Latvia (as is demonstrated in the exploration of constructive-discursive strategies).

Once the data from the two media monitoring periods was collected it was possible to look more closely for trends and main themes within the media discourses by comparing the highlighted portions of the articles that were deemed significant. Through this process certain themes emerged as commonly occurring points of interest for the Russian-language media. In terms of an anti-discursive strategy it was possible to sub-divide anti-discursive strategies into three main categories: (1) articles and rhetoric which queried and mocked Latvian notions of Europeanness; (2) efforts to deconstruct the Latvian myth of restoration; and (3) assertions that Latvia is a democratically deficient country which actually has more in common with the Soviet Union than many would care to admit. Each of these three areas represents a key nodal point for Latvian post-Soviet statehood and have all provided major discursive imperatives for Latvia to adopt its current form of statehood. It is therefore perhaps no surprise that these are the three main targets for Russian-speaking anti-discourse.

Russian-speaking discourses of Latvia's anti-Europeanness

As Eglitis (2002) has documented, during the times of *Atmoda*, Latvian narratives and many Latvian activists claimed that they were restoring normality to Latvia by restoring it to its natural European, democratic, and civilised state. These ideas are therefore immediate targets for Russian-speaking discourse in Latvia. Whereas the spatial narrative of Latvia's development, as described by Eglitis, posited that Latvia was rightfully a member of the European family of nations, numerous examples were found of journalists and politicians using Europe to shame the Latvian state. In this sense there was an evident desire to alter the meaning and associations of the linguistic sign 'Europe' to the extent that it would no longer be able to support and anchor certain Latvian discourses. Articles in *Chas* often highlighted differences between 'civilised' Europe and 'backwards' Latvia: 'And how many times have our [politicians] led a *baffled Europe* into bewilderment that a country that considers itself democratic can pass discriminatory, at times overtly racist, laws?' (*Chas* 20 February 2009, emphasis added).

Latvia's membership of the EU further facilitates the articulation of this anti-discourse. Tatjana Ždanoka, Member of the European Parliament since 2004, and re-elected in 2009 and 2014, who represents the Russian Union of Latvia (previously called For Human Rights in a United Latvia – FHRUL)[6] was foremost among those using Europe as a means to discredit Latvia's claims to Europeanness within the pages of *Chas*. Ždanoka is a controversial figure in Latvia, and for some (including some Russian speakers) represents a more extreme political viewpoint. (Under Latvian law she is prohibited from being elected to the *Saeima* due to her former ties with the Communist Party and her opposition to Latvian independence.) Nevertheless, her views are often published in Latvia's media, and as one of only eight Latvian representatives in the European Parliament, she is able to use her position to gain national and even international attention, especially on and around 16 March during the commemorative marches for the Waffen SS legionnaires (see below).

In this respect the fourth node of Brubaker's expanded quadratic nexus, international organisations, is highly salient. Using this updated model, it can be anticipated that the identity of Latvia's Russian speakers will be influenced not only by their relationships to both the Latvian and Russian states, but also by European structures and institutions. On a discursive level, if Russian-speaking politicians and journalists can demonstrate that the 'Europe' that Latvia has wanted to return to is in fact irreconcilable with 'actual' European norms, then this effectively serves partly to del-egitimise the current Latvian state, especially its 'return to Europe'.

Thus, when Tatjana Ždanoka can convince European politicians of the need to hold a plenary session in the European Parliament devoted to 'voting-rights of Latvia's non-citizens in local elections', not only is an issue of fundamental importance to her and her party being underlined, but differences between 'civilised' Europe and 'backwards' Latvia are also able to be highlighted. Ždanoka is quoted in *Chas* as saying, 'the fact that the European Parliament, in one of its plenary sessions, is examining the question of the discriminatory position of a concrete group of people in an actual EU country, is a unique event' (*Chas* 2 February 2009). Here Latvia is held up as an example of a country in direct opposition to the values of the EU. The perceived uniqueness of this discrimina-tion suggests that Latvia is out of tune with European conventions and standards. Alena Vysotskaya (2005: 1) also notes how representation in the European Parliament provided new opportunities for FHRUL, noting that,

[FHRUL] can now refer to previous precedents and norms of those old member states that have developed legal traditions of protection of their often regionally concentrated minorities . . . At the same time, minority activists can also demand more engagement from the part of the EU to defend their rights *versus* their own governments.

Another method that the Russian-language media use in order to further the idea that Latvia is far from being a 'normal' European country is through its scrutiny of Latvia's attitudes towards the holocaust and towards Nazi Germany. Accusations of Latvia's fascistic and Nazi tendencies inevitably come to the fore around the highly charged dates of 16 March and 9 May. As discussed above, each year on 16 March a number of Latvians meet in central Riga to lay commemorative wreaths in honour of Latvian veterans who fought and died in the Second World War within the ranks of the Waffen SS.

Although the events and circumstances surrounding the veterans' decisions to volunteer for the Waffen SS are highly complicated, the Russian-language press treats the whole affair with unwavering disgust. There is no attempt in the Russian-language print media to examine the 16 March events from anything but a position of moral indignation. This is because the events form a background for Russian-language newspapers to create, and each year reinforce, symbolic boundaries between Latvians and Russian speakers. Moreover, by treating the 16 March events with such one-sided disgust, newspapers are able to reinforce the notion that 'they' (Nazis, Latvians, fascists) are in direct opposition to 'us' (anti-fascists, Russian-speakers, liberators). In a *Chas* article on the 16 March commemorations, the final paragraphs expound the views of the two main parties the paper supports. The final paragraph, under the heading 'FHRUL: strong opposition' reads:

Vladislavs Rafaļskis, member of the Rigan city council, outlined FHRUL's position at a press conference. The position is effectively a strong opposition to any form of neo-Nazism and Russophobia. The appeal to ignore criminal, fascist ideology testifies to apathy and condones what is going on in the country. (*Chas* 13 February 2009)

'Neo-Nazism' is here directly linked to 'Russophobia', and is used to portray Russian-speakers as enlightened 'anti-fascists'. The term anti-fascist is used repeatedly in the Russian-language press in conjunction with the activities of prominent politicians and activists, with 'anti-fascist' groups outside of Latvia being of prime symbolic importance. Headlines in *Chas* and *Vesti Segodnia* announce, for example: 'Finnish anti-fascists oppose legionnaire marches' (*Chas* 17 February 2009) and 'Estonian anti-fascist calls Latvian authorities to account' (*Vesti Segodnia* 25 May 2009). Tatjana Ždanoka also devotes a great deal of her time to 'anti-fascist' activities and her image is enhanced by the media exposure afforded to her meetings with foreign anti-fascist organisations (for example *Chas* 17 February 2009 and 17 March 2009). This strategy has positive value as it allows Russian speakers to find a meaningful and morally justifiable status within Latvian society. At the same time, however, it further reinforces discursive boundaries by suggesting that Latvians are historically susceptible to fascist tendencies.

If it is possible to talk of the 16 March commemorations as constituting a profound symbolic othering of Latvians and 'their' value system, then 9 May is another significant date which symbolically helps to further create or embellish positive notions of Russian-speaking identity. Victory Day, on 9 May, is a holiday of extreme political and social importance for many Russian speakers, as it commemorates the Soviet Union's victory over fascist Germany in the Second World War. For the Russian-language media this is therefore the polar opposite of 16 March. If 16 March represents the totalitarian evils of Nazism for the Russian-language press, 9 May is seen unreservedly as representing liberation for Latvia and the Soviet Union from such evils. The historical interpretations of the Second World War therefore form a backdrop with which Russian speakers can claim to have a legitimate place in the modern Latvian state. For the Russian-language press this is a clear-cut issue and no shades of grey can be permitted to permeate the popular perceptions of Soviet 'liberation' and Nazi 'collaboration'. It is therefore a matter of grave concern for the Russian-language media that Latvian politicians and public figures are silent on the achievements of the Soviet soldiers ('liberators') who are so important to the identity of Latvia's Russian speakers:

> The silence regarding the heroic achievements of Soviet soldiers
> . . . is occurring against the backdrop of an effective glorification of
> the Waffen SS Latvian Legion. (*Chas* 21 January 2009)

> It is saddening that the self-assertiveness of the Baltic states is
> progressing exclusively along the path of exalting fascism . . .
> Meanwhile the Baltic prefers to count the cost of Soviet occupation. (*Vesti Segodnia* 11 July 2008)

Debunking the myth of restoration

In terms of the temporal narrative employed by Latvian nationalists in the years of the Awakening, a great deal of material was found that was devoted to dispelling ideas of the contemporary Latvian state as a continuation of the interwar republic. The temporal narrative stressed that the Soviet Union had destroyed and occupied the Latvian state, thereby perverting its natural political, economic, and social progression. For this reason the state and its attendant institutions were to be restored to their pre-1940 condition following Latvian independence in 1991. Thus, as documented above, in the immediate years following independence restorationists held sway in Latvia's domestic politics. This was evidenced most strikingly in the restrictive citizenship laws of the time that initially resulted in original Latvian citizenship being granted only to people who had been citizens in 1940 and to their descendants. Without doubt this narrative of legal restoration (or at least its active implementation) has had a very real impact on Latvia's non-titular population who have often felt victimised as a result of their non-Latvian roots. In many ways the narrative is seen by many as a vindictive and spiteful measure to punish Russian speakers for the ills of the Soviet period. Indeed, in 1993, while discussing the country's demographic situation, Georgs Andrejevs, the then foreign minister, commented on the need for 'affirmative action for Latvians to compensate them for the discrimination they have experienced in their own country' (as cited in Budryte 2005: 109–10). This 'affirmative action' has perhaps understandably been seen as highly discriminatory by many Russian speakers.

Since 1995, with the implementation of a naturalisation law, and 1998, when the process was sped up considerably, the restorationist tendency has somewhat receded in importance. However, the discourse and its consequences remain. Thus, the constructed group of Russian-speakers are constantly reminded by political elites and journalists of the inequalities in Latvia caused by the questions of citizenship and language. In order to debunk this Latvian discourse of restoration and temporal normality, a number of strategies were observed in this research. One major strategy was to cite numerous instances of Russian culture and influence existent in Latvia *before* the inception of the interwar republic. Therefore, instead of having to accept being labelled as occupiers and colonists, whose presence is somehow abnormal, *Chas* often printed articles arguing that 'We have always been here' (3 January 2009).

Russian schools are a central element in this search for historical legitimacy. In 2003–4 there was a great deal of agitation and tension surrounding the implementation of reforms to Russian upper second-ary schools which required 60 per cent of all teaching to be conducted in Latvian. This greatly exacerbated the tendency for language to become one of the most important markers of ethnic identity in Latvia. It also has meant that the issue of language has become one of the most important battle grounds in identity politics and in identity formation. Before this time language may have been a relatively important marker of national and ethnic identity but it was not until the school reforms that it became the most important marker. Mark Jubulis noted in 2001, for example, that 'the heterogeneous makeup of the Russian community [in Latvia] has hindered the development of a unified group consciousness, which could then provide the basis for group mobilization' (2001: 151). However, in 2003–4 the Russian language became an issue that was able to provide the symbolic basis for group mobilisation. Indeed, it was at this point that the term 'Russian-speaker' became the undisputed lin-guistic signifier of choice for journalists and politicians alike (see above). Not only was this useful in order to create an imagined community which was much neater than the previously used tags (Russians, Russian diaspora, Russophone community, Soviet-era migrants and so on), it also provided the opportunity to highlight 'language discrimination' as a means to promote the identity of Russian-speakers.

While much of the furore surrounding the language reforms has now subsided,[7] Russian schools are still portrayed as 'the cornerstone of Russian culture'. It is therefore with some pride that at the bottom of an article devoted to the 140th anniversary of 'one of the oldest Russian schools in the country' the author adds:

> P.S. it was only very recently, in December 2008, when the oldest Latvian [*latyshskaia*] secondary school celebrated its anniversary: Ventspils Gymnasium was 90 years old. That means that the tra-dition of Russian education in Latvia is half a century older than Latvian education! (*Chas* 26 January 2009)

Russian speakers' presence in Latvia is therefore framed and legitimised historically, allowing it to be seen as a temporal normality rather than an abnormality. For this reason the Napoleonic Wars suddenly take on a new significance for Russian speakers in Latvia. *Chas* reports on a monu-ment to the Russian Empire's victory over Napoleon which now lies in ruins in a 'forgotten' part of the country's capital. The paper draws its readers' attention to Latvia's selective historical memory, noting with some irony:

In Soviet times there was a full exhibition devoted to the 1812 war in Riga's Museum of History and Navigation. This exhibition is no more. It turns out that the city's history ended in 1710, when Peter the First took Riga, and then started up again in 1857 when the city's fortifications began to be torn down. A full 150 years have been missed out. (*Chas* 20 November 2008)

Another means by which the Russian-language press seeks to debunk the myth of restoration is through a selective historical examination of the events leading up to Latvia's incorporation into the USSR. Again it is possible to see that the occupation question is one that constantly looms large over Latvian politics and over questions of ethnic relations between Latvians and Russian speakers. If occupation is not accepted then it is also impossible to accept the idea of legal restoration, which is explicitly founded upon the understanding that Latvia was illegally occupied by the Soviet Union. In one *Chas* article attention is therefore drawn to the actions (and inaction) of the Latvian authorities in 1940. Historian and *Chas* journalist Igors Vatoļins contrasts the experience of Finland with that of Latvia noting that:

It was very different for Latvia. When, in 1940, the Soviet Union issued its ultimatum to the Latvian government, the political elite actually gave up the country. There was no kind of resistance. Additionally they organised no form of defence – not even a purely symbolic fight for a particularly important object, even if it was for an hour. There was an exchange of fire at the border but in the end they gave the country up without a fight. (*Chas* 22 July 2010)

This reading of the events of 1940 therefore allows Russian speakers to question the discourse of the restoration of Latvia's independence. If the Latvian authorities essentially agreed to the Soviet ultimatum and did not put up any resistance, even at the symbolic or diplomatic level, then it is less feasible to talk of Soviet occupation. This therefore puts into question the very idea of legal restoration and continuity.

Interestingly, the fact that Latvia had been ruled by the dictatorship of Kārlis Ulmanis from 1934 to 1940 was very seldom highlighted in the press analysis. Logically this fact could be used to question the restoration of Latvian statehood. If the principle of legal continuity is accepted as legitimate then Latvia should not have elected a fifth *Saeima*, but rather installed a dictator of the Ulmanis ilk. The new citizenship law, for example, ostensibly aimed to recreate the institutional arrangements that had existed in 1940. The parliamentary arrangements, however, opted for a system that had last been used in 1934, when Ulmanis dissolved parliament. While this argument was absent from the pages of *Chas*, the actions of president Ulmanis did came under greater scrutiny. Historian Vladimirs Simindeijs, in an extensive interview with *Chas* states:

> We need to bear in mind that [in 1940] the Latvian nation had already been deprived of the opportunity to participate in democratic elections for six years. In the course of the coup on 15 May 1934, the Latvian prime minister Kārlis Ulmanis dissolved the *Saeima* and abolished the Constitution . . . He, as the dictator, took full and complete responsibility for the Latvian nation.
>   . . . He did not utter a single word of protest against the events which were unfurling in the country. In his famous radio speech he called upon the people of Latvia 'to remain where they were'. It was he who provided all aspects of legitimacy for the advance of Soviet troops into the country. (*Chas* 5 August 2010)

The portrayal of Latvia as an anti-democratic and totalitarian state

Linked to a dismissal of both the temporal and spatial narratives of normality is a far more provocative approach that could be seen in the pages of *Chas* as well as in the political rhetoric of Latvia's Russian-speaking politicians. Just as Latvian activists had sought to depict the Soviet Union as totalitarian, and therefore inhumane, during the years of perestroika, certain of Latvia's Russian-speaking elites now also attempt to perpetuate the idea of contemporary Latvia as totalitarian. Although it may seem absurd, upon first inspection, to compare today's democratic Latvia with the authoritarian/totalitarian Soviet Union, this tactic should be viewed in the context of Latvian discourses of democratisation, human rights, and a return to such freedoms. These comments should not be viewed as actually trying to create an image of a totalitarian Latvia along the lines of, for example, Friedrich and Brzezinski's (1966) paradigm.[8] Rather, it should be seen as a critique, not only of the current Latvian state, but of the discourses which legitimised it in the first place. In the Russian discourse found within *Chas*, recourse to totalitarian imagery and accusations is most commonly seen in response to Russian speakers' status as non-citizens, and their perceived lack of rights to use Russian language and culture in Latvia's economic and political space. In *Chas*, under the heading 'Who's last in the language queue?' the article reads:

The paradox is that the government is increasing the requirements for knowledge of the state language at the same time as reducing the budget of the organization which gives out the critically important '*apliecības*' [certificates][9] . . . Who does this benefit? It benefits those who don't need to pass an exam and who have, in the mean time, managed to secure a plush position in the state structure and local government. (*Chas* 26 February 2009)

Clearly there is an effort to depict Latvian political elites as a ruling class that is not only exploiting Russian speakers for their own ends, but which is also deceiving Latvians as well. This discursive strategy is reminiscent of criticism levied at the Soviet regime and its nomenklatura comprised of bureaucrats and high-ranking party officials, who enjoyed access to goods and services unavailable to ordinary Soviet citizens. In place of the Soviet nomenklatura, Latvia now has its own ruling class: the 'professional Latvians':

[The ability to choose to speak Russian] is a threat, but not to integration or to the rights and interests of the Latvian nation. Rather it is a threat to the '*professional Latvians*' who, for two decades, have been feeding themselves on a crop of 'defence' of the single state. (*Chas* 16 June 2010, emphasis added)

Furthermore, explicit comparisons with totalitarian Latvia during the Soviet era and contemporary Latvia are gleefully reproduced in the Russian press. Again, this is most commonly associated with Latvia's language and citizenship laws. The Latvian state is portrayed as the vehicle by which Russian speakers are now discriminated against. Instead of the KGB during Soviet times, Latvia now has its own 'inquisitors' (*inkvizitory*) – the language inspectors (*Chas* 10 February 2009). Instead of Russians having a privileged position in Soviet structures, it is now the Latvians: 'The language inspection's vindictive operations are well-known far beyond Latvia's borders. In Europe they are in shock over the actions of this structure' (*Chas* 16 September 2010).

Of course, although this analysis of anti-discourse has been divided into three subsections, it does not necessarily follow that each of these subcategories is wholly separate from the others. In the above example, not only is the journalist pouring scorn over Latvia's supposed democracy and democratic norms, but he is also mocking Latvia's claims to be European. In this sense most of the examples which have been categorised as anti-discourse can be linked to other discursive strategies. Contemporary Latvia is not a fully democratic state, the argument goes, and therefore it is not European; contemporary Latvia has a certain amount in common with the Soviet Union, and is therefore neither democratic nor European.

SYNTHESIS WITH LATVIAN DISCOURSE

The main ways in which the Russian-speaking press attempt to dismantle Latvian narratives and discourses have been outlined above. There are, however, also clearly observable trends for the Russian-language press to also pursue integrational discursive strategies. It is argued that Russian-speaking identity is not formed solely in opposition to Latvian narratives and discourse, and is not solely a negative phenomenon which relies on the othering of 'Latvian nationalists', 'professional Latvians' and so on. Rather, it is also a negotiated synthesis between competing Russian, Latvian, and, to a certain extent, European discourses.

Many people (including a politically significant and vocal group of Latvian nationalists) see Russia as one of the, if not *the*, main poles of identification for Russian speakers in Latvia. This can be evidenced in claims that HC and FHRUL are in fact 'pro-Russian' and 'anti-Latvian' parties.[10] On one level it would seem logical that Russia would exert some form of symbolic influence over its so-called 'diaspora' or 'compatriots abroad' in Latvia. Russia is, after all, the country from which most people's families emigrated to Latvia during Soviet rule, and can therefore be seen as a historic homeland in the way that Brubaker's triadic nexus anticipates. The extent of this influence is addressed in more detail in Chapter 8.

However, even if Russia does play a major role in influencing Russian-speakers' identity, this research argues that this influence does presuppose that Russian speakers will not be loyal to Latvia and the Latvian state. Adopting the quadratic nexus approach, it is necessary to also look towards Latvia's titular discourses and narratives for a fuller explanation of contemporary Latvian–Russian identity. Latvia, as the nationalising state in which Latvia's Russian speakers reside, must also have a powerful influence on the formation of Russian-speaking identity. Indeed, as this research suggests, Russian speakers in Latvia are increasingly attempting to integrate their own discourses within already established discourses of the Latvian state. As such, the strategies employed within the media space are not exclusively anti-discursive ones.

The impact of Latvian narratives and discourse on Russian speakers

In this research I found a number of instances where the Russian-speaking community, instead of portraying themselves as a poorly treated and discriminated group, was *positively* framed in relation to Latvian narratives, discourses, and symbols. This must therefore be seen as a negotiated result of the dialectic relationship between competing identities and narratives that Latvia's Russian speakers are faced with. For example, on a very basic level there was often a geographical solidarity with Riga and Latvia rather than Russia. Thus, reporting on a hockey match between Dynamo Moscow and Dynamo Riga, *Chas* laments the loss of 'our' (*nasha*) team, referring to Dynamo Riga (2 March 2009). Moreover, there is a generalised conception of 'our people' (*nashi*) which does not always revolve around ethnocentric conceptions of Russianness and/or Russian language. In an article entitled 'Our people come top in Italy', 'our people' refers to two Latvian sculptors with particularly Latvian names, but this does not prevent the paper from taking pride in their international achievements (*Chas* 27 January 2009). Similarly, in a piece on the renowned Latvian opera singer Kristīna Opolais, the singer is referred to as 'our compatriot' (*nasha sootchestvennitsa*) (*Chas* 8 July 2010).

However, more than a geographical solidarity, this research found evidence of an acceptance of Latvian symbols and ideals centrally located within Latvian discourse. Latvian festivals were unanimously treated positively in *Chas*. For example, the traditional Latvian, pagan summer solstice *Līgo svētki* was described in very poetic terms: 'The bouquets of flowers fade away, along with the ferns and the Līgo beer, but the festival is always with us!' (*Chas* 25 June 2010).

A very significant symbol which is co-opted by the Russian-language press is that of the Freedom Monument. The monument in Riga, which stands as a pre-eminent symbol of Latvian nationhood and independence, is an obvious rallying point for Latvian nationalistic movements, and was central in the *Atmoda* years as a symbol of hope and Latvian pride, as well as serving as a practical location for demonstrations against Soviet power (Karklins 1994a: 67). Notwithstanding the statue's place in Latvian nation-building and symbolism, the Russian-speaking discourse in *Chas* also embraces and co-opts this symbol of Latvian nationalism, which is inscribed with the words, 'For fatherland and for freedom' (also the name of the nationalistic party ever so keen to portray Russian-speakers as disloyal and alien to the state). Discussing the actions of a number of foreign visitors to the nation's capital who have been arrested for urinating on the Freedom Monument, *Chas* states, 'the inhabitants of Riga constantly have to deal with the rowdy behaviour of drunken tourists who come to Latvia to spend a jolly weekend. There is always one of these fun-seekers trying to defile *our indestructible symbol* – Milda' (*Chas* 2 December 2008, emphasis added).

Milda is the commonly used name by which Latvians affectionately refer to the Freedom Monument. It is therefore striking that for Russian speakers this is also portrayed as 'our indestructible symbol'. The adoption of this and other symbols of Latvianness highlight the complex nature of the public discourse of Russian speakers. While they may display a keenness to remember and preserve links with 'Mother Russia', they also acknowledge Latvia as their actual homeland (*Rodina*) (for example, *Chas* 3 December 2008). Similarly Mihails Rodins, in his research, also finds a great degree of co-option of Latvian symbols among the country's non-Latvian population which reveals 'a unification of patriotism and loyalty among the whole population of Latvia' (2005: 49).

Perhaps one of the most striking aspects of the synthesis with Latvian discourse lies in the insistence that Latvia's Russian speakers have always been fervent supporters of Latvian independence and the then-stated goals of *Atmoda*. In many respects this assertion runs contrary to the discourse of certain Latvian nationalists, who hope to persuade Latvians that Russian speakers' allegiances lie, and have always lain, with Russia and the Soviet Union. There were many noticeable instances in this research which revealed a solidarity and affection for the *Atmoda* years. *Chas* reports on a protest meeting in Daugavpils, a city mainly populated by ethnic Russians, against the Latvian government. Here the reader is introduced to pensioner Valentina Bogdanova who shows a cut-out from a local newspaper from 1990, explaining:

It's a meeting in support of an independent Latvia which took place on this very spot 18 years ago. There I am in the photograph. Then I, along with other people from this city, went along to support the Popular Front. Dobelis[11] spoke, and in Russian, saying that in a free Latvia all inhabitants would be able to live dignified lives, that there could be no question of a division between Russians and Latvians ... And I believed it; I applauded, and I voted for an independent Latvia. We have all been deceived. (*Chas* 23 February 2009)

Russian-speaking discourse in Latvia appears to be keen to stress Russians' loyalty to the Latvian state and to an independent Latvia. This runs contrary to the stereotype of Russians, as presented by Latvia's nationalist parties, as a direct threat to the sovereignty and integrity of the state. Indeed, although there are historical references to the achievements of the Soviet Union in the Russian-language press of Latvia, there is a noticeable absence of calls to restore any of the institutions of the Soviet period.

During the years of *Atmoda* a reactionary neo-Soviet narrative (Smith et al. 1998: 10) which supported the maintenance of Soviet norms and institutions was the staple for the Interfront movements within the Baltic republics. Modern Russian-speaking discourse in Latvia, however, chooses to focus on the support for the Popular Front of Latvia from Russian speakers. To a large extent this is illustrative of the need to understand the selective power of discourse in the emergence of Latvia's post-Soviet identities. Karklins estimates, for example, that in a republic-wide advisory poll in March 1991, 47 per cent of non-Latvians voted 'yes' in answer to the question, 'Are you in favour of a democratic and independent Republic of Latvia?'(1994a: 101–2).[12] It is interesting that in the rhetoric of Latvia's 'Russian' political parties and the media, the focus now is necessarily on the 47 per cent of non-Latvians who supported independence.

The prominence of the pro-Soviet Interfront organisations during the *Atmoda* years in providing a representative voice for non-Latvians can therefore be seen as disproportionately high. Soviet bureaucrats and similarly interested parties were able to wield their positions of influence, and their places in the structures that existed at the time, to articulate their positions much more effectively and coherently than any other group of Russian speakers. Added to this, the voices of many 'Russian-speakers' who were supportive of Latvian independence were largely indistinguishable from the 'Latvian' discourses of the time that supported the Popular Front movement (Lapsa et al. 2007: 171). As discussed in Chapter 3, support for the Popular Front was actually significantly higher among Russians than support for the Interfront. Therefore, irrespective of the diffuse positions within the non-Latvian community, it is possible to see just how easily public perceptions can be manipulated, and just how important discursive positioning is to the subsequent legitimacy and identity of any given group.

Thus even contemporary academics working on the issues of identity politics in the Baltic states can fall prey to the quite incorrect assumption made by Magdalena Solska that 'the majority of the Russian-speaking population in all three [Baltic] countries supported the pro-Moscow and anti-independence Interfronts during the independence struggle' (2011: 1093). Survey data from the *Atmoda* period suggests that the Latvian Interfront movement actually had relatively little support. For example, in 1990 one survey reported that only 9 per cent of Russians in Latvia were willing to support Interfront candidates in the upcoming elections to the Latvian Supreme Soviet. Support for the Communist Party and the Popular Front among Russians stood at 23 per cent and 18 per cent respectively (*Atmoda* 13 March 1990).

In recent years survey data have suggested that an increasingly high proportion of Latvia's Russian speakers have a significant attachment to Latvia. In the 2004 Baltic Barometer, for example, Latvian Russian speakers were more than seven times more likely to identify themselves primarily with Russia than with Latvia (Rose 2005: 22). In contrast, in a 2014 survey (SKDS 2014: 10), non-Latvians in Latvia were almost five times more likely to feel a very close sense of belonging to Latvia than to Russia (50.7 per cent and 10.6 per cent of respondents respectively). While these surveys are not entirely comparable,[13] they provide support for the idea that Russian-speakers have considerable attachment to Latvia. While some data suggests that attachment to Russia has increased in certain periods, surveys consistently show far higher sense of belonging to Latvia than to Russia for the majority of Russian speakers.[14]

Certainly this is why an understanding of the synthesis between Russian and Latvian discourse is now so salient to this analysis. There is some evidence that many Russian speakers are now responding to, as well as creating, increased feelings of loyalty to Latvia (see also Rodins 2005). Importantly, as opposed to the *Atmoda* period, elites are choosing to articulate this loyalty in a more coordinated manner, in a way that claims to represent the discursively constructed group of Russian-speakers. In order to reflect this loyalty *Atmoda* is chosen as a frozen point of time which symbolically represents the Russian-speaking community's full acceptance of the idea of an independent Latvian state. This is the period where Russian speakers claim to have been working together with Latvians, 'when unity was not just an empty word' (*Chas* 12 January 2009).

CONSTRUCTIVE DISCOURSE AND THE ARTICULATION OF COUNTER-NARRATIVES

The third discursive strategy which was enumerated above was constructive discourse. As has been seen, Russian-speaking discourse has first rejected and then adopted certain aspects of Latvian (as well as Russian) discourse. Here it is argued that there is an increasingly coherent vision and ideal of how an ideal Latvia should look, from the perspective of the country's Russian speakers. This ideal is a result of a negotiated synthesis between the main Latvian and Russian discourses, narratives, and historical interpretations.

Because Europe plays such a significant role as a legitimising factor in both Russian-speaking and Latvian discourses, it should come as no surprise that Europe again figures strongly in this stage of the formation of Russian-speaking discourse. 'European norms' of multiculturalism are often invoked as positive examples for Latvia's political, cultural, and economic development. Such documents as the Council of Europe's *Framework convention for the protection of national minorities* provide a solid basis for Russian speakers to claim the right to practice and celebrate their particular traditions and cultures: 'The Parties undertake to promote the conditions necessary for persons belonging to national minorities to maintain and develop their culture, and to preserve the essential elements of their identity, namely their religion, language, traditions and cultural heritage' (Council of Europe 1995).

In light of this 'European' understanding of multiculturalism *Chas* chides Juris Asars, the then head of the Secretariat of the Special Assignments Minister for Social Integration, for not being aware of the content of 'fundamental documents in the field of social integration' (11 December 2008). Asars is quoted as saying: 'Our greatest mistake has been that we have allowed national minorities to express themselves and preserve their own cultural traditions with state money.' *Chas* notes, however, that the Secretariat for Integration Affairs itself is a product of EU money and was established as part of the Year of Multicultural Dialogue.

Utilising this multicultural vision for contemporary Latvia, *Chas* is keen to cite examples of Latvians and Russians going out of their way to explore the other ethnos' culture and language. The example of schoolgirl, Santa Getmančuka, is illustrative of this. At a gala concert to celebrate Tatiana Day, a celebration of Russian culture, *Chas* reports on Santa's rendition of a Russian song: 'Notwithstanding it being very difficult for her to speak Russian, and her Latvian accent which could be heard while she was singing, she performed the song with such feeling and enthusiasm that the hall simply exploded into applause.' The girl in question is also quoted as saying: 'I liked the fact that at this festival, even when you belong to a different culture, you don't feel like an outsider' (*Chas* 26 January 2009).

In one article entitled 'Ok, labi, давай' *Chas* editor Aleksejs Šeiņins, who was also a candidate for the political party For a Good Latvia, expresses his delight at hearing Latvian, Russian, and English being used interchangeably on the streets of Riga, citing numerous colourful examples of the three languages being used simultaneously (*Chas* 6 September

2010). Unfortunately for the purposes of this analysis they are largely untranslatable (see Appendix 1:5).

Likewise, *Chas* writes highly favourably of Latvian arts and culture. For example, an album by famed Latvian composer, Raimonds Pauls, is singled out for particular praise, with the author commenting that, 'surely, irrespective of nationality, everybody living in Latvia who loves nature and the country's unique landscapes can learn more about its cultural heritage thanks to these incredibly melodic modern performances of the Latvian nation' (*Chas* 2 March 2009).

For Russian-speaking discourse, this approval of Latvian culture plays an important discursive function. For Russian speakers this is used to highlight the desirability of a multicultural society. For this reason a number of integrational strategies which have been identified above are in fact simultaneously constructive strategies. Russian-speaking media discourse may well have been attempting to integrate within already existing discourses (for example in expressing appreciation for and claiming ownership of certain 'Latvian' symbols). However, this is also linked with a desire to create new realities and to propagate new discursively meaningful identity frameworks. In this example, integration within Latvian discourses is used as a means to support calls for a more multicultural Latvia. As part of this call, support is voiced for Latvian culture and Latvian language. At the same time, this is also part of a strategy that stresses the unique position of Russian speakers as a cultural (and economic) bridge between Latvian and Russian cultures.

Russian speakers as a bridge between Europe and Russia

Because Latvia's Russian speakers straddle competing discourses from Russia and Latvia, an effective way in which to come to terms with the inherent contradictions of their position is to create a unique space that can only be inhabited by 'Latvian–Russians'. There is evidence that Russian speakers from the Baltic states often feel like strangers when they visit Russia (Vihalemm and Masso 2003; Fein 2005; Zepa 2006). As such their sense of belonging to Russia is weaker than some people would like to suggest. However, their belonging to Latvia is also frequently put under question.

A feeling of belonging within any politically defined territory is inevitably closely connected to the state, and to the reciprocal relationship between any given state and it citizenry (Croucher 2004). For Russian speakers their relationship with the state is often subject to strain; a tendency which is often exaggerated in the media and by political parties. Russian speakers' sense of belonging is consequently also subject to question. Many Russian speakers were initially denied citizenship rights at the outset of the newly formed independent state, which can understandably have led to a feeling of inferiority in terms of their citizenship status (Aasland and Flotten 2001: 1028). The findings of the survey 'On the path to civil society' reflect this; whereas 93 per cent of Latvian citizens reported that they felt a personal sense of belonging to Latvian society, only 67 per cent of non-citizens shared this feeling (Zepa et al. 2001: 83).

One way in which Russian-speaking elites attempt to combat this perceived lack of belonging is to stress the group's unique function as a bridge between Russian and European (including Latvian) civilisations and cultures. This enables the country's Russian speaking population to create a unique identity that is able to embrace both cultures without losing either. Moreover, it facilitates the formation of an identity that has a distinctive purpose, and therefore sense of belonging. This is also a central tenet of Latvia's 'Russian' political parties. In their Founding Declaration HC declare:

> We are for a 'large' Europe which cooperates with its Eastern neighbours, including Russia, Ukraine, Belarus, and the countries of the CIS [Commonwealth of Independent States]. Latvia must become a leader for constructive dialogue with Russia and the CIS, and become a bridge between the EU and Russia. (Harmony Centre 2005)

Therefore, while the Latvian spatial narrative places Latvia firmly on the side of Europe, the Russian-speaking narrative spans both East and West. Moreover, it enables Russian speakers to be an integral part of the post-Soviet Latvian Republic. This is most visibly demonstrated in the political arena. A forum in Brussels entitled 'The EU and Russia: New Challenges' attracted much attention in the Russian-language press. *Chas* applauds Tatjana Ždanoka for her ability to bring together sides from Europe and Russia:

> The only Russian-speaking European Member of Parliament, Tatjana Ždanoka, has achieved the unachievable: bringing together in one hall people who had literally been on different fronts of the conflict in the Caucasus, namely politicians from Russian and from the EU. (*Chas* 12 December 2008)

HC's success in the Riga mayoral elections of 2009 and 2013 has provided more opportunity to articulate this vision of being a bridge between Latvia and Russia. Nils Ušakovs, the HC mayor of Riga, has stressed his desire to renew contacts with Russia both economically and culturally. The Riga government has hosted numerous delegations from its Russian counterparts and HC representatives have also been officially hosted in Russian cities. In many respects HC have attempted to market Latvia, and specifically Riga, as an economic and cultural gateway to Europe for Russia.

For some, the concept of Latvia as Russia's gateway to Europe is simply another manifestation of Russian chauvinism. Kristīne Doroņenkova, in her study of Russian media depictions of Latvia, observes how the concept of the Baltic as a 'window to Europe' is often propagated in the Russian (*Rossiiskie*) media. She notes that, 'to intellectual Russians, the Baltic states are not just a window, but a bridge between Russia and Europe, constituting "our Europe"' (2008: 109) In Russian (*Rossiiskii*) discourse the Baltic states can be conceptualised as 'our Europe' because Russian speakers, or Russian 'compatriots' abroad are often seen as a natural extension of the Russian nation, as visualised in neo-imperial terms (Morozov 2004: 319). Nevertheless, it is important to make a distinction between the discourses that emanate from the Russian Federation, and those that are generated and propagated from within Latvia.

From the perspective of Latvia's Russian speakers, the 'bridge' discourse is not simply conceptualised as a one-way conduit bringing Russian culture and traditions to the Baltic states. Rather, Russian-speaking discourse increasingly stresses its nascent Latvian values and inheritance and places emphasis on the multicultural nature of Russian-speaking identity within Latvia.

HC politicians are accordingly increasingly eager to speak Latvian in public interviews, even when a number of them have had, especially in the past, obvious difficulties in doing so.[15] In 2009, for example, Nils Ukašovs even greeted a visiting delegation from Moscow's city council in Latvian before continuing talks in Russian. It is therefore apparent that the Russian-speaking counter-narrative should be seen in the context of the processes of syntheses that are occurring between Latvian and Russian discourses.

THE EVOLUTION OF RUSSIAN-SPEAKING DISCOURSE

The discourses observed in *Chas* have been divided into three broad categories. This does not mean, however, that the discourses are equally used, nor that conflicting discourses (both negative and positive) are not employed by the same people simultaneously. For the sake of academic study there is a clear methodological rationale behind making such divisions. It is unlikely that such abstract distinctions are made by journalists and politicians. As a result, there is an inevitable overlap between the three strategies. While there was considerable overlap between the three discursive strategies, there were a number of observable trends within the individual anti-, integrational, and constructive discursive strategies.

An important observation from this monitoring period was that although anti-discourse constituted a significant proportion of the total discursive material that was analysed, the number of instances when it was employed generally fell. This downward trend was fully observable in the two comparable periods of this analysis (15 November 2008 to 15 May 2009 and 15 May 2010 to 15 November 2010). In the second period of analysis there were noticeably fewer articles or sentiments devoted to the discrimination of Russian-speakers in Latvia. Anti-discourse was still present, including the usual staple of articles detailing perceived language discrimination, caricaturing Latvian nationalists, and railing against the incivility of the Latvian state. The number of such articles, however, was certainly fewer. Instead there were even instances of journalists claiming that being a Russian speaker was actually an advantage in Latvia. One commentator states:

> There has been a thorough change in priorities. For Russian-speakers the so-called ethnic problems: language, education in one's native language, voting rights for non-citizens etc. are no longer so heated ... Today graduates of Russian schools sometimes speak Latvian better than their Latvian counterparts, and have therefore become more competitive on the labour market. (*Chas* 6 October 2010)

This is indicative of a more pragmatic approach to identity formation for Russian speakers. Language continued to be an important issue, and measures to curb the public use of Russian were still met with frank condemnation. There was, however, a shift towards seeing Russian as an economic commodity which placed Russian speakers in a unique position. Indeed, Russian was seen as a means to ease the effects of the economic crisis in Latvia. For example, the head of Daugavpils University is quoted as asking, 'If we can export sprats to Russia, why can't we also export higher education [in Russian]?' (*Chas* 28 June 2010). In the same article the journalist even proposes a pragmatic solution to those who fear the use of Russian in Latvian higher education: 'The law could be passed in such a way that only foreigners could be accepted for courses in Russian rather than our native students.'

A further evolution of *Chas* discourse was evident in the partial soften-ing of discursive strategies linked to the othering of Latvians. Although there were still numerous instances of *Chas* provocatively highlighting certain actions of 'Russophobic' Latvians, there were also new portrayals of Latvians who were more sympathetic to the position of Russian speak-ers, or at least not anti-Russian. One journalist noted that 'Generally the Latvian political elite are already moving away from national stereo-types' (*Chas* 26 August 2010). Amazement was expressed at the former President Vaira Vīķe Freiberga's sentiments that it would be for the good of society if Russian-speaking politicians were to be part of the new government, announcing that she 'unexpectedly has fallen in love with Russians' under the subheading 'metamorphosis' (*Chas* 7 October 2010). There was therefore a noticeable decline in anti-discursive strategies during the second monitoring period. At the same time, it is important to note that negative discursive strategies, such depictions of 'professional Latvians' and nationalistic, Russophobic, 'anti-European' Latvians, did not disappear during this period and continued to be used as important discursive reference points.

Within texts that may be categorised as representing integrational discourse there was also a noticeable increase in the number of instances when *Chas* journalists reported a solidarity and affection for Latvia and Latvian culture and language. For example, the Latvian school festival of song and dance, in which participants dressed in traditional Latvian cos-tumes and danced traditional Latvian dances, was described as 'an event for children and for adults, and for the country as a whole' under the heading 'The song which unites' (*Chas* 12 July 2010). Certain symbols of Latvianness were therefore co-opted simultaneously as symbols of Latvia's ethnic unity.

In the second monitoring period, however, there were fewer refer-ences to the *Atmoda* period than in the first period of analysis. This perhaps underlines the greater confidence felt by Russian-speaking elites in Latvia, who instead of looking to the past, were increasingly optimistic about their current and future status in Latvia. One article highlighted this in reflecting on the success of the 'Russian Duma' – Riga's municipal government which was led by the 'Russian' HC party:

> It was [Riga's municipal government's] fate to show the Latvian electorate that Russians in power not only do not pose a threat to the Latvian state, but dare I say, they can get on with things better than the Latvian ethnocrats [*etnokraty*], even when the govern-

ment are constantly throwing a spanner in the works. (*Chas* 4 June 2010)

Linked to this rise in optimism was also a rise in the number of direct and indirect references to Russian speakers as a bridge between Latvia and Russia. A great deal of attention was given to Ušakovs' visits to Russia and his calls for greater economic ties with Latvia's largest neighbour. Added to this, articles on Latvia's economic crisis often focused on the country's unique 'advantageous, geographical position' (*Chas* 27 August 2010). As FHRUL MEP Tatjana Ždanoka states in one article, 'Latvia, who best knows the peculiarities of Russia, needs to utilise its [linguistic] advantages and become a mediator for business contacts and to strengthen relations between the western countries and Russia' (*Chas* 20 September 2010). It was therefore apparent from the media analysis that the focus of Russian-speaking discourse in *Chas* was gradually moving away from singular efforts to dismantle Latvian discourse and was increasingly focusing on the more positive elements of identity construction.

CONCLUSIONS

The analysis of *Chas* points to a complex picture of how the publically constructed identity of 'Russian-speakers' is being negotiated in the context of over twenty years of Latvia's post-Soviet statehood. Naturally, an investigation of only one newspaper cannot tell us everything and the limitations of such a discursive approach to studying identity formation need to be borne in mind. This discursive approach does, however, allow for an observation of general trends in the identity strategies and positioning of 'Russian-speakers' by certain elites.

Using Brubaker's (expanded) nexus it has been possible to see how the conceptualised ideals of Latvia, Russia, and Europe are all invoked at different times to cement and legitimise Russian-speaking discourse. It is important, therefore, be very wary of assertions that Latvia's Russian speakers are simply an extension of Russian chauvinism, or that they, as 'compatriots' of Russians in Russia, represent a loyal 'fifth column' with more loyalty to Moscow than to Riga. Such accusations must be understood primarily to belong to the realm of the hegemonic desires of certain Latvian nationalistic forces.

Instead, a dynamic process is emerging whereby the relationship to the Latvian state appears to be increasingly important to Russian speakers. That is not to say that Russia is not an important element or even sponsor of Russian-speaking identity in Latvia (see Chapter 8). However, the Russian-speaking community has been forced to adjust to the discursively proscribed conditions that it now finds itself in. Indeed, because of the power of discourse to become cemented into social consciousness, it has been possible to see how certain concepts have become central in the discursive posturing of the imagined community of Russian-speakers.

For the case in hand, such nodal points are abstracts ranging from 'democracy', 'Europe', and 'loyalty', to historical interpretations of Latvia's past. It is because these points of reference are so central to the construction of Latvian identity in the first instance (see Chapter 3) that Russian-speaking discourse is forced to engage actively with them. However, it is through the process of antagonism and discursive posturing that these concepts are being challenged/negotiated and meanings are being purposefully altered. Therefore the Europe of Latvian discourse is a subtly different Europe from that invoked by Russian-speaking discourse.

There are, however, a number of paradoxes inherent in the Russian-speaking position. Although the othering of Latvians is essential to the internal unity of 'Russian-speakers', there is a visible desire and trend to portray themselves as Latvian–Russians, rather than Russian–Russians. Indeed, great efforts are made to stress the loyalty of Russian speakers to the Latvian state, its independence, and its ongoing democratic development. Nevertheless, the constant overemphasis on the actions of Latvian 'nationalists' (usually at the expense of portrayals of moderate Latvians) can leave no doubt that Russian speakers still define themselves in opposition to the discursive representations that 'Latvians' give to them. This 'self-marginalising strategy' (Golubeva et al. 2007) thus maintains the distinctness of the two groups while allowing 'Russian-speakers' to retain their internal unity.

However, in order to marginalise the Latvian hegemonic position, 'we', for Russian-speaking discourse, often embraces the 'civilised' nations of old Europe. By linking their own discourses with supposedly European discourses of equality, racial and cultural tolerance (which are in fact Russian-speaking discourses as much as they are somehow real European facts), Russian-speaking elites attempt to shift the relational nodal network that Russian speakers are attempting to operate within.

On the other hand, Russian-speaking elites have carefully been crafting out a space for themselves within the narratives of an independent, post-Soviet Latvia. In order to find such a place, they have been forced to adopt many positions congruent with Latvian discourses. In so doing, they have moved further away from wholesale 'pro-Russian' and 'homo-Sovieticus' identities and instead have sought a meaningful role as Latvian Russian speakers.[16] The analysis suggests that it is this dual, or 'bridge' identity which Russian-speaking elites are increasingly attempting to promote.

NOTES

1. Available at <http://www.ves.lv> (last accessed 17 July 2013).
2. An expanded version of this section was published as Cheskin, A. (2010) 'The discursive construction of "Russian-speakers": The Russian-language media and demarcated political identites in Latvia' in, M. Golubeva and R. Gould (eds), *Shrinking citizenship: Discursive practices that limit democratic participation in Latvian politics.* Amsterdam: Rodopi, 133–54. I am grateful for Rodopi for granting permission to use extensive parts of this chapter in this book.
3. For example in 1991 approximately 49 per cent of non-Latvians supported Latvian independence (see Karklins 1994a: 102).
4. For the sake of consistency, official Latvian names of individuals from Latvia are used in preference to their transliterated Russian versions. So Valērijs Agešins and not Valerii Ageshin, Irina Cvetkova and not Irina Tsvetkova.
5. The results of this analysis were originally published as Cheskin (2012b).
6. FHRUL was officially renamed the Russian Union of Latvia (RUL) in 2014, representing a shift towards a more ethnicised and radical programme. See Chapter 8 for more discussion of RUL.
7. New legislative initiatives were, however, introduced in 2014 that sought to move to 100 per cent teaching in Latvian by 2018. See Chapter 3.
8. Friedrich and Brzezinski (1966: 9) outline six main traits of totalitarian regimes, namely: an elaborate ideology, a single party typically led by one man, terroristic police, a communications monopoly, a weapons monopoly, and a centrally directed economy.
9. In the original article the Latvian word *apliecības* was used instead of its Russian-language equivalent.
10. See, for example, two blog articles published online at *Diena*'s internet portal by representatives of *Visu Latvijai!* [All for Latvia!]: 4 June 2009, *Par latviešu (ne) vienotību* [On the (dis)unity of Latvians]. <http://www.diena.lv/lat/tautas_balss/blog/raivis-dzintars/par-latviesu-ne-vienotibu> and 5 June 2009, *Divi no astoņiem Eiroparlamenta deputātiem būs krievu šovinisti* [Two out of eight Members of the European Parliament will be Russian chauvinists]. <http://www.diena.lv/lat/tautas_balss/blog/martins-kalis/divi-no-astoniem-eiroparlamenta-deputatiem-bus-krievu-nacionalisti> (last accessed 12 December 2010).
11. At the time of the article's publication a *Saeima* deputy for the nationalist party For Fatherland and For Freedom/LNNK.
12. This figure is based on census data and Karklins' assumption that 90 per cent of eligible Latvian voters participated in the referendum, with 95 per cent voting yes. This would mean that approximately 47 per cent of non-Latvians would have also voted yes. See Karkins 1994a: 113, footnote 52.
13. The Baltic Barometer respondents are people who chose to answer in Russian. In the SKDS survey the respondents are 'national minorities', of whom 79.6 per cent

reportedly spoke Russian at home, 8.4 per cent spoke both Latvian and Russian, and 9.6 per cent spoke Latvian (SKDS 2014: 5).

14. For example, in a 2004 survey 74 per cent of Russians expressed a sense of belonging to Latvia compared to 25 per cent who expressed similar sentiments towards Russia (Zepa et al. 2005b: 60). In a 2010 survey, the respective figures among Russians were 72 per cent and 33 per cent (Zepa 2011: 22).

15. The most notorious case of HC politicians struggling with Latvian was that of *Saeima* deputy Valērijs Kravcovs. In 2010 the National Alliance asked for his parliamentary mandate to be removed on the grounds that he had minimal knowledge of Latvian. At the time there was much debate about the legitimacy of Kravcov's Latvian language qualifications (a requirement for *Saeima* deputies). Kravcovs did not stand for re-election in the 2011 snap elections, and has since devoted a great deal of time to learning Latvian, even conducting interviews in Latvian with journalists. See *Diena* 16 July 2012: <http://www.diena.lv/latvija/politika/kravcovs-parvarejis-bailes-runat-latviesu-valoda-13957809> (last accessed 1 October 2014)

16. Of course, as explained in Chapter 3, we should also be careful not to assume that a majority of Russian speakers in the late 1980s/early 1990s simply held to such 'homo-Sovieticus' positions.

CHAPTER 5

Examining Russian–Speaking Identity from Below[1]

В гостях хорошо, а дома лучше
It's nice to be a guest, but it's better to be at home.
(Russian saying)

METHODOLOGY

A potential pitfall of a discursive approach to the study of national identities is that it can be easy to get carried away with a narrow focus on selected discourses. For example, there might be a temptation to study media discourses in isolation from any consideration of how these discourses are actually integrated into the identities of those people who read (or even those who do not read) the discourses in question. In many respects this again invokes the question of media effects – that is, how much impact do media discourses actually have on people's attitudes and behaviour? Most commonly a discursive approach is based on the ontological assumption that discursive actors create meaning. This, in turn, would indicate that it is important to study the discursive content of specific discursive agents, be they journalists, politicians, academics or any other socially important actors. While this research adheres to a constructivist position, it is also acknowledged that the sheer number of potentially creative agents means that it is impossible to conduct a comprehensive study of discourse for any given topic. It is precisely for this reason that CDA has traditionally focused on the areas deemed to be most discursively significant: the fields of politics and the media. This makes logical sense when consideration is given to the outreach and exposure politicians and journalists can potentially enjoy. Nevertheless, this traditional focus is not without its problems.

The most obvious potential problem is that, by focusing solely on the moment of *production*, we can miss the importance of the moment of *consumption* – for Stuart Hall (1980) encoding and decoding respectively. That is to say that it is possible to examine why and how discursive agents create specific discourses without considering how these discourses are interpreted by their audiences. Moreover, by privileging the moment of production when trying to map out the contours of group identities, there is the possibility of effectively trying to speak on behalf of large groups of individuals without letting them have any input into the conclusions that are drawn. In short, just because a group of people is written about or constructed in a particular way by a small group of 'powerful' individuals, this does not necessarily mean that this group actually shares the views and behavioural patterns ascribed to them.

In light of this potential pitfall, attention was turned to focus groups in order to assess the process of consumption (decoding) of media and political discourse by Russian speakers in Latvia. The focus groups were conducted in Riga, with the assistance of the Baltic Institute for Social Sciences, and consisted of three groups of participants. The first group (n=10) were aged between nineteen and twenty and were all undergraduate students enrolled on various degree courses in Riga. The second group (n=8) were post-graduate students from Riga, aged between twenty-two and twenty-five. The third and final group (n=10) were aged between forty and sixty and were all permanent residents of Riga. All participants were native speakers of Russian, where Russian was considered as their first language.

Inevitably there is a certain amount of sample bias as a result of these group compositions. However, it was felt that this sample bias was offset by the findings of the survey data (see Chapter 6) which was able to cover a broader cross section of Russian speakers and pointed to a number of similar trends among the population. Additionally, the parameters for these groups were deliberately chosen in order to focus primarily on younger Russian speakers, especially those who had been school children during the mass protests against Latvia's education reform in 2003–4. During these protests the participants of the first group would have been aged between eleven and twelve. Participants in the second group would have been aged between fourteen and seventeen. This period of time (2003–4) could consequently have been a formative one in their attitudes towards the Latvian state and the Latvian language. The group of undergraduates would also have been directly affected by the actual implementation of the education reforms in the classroom.

Another reason to focus on this younger, and more educated, cohort was that previous research has shown that younger Russian speakers are more likely to possess advanced language skills in Latvian (Zepa et al. 2008b), and that language knowledge is positively correlated with a preference for integration (Pisarenko 2006). Russian speakers enrolled on undergraduate and postgraduate courses at a Latvian university would necessarily have to possess a high level of competency in Latvian. In order to understand how Russian speakers were, or were not, able to integrate Latvia and Russia's official discourses and narratives, it therefore made logical sense to focus on this group, who would theoretically have a greater desire to integrate into Latvian society, and who were already in a linguistic position to do so. The older group of respondents was also chosen in order to contrast the opinions of people who were already adults (aged, as they would have been between twenty and forty) when the Soviet Union collapsed.

In the course of these focus groups the respondents were asked how they felt in relation to Latvia, Russia, and the Soviet Union, and to various aspects of their identity and sense of belonging. In general the questions arose from the discourse analysis of the country's Russian-language media and represent the main topics that were identified during this process. It was felt that it was important to compare the discursive content of the Russian-language press with the actual attitudes displayed by Russian speakers.

In an attempt to further examine the decoding process, the participants were all presented with a series of five extracts from *Chas* which they were then asked to read and to then to make comments regarding the contents of what they had read (see Appendix 1 for a full reproduction of all of the texts used). The participants were also asked to read and comment on an extract from a series of political proposals found on HC's website (also included in Appendix 1). It was felt that this would be an ideal opportunity to experience first-hand the decoding process, and to see to what extent these groups of Russian-speaking individuals would, or would not, critically and unquestionably consume the presented discourses.

KTO BЫ? WHO ARE YOU?

The first question that was posed to all three of the Russian-speaking focus groups was how they would characterise their nationality (*kto vy po natsional'nosti?*). Before moving to an analysis of the answers that were given by the respondents, it is important to bear in mind the historical connotations and usage that have been sedimented within this linguistic sign 'nationality' (Russian *natsional'nost'*, Latvian *tautība*) in its Latvian context. During the Soviet period, although everyone was a citizen of the USSR, 'nationality' was not defined by one's citizenship. Instead, in every Soviet citizen's passport the individual nationality of the bearer was recorded. The person could choose to record the nationality (sometimes translated into English as ethnicity in this context) of either one of their parents, but could not choose to denote nationality based on their residence. Thus, even if a person was resident in, for example, the Soviet Republic of Moldova all their life, and felt a genuine attachment to that republic, yet their parents were both 'Russian', then they had no choice but to also be officially classed as Russian.

The complexities of this Soviet categorisation of nationality were clearly seen in the responses to this initial question, especially among the older generation of respondents:

> You have to understand, it's very complicated. For example, my bloodline (*rod*) is so mixed up that I can't say what my nationality is. I have Poles in my bloodline, I have Russians. In spirit I'm a Russian insomuch as my language is Russian and I consider myself to be Russian. (Respondent aged between forty and sixty)

Nevertheless, even taking into account the complexities of describing their nationality, the vast majority of respondents in this age group preferred to refer to themselves as Russian:

> I'm Russian and very proud of it, although I have various mixed ancestry everywhere. But I consider my identity as Russian. (Respondent aged between forty and sixty)

One of the most interesting things about this identification within this age group was that, even with such an apparent affinity and attachment to being Russian, there was a near unanimous disapproval for the term 'Russian-speaker'. When asked if they approved of the term 'Russian-speaking community' (*Russkoiazychnaia ili Russkogovoriashchaia obshchina*) only one person indicated that they had no objections to the term. The other respondents in this age group expressed a great deal of unease at the term: 'No, please tell me, there's the word 'non-citizen' right? That's the word they thought up for us, and here they thought up 'Russian-speakers' . . . They invented it that's all!' (Respondent aged between forty and sixty).

In the two groups of undergraduate and postgraduate students a small number of respondents expressed a similar complexity of being able to state their nationality. However, there was a lack of any in-depth discussion of family histories, bloodlines, or the different nationalities in the respondents' family trees, as witnessed in the older age group. Instead, the younger participants seemed to be far happier simply to state that they were Russian, with perhaps a fleeting indication that their genealogy was somewhat mixed: 'Russian is the generally accepted marker of identity because, in actual fact, most people have mixed blood' (Postgraduate respondent).

It was also notable that the younger groups of participants, in contrast to the older age group, did not voice any concerns with the term 'Russian-speakers' as a valid signifier. Not one person in either of the undergraduate or postgraduate sample groups stated any problem with this term when asked if they approved of it: 'Well it's our term! (laughter)' (Postgraduate respondent).

This contentment with the term Russian-speaker for younger generations of 'Russian-speakers' is highly significant. As discussed in previous chapters, the term 'Russian-speakers' has been used with increasing frequency by the media and by political elites in Latvia, who have invested a lot of effort into creating and strengthening this group. Based on this research's small sample of focus groups, there is therefore evidence that this political and journalistic trend may have influenced the way young, educated Russian speakers feel about and imagine themselves as a group of people. This concurs with Vladislavs Volkovs' research which highlighted that 'the majority of Russian youth have a language identity. Their language identity appears to be the most significant national self-confidence factor, even more important than the factor of ethnic origin' (as cited in State Language Commission 2008: 137).

Even though the participants of the focus groups were generally happy to conceptualise themselves as Russians, or (primarily for the younger respondents) Russian-speakers, they also drew a sharp distinction between Russia and Europe, and interestingly placed themselves firmly on the side of Europe:

Here we have the contradistinction of Europe and Russia. This goes for Russians in Estonia and Latvia. (Postgraduate respondent)

Because Latvia is Europe and Russia isn't Europe, the standard of living naturally differs. (Undergraduate student)

It is interesting that the concept of Europe was used in a fundamentally different way from the way it was used in the Russian-language press. Instead of Europe being used as a benchmark with which to judge Latvia's claims to civility and enlightenment, the Russian-speaking respondents in this research used Europe as a *positive* means to distinguish between Latvia and Russia. In other words, instead of 'Europe' representing an anti-discursive mechanism, here it has an integrational-discursive function. Here, the Europe of Latvia's state-building project finds much greater accord with the actual discourse and understandings of Russian speakers than found within the media. Indeed, in every instance where the words 'Europe' or 'European' occurred in all three focus group discussions (a total of forty-one instances), never was this in connection with a negative, anti-discursive portrayal of Latvia. Instead, it was most commonly linked to an integrational discursive strategy linking Latvia with Europe, and even an othering function of depicting Russia, and Russians in Russia, as non-European and somewhat backwards.

> I don't know, I think Russia has become outdated. (Respondent 1)

> Sovietdom (*sovdepiia*)! (laughter) (Respondent 2)

> Well it's different there. Europe is Europe. There are European standards and quality products. (Respondent 3) (Three undergraduate respondents)

It was among the group of undergraduates where the connection between Latvia and Europe was most pronounced. Thoroughly in line with the narrative of the 'return to Europe' (see Chapter 3), one undergraduate stated that 'It's a straightforward fact that [Latvia] is a more modern country than Russia. Latvia was always more modern and that's why people came over here to live.' Members of the postgraduate group also expressed an understanding that Latvia was far more European than Russia.

In contrast, the participants from the older group of respondents only mentioned Europe or European on five occasions and four of these were more neutral references to people moving to European countries. Admittedly these 'neutral' references could also be seen as significant – that is, Latvia is considered distinct from the 'Europe' of these instances. Nevertheless, among this group, there was again a distinct absence of any negative use of the term European in relation to Latvia. Tentatively then, it could be posited that, among younger, more educated respondents, the higher frequency of positive, discursive geographical alignment with Europe points to an increasing integration of Russian-speaking discourse within official Latvian discourse.

THE INFLUENCE OF RUSSIA: POLITICS, CULTURE, AND HISTORICAL MEMORY-MYTHS

One thing that came across very strongly in all focus groups was that the Russian-speaking respondents considered themselves to be fundamentally different from Russians in Russia. In all of the groups this was a unanimously accepted position:

> We're completely different; like they say and joke about 'vodka and *vobla*'. They're so different there . . . we've somehow become Europeanised . . . When you arrive in Moscow everything is different. (Respondent 1)

> And they're different. (Respondent 2)

> They're different culturally. We're more reserved, not like Russians in terms of temperament – they're more emotional. (Respondent 3) (Three respondents aged between forty and sixty)

This difference was unequivocally outlined in all three focus groups. Interestingly, alongside the geographical division of Europe–Russia, a number of additional stereotypes were invoked in order to further distance Russians in Russia from Russian speakers in Latvia. In the above example the first respondent makes mention of 'vodka and *vobla*'. This is a reference to an infamous statement made by ex-Latvian president Vaira Vīķe-Freiberga. President Vīķe-Freiberga gave a radio interview in 2005 in which she discussed 9 May and the attitudes of a number of Russian-speaking people in Latvia, in which she stated: 'Of course, we won't change the conscience of those old Russians who on May 9 will wrap their *vobla* in newspaper, drink *vodka* and sing *chastushki* while remembering how they heroically conquered the Baltics' (*Baltic Times* 9 February 2005, emphasis added).[2] Notwithstanding the conversation being in Latvian, President Vīķe-Freiberga purposefully used the words *vobla* (dried and salted roach usually drunk with beer), *vodka*, and *chastushki* (traditional Russian folk songs) in Russian. However, these stereotypes are here turned around and used in reference to Russians *in Russia*. Another participant joked that the difference between Russians in Russia and Russians in Latvia was that, 'we don't throw [sunflower] seeds[3] on the streets and bottles on the Metro (laughter)' (Respondent aged between forty and sixty).

Nevertheless, even with a clear distinction for most respondents between Russians in Russia and Latvian Russians, the abstract concept of Russia still exerted a meaningful attractive force. Within Brubaker's triadic nexus, one of the main poles of attraction for national minorities is their 'historical homeland'. For Russian speakers in Latvia this is generally presumed to be Russia (although, of course, there may exist numerous historical homelands: Belarus, Ukraine and so on). When asked what the respondents considered to be their homeland (*rodina*), they were unanimous in citing Latvia as their homeland. Then asked if Russia also represented some form of homeland, the participants agreed that it did. One undergraduate referred to Russia as their 'secondary homeland', others as their 'spiritual homeland':

> As far as the question of [our] relationship with Russia goes, it's a question which in principle has two sides; because in the grand scheme of things there are two Russias. One Russia as a certain, you could say, *spiritual homeland* primarily because of the Russian language and literature which we've learnt at school from a young age – all the writers of Russian literature, and also our parents being from there. And then there's Russia as a modern state – the Russian Federation. I think that the majority of Russians in Latvia don't have any concrete ties with the state, with the Russian Federation, or with the political class. But the ties with Russia as, I don't know, the Russian hockey team, May 9 and so forth are much stronger and much deeper. (Postgraduate respondent, emphasis added)

This distinction between the two Russias: one a political entity, the other a historical, cultural, and symbolic entity, seemed to sum up the general attitude towards 'Russia'. This was underlined by the responses elicited by an excerpt from *Chas* which was distributed among the participants for discussion. In the article Konstantin Kosachev, the then chairperson of Russia's Duma Committee on Foreign Affairs, was quoted as saying:

> We should not restrict our campaigning for the Russian world simply to its cultural and historical aspects. It is all good and well if people love Russia, speak Russian, and play Russian folk instruments. But this is not enough.
> Does not every diaspora lobby for the interests of its fatherland from the country of its residence? (*Chas* 11 December 2008, see Appendix 1:4)

The assertion that Russian speakers in Latvia could be used as some form of lobbying group for the interests of the Russian Federation was generally met with a mix of amusement and derision:

It's incredible that such an educated person can say such funny things. (Respondent aged between forty and sixty)

In all honesty I probably consider myself a Latvian (*latviika*). . . Yes Russia is my historical homeland, but I have never been there, and if the truth be told I'm not going to fight for them. (Undergraduate respondent)

Nevertheless, in the same *Chas* article Mr Kosachev refers to 'the Russian world'. This collocation has become widely used in recent years. Not only is it the name of Russia's state cultural outreach programme (Russia's equivalent of the British Council), it also represents a transnational, civilisational space (Wawrzonek 2014). For Kosachev, this space clearly includes Latvia. Asked whether the respondents were in fact living in this so-called Russian world the answer came back that, yes, indeed they did inhabit such a space: 'It's our world, the world of Russians in Latvia' (Respondent aged between forty and sixty). Again, however, the distinction was clearly drawn between the cultural Russian world and the political Russian world: 'The Russian world (*russkii mir*) but not the world of the Russian Federation (*rossiiskii mir*)' (Postgraduate respondent).

Politically, the responses of the focus group participants hint at the negligible potential for the Russian Federation to have any meaningful impact on Latvia's Russian speakers. Culturally, however, there is an obvious link between the 'historical homeland' of Russia and the world inhabited by contemporary Russian speakers in Latvia. As discussed in Chapter 3, one of the main stated areas of concern for the Russian Federation in respect to its foreign policy has been a desire to strengthen its historical interpretation of the Second World War. For this reason it was interesting to note how the participants responded to the question of Soviet occupation. In truth there was a wide range of responses in answer to whether it was fair to talk of Soviet occupation in the Baltic states.[4] Some expressed a straightforward acceptance of the occupation: 'It's a political game. There was an occupation. What, in 1940 did someone invite [the Soviets] in? That's all nonsense' (Respondent aged between forty and sixty). Others were more inclined to defend the actions of the Soviet Union:

Latvians think that the Russians should have liberated this country and then just left. In reality, if we think about it logically, what would have happened if the Germans had remained here all this time? They would have set up concentration camps and killed the

Latvians in these camps. After all that it's just funny to hear that the Latvians aren't happy. (Undergraduate respondent)

On the other hand a number of people also adopted a fairly noncommittal stance towards the question of occupation, perhaps seeing it as an issue that should simply be put to rest: 'There are always two sides to anything and so there's never one opinion. That's why people are never satisfied . . . and why it's completely senseless' (Undergraduate respondent).

Generally speaking, even if the concrete question of whether or not there was a Soviet occupation was seen primarily as a 'problem of terminology' (postgraduate student), the respondents were far more eager to point out that the Soviet Union was not an entirely negative phenomenon for Latvia. Examples were given of factories that used to operate in Soviet times which have since been closed, and of a life that was, in many respects, better than at present. The question of the occupation was therefore treated on two levels. On one level there was the academic question of a correct legal and moral definition for the events of the Second World War. On another level there was a discussion of the ways in which the acceptance of occupation was manipulated by certain political forces:

> If we just look at the terminology [of the word occupation] then I'm completely tolerant of it and think it's fine. But for Latvians occupation is a real kind of hurt.

> well at the moment, I don't know, I think that now they only talk about it to turn Latvians against Russians. (Two undergraduate respondents)

It would seem therefore, that the respondents were wary of the Latvian discourse of occupation, which is so observable in media and political discourse. According to the official discourse, as implemented in the country's official policies on citizenship, the majority of Russian speakers are a direct consequence of occupation. Therefore, for the majority of Russian speakers, to admit to occupation is to admit to being an occupant:

> Well it's not nice to be occupants of course, but you get used to it. (Respondent aged between forty and sixty)

> Latvians are always saying, and I hear it, "'Russian occupants (Krievu okupanti)' and so on. (Undergraduate respondent)

In terms of placing themselves neatly within the official discourses of the Russian Federation or of Latvia, Russians speakers are thereby placed in a difficult position. If they were to adopt a fully integrational discursive approach to the question of occupation then it would also paradoxically serve to delegitimise their position within Latvia and push them 'back' towards Russia – it would be tantamount to admitting that they have no morally or legally justified place in modern Latvia. On the other hand, as has been shown, the attraction of the Russian Federation is actually rather weak, even if the more abstract attraction of 'cultural Russia' is relatively strong.

Notwithstanding this tension, official Russian discourses of the Second World War were largely supported by Russian speakers in Latvia. In many ways the memory-myths of the war appear to have been passed down from parents and grandparents to the younger generations of Russian speakers. For this reason the respondents related the great importance they attached to 9 May (Victory Day). A number of people noted that their parents or grandparents participated in the war and that they had a duty to pay their respects for the sacrifices that were made for them. The discursive bonds of family should not be underestimated here. For Russian speakers to integrate into the official Latvian discourse of occupation, this would necessarily entail admitting that the heroic achievements of their parents and grandparents were perhaps not as heroic as some have suggested:

> My great-grandfather and great-grandmother, who are now in heaven, lived through the war. And my grandmother and grandfather both were alive at the time of the war. People lived and [Victory Day] is about remembering. They liberated us from fascism. They aren't occupiers but liberators! (Postgraduate respondent)

One has only to tune into Russian (*rossiiskii*) television for a few days to see how Red Army veterans are treated with the utmost reverence in Russia. Russia's cultural space is full of broadcasts, documentary and feature-length films devoted to the theme of the Great Patriotic War. As was evidenced in the *Kononov* v. *Latvia* case in the European Court of Human Rights (see Chapter 3), even when there is evidence to suggest that an individual in the Soviet army committed heinous crimes during the war, that is not enough for everyone to doubt his heroism and honour, for he was fighting for a sacred cause.

It therefore seems 'natural' that Russian speakers would not wish to defile the sacred memory of their relatives by debasing their heroic achievements. For this reason a number of subsequent positions are also maintained. As was noted above, a number of respondents pointed to the positive achievements of the Soviet Union in Latvia, not least saving the country from the despotism of fascism, but also its positive achievements in Latvia's social and economic development: 'Yes in principle, almost all of what was built in Latvia was built when the Russians were here, when we had the Soviet Union. But they still whine about it today (laughter)' (Undergraduate respondent).

As outlined above, autobiographical memory is a distinct phenomenon from historical memory. In the context of Russian speakers in Latvia, the autobiographical memories of the Second World War have been (mostly) buried with the parents and grandparents of today's Russian speakers. In its place we now have a generally accepted collective memory of the war. This memory, instead of representing a view from one point in time, contextualises and justifies the actions of a particular time within the understandings of the subsequent history which followed the war. Thus, the collective memories of the Second World War seem to be an extremely important nodal point in the consolidation of Russian-speaking identity in Latvia. To this end, the role of the Russian Federation is significant for the maintenance of such memory-myths. It is primarily within the mythscape of the Soviet Union and subsequently the Russian Federation where this memory has been cultivated (Weiner 1996; Tumarkin 1987). Nevertheless, this is not to say that there was not an observable influence also from the Latvian state and from various Latvian sources.

THE INFLUENCE OF LATVIA: INTEGRATIONAL OR ANTI-DISCOURSE?

The data gathered from the focus groups, just as with the data from the media analysis, points to a complex relationship between Russian speakers and the Latvian state. In both instances there were occurrences of both anti- and integrational discourse in relation to Latvian state discourses and narratives. To deal with this complex issue it is important firstly to outline the ways in which Russian speakers employed integrational discourse within the focus groups, followed by an examination of instances of anti-discourse. This data is then compared to the data from the media analysis in order to determine whether there is a clear link between the discursive strategies found within the Russian-language media and the observed, discursive attitudes of Russian speakers.

In the media analysis of Latvian newspaper discourse a great deal of integrational discourse was found whereby Russian speakers were linked into historically established, Latvian discursive relations. In the course of the focus groups which were conducted there were also numerous instances where Russian speakers attempted to integrate into Latvian discursive understandings. On the topic of 9 May, the respondents generally adhered to the standard official interpretation of historical events of the Russian Federation. There were, nonetheless, a few participants who were happy to say there was an occupation. Added to this, there were indications that the respondents were generally aware that the history of the Second World War was perhaps not as straightforward as it was often presented in either the Russian or Latvian official versions. This was evident in the discussions of the 16 March marches in remembrance of the Latvian Waffen SS legionnaires. Instead of condemning the marches wholesale, the participants expressed acknowledgement that history was complicated:

> It's actually complicated. Everyone has their own truth. (Respondent 1)

> It's their right [to march]. We can't condemn these old men who participate. They were alive back then. (Respondent 2)

> They have their rights, they see things in their own way. They were on the other side. It's really complicated when we judge them on various grounds. But those people have it stuck in their minds. They were on the other side, and they see things completely differently. (Respondent 1)

> We can't condemn them. (Respondent 3) (Three postgraduate respondents)

There were also many other instances where the Russian-speaking participants of the focus groups expressed opinions which could be categorised as integrational discourse. Firstly there was a deep affection for Latvia as a beautiful and good place to live: 'Well personally I like it in Latvia; it's a beautiful place Riga, and Latvia' (Undergraduate respondent). Moreover, in response to the question, 'Do you identify more with Russia or Latvia?', every single respondent answered that they identified more with Latvia: '[I identify more] with Latvia most likely. Russia is somehow far away and there are so many people there that you don't have any real place. But in Latvia you feel needed' (Postgraduate respondent). Added to this there was not a single instance of any respondent in any of the three groups who expressed a negative opinion towards Latvian culture or towards the Latvian language in and of itself. Instead there was a widely accepted belief that everyone in Latvia should learn Latvian, and should also respect Latvian culture:

> This is an extremely beautiful country and without the Latvian language it wouldn't be Latvia. And I would have thought that, in principle, most people sitting here also wouldn't want Latvian to disappear. (Undergraduate student)

> The state language is Latvian and we should know Latvian. (Respondent aged between forty and sixty)

One of the main state mechanisms which has been utilised in order to secure the status of the Latvian language has, of course, been Latvia's education reforms which came into force in 2004. Contrary to expectations, the respondents did not condemn the 2004 education reforms which affected Russian-speaking schools. It should be remembered that the respondents from both the undergraduate and postgraduate group were of an age that they would have been pupils in 2003–4 during the furore surrounding the education reforms. Indeed, many of them recalled attending the protests. However, when questioned about their views on the reforms, most people were actually rather stoical about the effects of the reforms, and even viewed them positively: 'It's good like it is now. Even if we've been coerced then at least we've been coerced. And if I know Latvian then it's thanks to this coercion which is set out by this law' (Undergraduate respondent).

Before getting carried away, however, with the extent of Russian-speakers' identification with Latvia, Latvian culture, and the Latvian language, it is also important to consider the numerous instances where Russian speakers had great difficulty integrating into Latvian discourse. The analysis of Russian-speaking media pointed to the continued use of anti-discursive strategies that highlight the marginalisation and discrimination of Russian speakers in Latvia. Notwithstanding the tendency for Latvia's Russian-language press to focus on personal stories and narratives in pursuit of this goal (Zelče and Brikše 2008: 92), the data from the focus groups revealed a particular nuance of Russian-speakers' existence in Latvia that was not so evident in the media analysis. In the Russian-language press the action of drawing attention to the discrimination of Russian speakers serves a useful othering function: 'look how "*they*" treat "*us*"!' When the focus group participants talked of instances where they have felt excluded from Latvia's social and political spheres, they did not necessarily link this with an attempt to depict a monstrous Latvian 'other'. Instead there was often simply sadness that at some level they did not quite belong in Latvia:

> I'm appalled by the words of my son, who, in a way, represents young people. He returns home and says 'Mum, at university in England, I talk with the guys from different European countries. They tell me about their homeland and I get the impression that they love their homeland.' And maybe he and others from Latvia miss certain things from home; they return home and 'Oh this is where I used to play', 'This is where I went to pre-school.' But they don't have that feeling of homeland and they find that hard. (Respondent aged between forty and sixty)

> I think that Russians feel more at ease abroad than Latvians . . . I'm saying this based on my friends and acquaintances, because this is our home country, but still it's not quite like that. The Latvian language and all the rest, and many people know Latvian, but still it's a little different. Latvians abroad miss Latvia. For them it's more of a homeland than for us. (Postgraduate respondent)

While these sentiments were emotionally charged, it was significant that they were not accompanied by any vitriol directed towards Latvians or any other group. In fact the respondents showed a great deal of empathy towards the position of Latvians – a phenomenon almost wholly absent from the pages of the Russian-language press:

> Well because in Riga it's roughly 50 per cent Russian and 50 per cent Latvian. You walk along the street and only hear Russian. It's not nice for Latvians which is why they make a fuss about it. Put yourself in their position – imagine I live in England and when I walk down the street there are only Latvians instead of people from England. Well it wouldn't be nice. (Undergraduate respondent)

On the other hand, many respondents cited instances where they had personally experienced discrimination against them for being Russian speakers. Sometimes this was more subtly expressed; sometimes it was more explicit. However, the anger expressed in the pages of *Chas* was notably toned down. Instead, Russian speakers generally expressed a sense of miscomprehension rather than anger at certain phenomena, not least the status of 'non-citizens' for a large proportion of the population:

My dad categorically refuses to learn Latvian because he was born here – he will soon be fifty. He pays a crazy amount of tax, but for some reason he's not considered the same citizen as, I don't know, the majority of people. And so he has this anger, he has his principles and so that's where the enmity comes from. *Well not enmity, rather miscomprehension.* (Undergraduate respondent, emphasis added)

Certainly it is significant that the respondent in the above quotation chose to qualify her father's position from 'enmity' to 'miscomprehension'. Indeed, in response to this statement another undergraduate student stated:

If I'm honest, then if he thinks like that, then I couldn't disagree more with him. It's just that I think it's a problem of the state. I'm also a non-citizen of Latvia but I'm going to take the exam, you know I want to be a citizen of this country and I don't really want to leave here. (Undergraduate respondent)

Here it is interesting that the problem is ascribed as a state problem rather than resulting from the discriminatory actions of certain nationalistic Latvians (as it is often portrayed in the Russian-language press). Moreover, the respondent above was more than willing to accept the state's conditions for naturalisation and had a real desire to have a meaningful and legitimate place in Latvia and the Latvian state.

Certainly one potential reason why Russian speakers seem to be more phlegmatic in assessing their perceived discrimination in Latvia is that they are able to differentiate between interpersonal and intergroup relations. Studies have often found a link between positive interpersonal contacts across groups and improved intergroup relations. The most developed literature in this regard comes from social psychology and intergroup contact theory. Indeed, in Pettigrew and Tropp's (2006) meta-analysis of 516 studies which employed such an approach, as many as 95 per cent reported a negative relationship between intergroup contact and prejudice. Additionally, friendships which transcend group boundaries have also been found to negatively correlate with prejudice (van Dick et al. 2004; Hewstone et al. 2006). In the course of the focus groups the respondents indicated that they had a fairly high level of contact with Latvians either at work or in a social setting, and that they had little or no problems interacting with Latvians:

When we're talking about an individual, when you take a concrete person, then in principle it's really easy, in my opinion, to talk with Latvians . . . I have some acquaintances, not like super-good friends, just good acquaintances and we study together, relax, I mean we all get on without any problems. There are jerks among Russians and among Latvians. (Postgraduate respondent)

Because of the relatively high level of contact between Russian speakers and Latvians, the respondents were able to acknowledge openly that the intergroup distance between Latvians and Russian speakers was most visible in the media and political spheres, and in everyday life the two communities were far closer. In terms of interpersonal relations, Russian speakers were thus much more inclined to suggest that, on the whole, relations were not too bad (or at least not as bad as portrayed by the press). This is a vitally important point to consider for this study. It would suggest that the distinctness of the two discursively proscribed communities seen within the country's media and politics is perhaps not as visible in the everyday interactions of Latvia's inhabitants.

Even though the focus group respondents were more balanced in their opinions than journalists, a number of them nevertheless expressed their displeasure at the way Russian speakers were sometimes treated in Latvia: 'Come on, let's be honest. It's simply that they have cast aside the Russians who voted for their homeland, for independence. They just took them and then cast them aside rather than giving citizenship to everyone who had come here' (Respondent aged between forty and sixty).

The most common gripe among the focus group participants was the issue of citizenship. For many people it would seem that the idea of non-citizenship is degrading and insulting. One man in the older age group joked that Russians were no longer lowly 'occupants' in Latvia: 'Now Russians have lessened that to the grand status of . . . non-citizens! (laughter)' (Respondent aged between forty and sixty). It would seem that the reason why the issue of non-citizenship is so offensive to Russian speakers, is that it represents the most visible and actual sign that they have no legitimate place in Latvia.

Admittedly, while group relations were generally seen in a positive light, there was a generally accepted notion that the Russian-speaking community was largely separate and distinct from the Latvian community. One undergraduate participant was particularly forceful in voicing her opinions. Asked whether the Russian-speaking community was very different from the Latvian community, she replied: 'They are completely different . . . That's why since 1991, when Latvia became a separate state, there's been a war between Russians and Latvians. You know, it's complicated for Russians in Latvia' (Undergraduate respondent).

Nevertheless, the participants of the focus groups generally saw interpersonal relations in a relatively positive light. While there was an abstract understanding that the two communities were very separate, there was still a great deal of empathy, open-mindedness, and collectedness displayed by the respondents in the face of potentially very emotive issues. Perhaps one respondent summed up the general mood: 'There are only two nationalities: a good person and a bad person' (Respondent aged between forty and sixty).

IN SEARCH OF HOMELAND: FINDING A LEGITIMATE PLACE FOR RUSSIAN SPEAKERS IN LATVIA

In the media analysis the third major area that was examined was constructive discourse. In the Russian-language press this was employed as an increasingly important discursive strategy which allowed Russian speakers to preserve many discursive connections with their 'Russian' heritage and cultural belonging, while also acknowledging their loyalty and belonging to Latvia. In the media discourse this was achieved by presenting Russian speakers as an economic, cultural, and political bridge between Russia and Latvia (Europe). Certainly this was a strategy that was also evidenced in the focus group discussions. It was, however, also accompanied by a counter-strategy – that of indicating that Russian speakers were *neither* Russian *nor* Latvian, and that they were a group of people stranded without a culture to call their own. On the one hand this could be perceived as a destructive, rather than constructive, discursive strategy. The discursive process of self-marginalisation, however, can also be seen as constructive, insomuch as it has potential to unite a group of people around the idea of marginalisation and differentness. When asked if they considered Latvian culture part of their culture, a number of postgraduate students indicated that they did not:

No. It's Latvian culture. (Respondent 1)

As regards the culture of Latvia, we hardly, I mean, we don't try to get into it (*proniknut'*). It's there and that's fine. (Respondent 2)

Just like they don't get into [Russian culture]. (Respondent 1)

It's not our [culture]. I mean from the outset we don't relate to Russia, although we relate to the Russian people (*narod*). But we don't relate to Russia, and neither do we relate to Latvian culture. So that's the sort of community we have here. (Respondent 2) (Two postgraduate respondents)

This lack of belonging to either Russian or Latvian culture is linked to the sense that many of Latvia's Russian speakers seem to lack a homeland, or do not feel completely accepted in Latvia as legitimate citizens. Nevertheless, although many Russian speakers may well feel at the margins of, or excluded completely from, Latvian culture, they still displayed a desire to maintain and cultivate links with *both* Russian and Latvian culture:

> I think that if there are Russians here then they shouldn't forget their own culture, and, how can I say this, well they should honour their traditions. But still they should know the Latvian language and shouldn't ignore it, like, I don't know, the majority of people over 40 who lived here in the Soviet Union who completely ignored it. (Undergraduate respondent)

Indeed, as this quote suggests, there was a sense that the younger Russian-speaking participants wanted to be more integrated into Latvian culture than their parents. There was a widely accepted acknowledgement that Latvian language and culture were largely ignored during Soviet times, and a wish to reverse that trend. Therefore there is evidence of a fairly strong desire to integrate into and learn Latvian culture. On the other hand, there was also a widespread feeling that Latvian culture is 'Latvian', that is, for 'Latvians' and not really their culture. This is compounded by the fact that Russian speakers often do not feel like Latvia is their genuine homeland. Further, there is an equally strong feeling that Russian speakers, while learning about Latvian culture, should not neglect their own Russian cultural heritage.

These three factors lead logically to the creation of a new discursive and symbolic position for Russian speakers in Latvia – the construction of a new identity which straddles both Russian and Latvian discourses, but which also creates a new identity. In the media discourse this was evident in the desire to point out the value of Russian speakers in Latvia, who could function as a bridge between Russia and Europe. In the focus group discussions the respondents were presented with a quote from *Chas* which championed the use of Russian as an economic resource for Latvia to build relations between the West and Russia (see Appendix 1:1). The respondents agreed entirely with this sentiment: 'Because [language] is a resource. If you don't use a resource then someone else will use it . . . But in principle Latvia has traditionally not utilised at all the resources which are here. So there's nothing surprising in this' (Postgraduate respondent).

As the conversation progressed from this quotation, one respondent agreed that Russian speakers were a bridge between Russia and Latvia: '[Russian speakers] are a bridge. All business relations are based on acquaintance, on family ties. All Russians work with Russia' (Respondent between forty and sixty). Admittedly, although the focus group participants were agreeable to the idea of Russian speakers functioning as a bridge between Russia and Latvia/Europe, they were not necessarily forthcoming in expressing this idea explicitly. Rather, the idea was somewhat elicited. In the above example, for example, the respondents were asked outright if Russian speakers could be considered as a bridge between Russia and the West. Nevertheless, the idea still had resonance with the participants. For most people it was desirable for Latvia to start to utilise its perceived geographical and linguistic advantages vis-à-vis Russia, and to put more effort into developing economic ties with Russia:

It would be better for Latvia and relations with Russia would be much better. That would be ideal.

Latvia would have contact with Europe and would be a bridge to Russia. Yes, and in terms of geography it's also in a good position. (Two undergraduate respondents in response to the question, 'What do you think of the idea that Russian speakers in Latvia can become a bridge between the West and Russia? Have you heard of this idea?')

It was also significant that almost the exact same sentiment was similarly expressed by the postgraduate group of respondents: 'Yes, the geographical position [is advantageous] – I mean Latvia as a bridge from Europe to Russia, that is, through Latvia, I mean, talking about freight, connections, and logistics – in that respect' (Postgraduate respondent in response to the question 'Would you say that Latvia was in an advantageous geographical position?'). Thus, in the first example from the undergraduate group, the prompt of a bridge between the West and Russia elicited an explanation that Latvia was in an advantageous geographical position. In the second example the prompt was the advantageous geographical position and the elicited response was that Latvia was a bridge between Europe and Russia.

However, in terms of national identity, Russian speakers seem to be more concerned with 'concrete' issues such as economics and social cohesion rather than ethnicity or language: 'For people now, well in our country in our situation it's important to solve all these economic problems. Language is already, I don't know, it's an anachronism' (Undergraduate respondent). For this reason the bridge between Russia and Europe is perceived less as a symbolic device which gives meaning and legitimacy to Russian speakers in Latvia, and more as a pragmatic approach to deal with Latvia's largest neighbour. This was largely confirmed by the respondents' reaction to the second of the *Chas* excerpts (see Appendix 1:2). The quote talked of how 'the so called ethnic problems' were no longer so important for Latvia's inhabitants, as economic concerns were far more important:

> We're used to it now . . . About five or six years ago [ethnic issues] were very salient. It all happened when there were these [education] reforms. (Respondent 1)

> Yes, and we even played an active role in them. (Respondent 2)

> Yes, we did then, but now we've become accustomed to it, we've got used to it, and we've come to terms with it. Well what can you do? It's just the way it is. But Latvians (*latyshi*) are also such a phlegmatic nation. (Respondent 3) (Three postgraduate respondents)

In this respect, HC's Riga mayor, Nils Ušakovs, was perhaps right to contend that the financial crisis in Latvia 'brought Latvians and non-Latvians closer' (*Diena* 20 April 2011). Whether this is or is not the case, it would appear that a number of Russian speakers in Latvia are at least coming to terms with their government's policies on education and citizenship. This potentially allows them to integrate much deeper into 'Latvian' discourses. Moreover, although Russian speakers (as of now) do not necessarily see the bridge function as a specific component of their identity, the idea nevertheless still seems to hold great appeal to them.

This pragmatic approach to ethnic relations within Latvia must therefore be understood as a useful means for Russian speakers to find their place in contemporary Latvia. There would seem to be a realisation that the state policies on language, education, and citizenship are hardly likely to change. It may be posited that the more 'ethnic issues' are removed from the political agenda, the less Russian speakers will feel estranged from all things 'Latvian'. To this end, a pragmatic and stoical approach to ethnic relations, with an increasing focus on the economic and social issues which affect all of Latvia's inhabitants equally, holds much potential for Russian speakers. This can be seen in the new optimism of Russian speakers observed in these focus groups. The discourse of self-marginalisation, which has traditionally been a staple of Russian-language media discourse since Latvia regained independence in 1991, stresses how hard it is to be a Russian-speaker in Latvia. However, as we have seen in the media discourse, Russian speakers are increasingly pointing to their advantageous position in Latvia.

> Respondent: Well if you take any job advertisement then it will have requirements for Latvian, Russian, and English for example. So Russian is always there now and employers want to have Russian workers, which means they won't pay full attention to whether or not you speak Latvian.
> AC: So, in terms of economics, in Latvia it's better to be Russian?
> Respondent: Yes. (Undergraduate respondent)

In response to the question of whether it was difficult to be a Russian in Latvia, the group of postgraduate respondents immediately pointed out that it was, in fact, more difficult for Latvians in many respects:

> It will probably be more difficult for Latvians.

> Because of this policy which has been carried out . . . then with their Latvian language, in principle, there's nowhere for them to go except for Latvia. Those who've learnt English are lucky, but many haven't even learnt English. If Russians can at least reorient themselves towards Russia, then Latvians can't. (Two postgraduate students)

This optimism with regards to the economic standing of Russian speakers stood in contrast to the resignation and concern the respondents expressed regarding their difficulty of finding symbolic acceptance and belonging in Latvia. Indeed, one thing that this optimism does enable is the partial disavowal of the self-marginalisation strategy that was identified within Russian-speaking discourse. The idea that Russian speakers are able to forge their own future instead of being held back by discrimination appeared to be an empowering concept. This was demonstrated when the focus group participants were shown an excerpt from *Chas*, in which the author railed against the people who have introduced Latvian language requirements for most professions (see Appendix 1:3). In the article the author, somewhat dramatically, links these language requirements with eventual homelessness: 'What follows is simple: no language, no job; no job, no income. That means poverty which means the street'

(*Chas* 26 February 2009). However, as one postgraduate participant responded:

> I would say that here it's actually pretty debatable. Firstly, because if you look where it was published – in the newspaper *Chas*, which is a radical enough Russian newspaper. Secondly, it also seems a little far-fetched that for twenty years Russians have been scream-ing that we haven't been given any opportunities. If it was 1995, then it would be understandable, but this is 2011, and twenty-one years have now passed. And it's worth saying that Latvians are forcing us to learn, but we forget that in this time Russians could have already leant Latvian. And for the many people who haven't in this time period, in actual fact, it's their problem. I would say that because for pupils, students, and everyone else it's no longer an inherent problem. (Postgraduate student)

MEDIA EFFECTS?

In the discussion with focus group participants it was clear that there was both disagreement and agreement with various aspects of the media discourses which were presented to them. In some respects the respondents were categorical in rejecting certain arguments relating to the discrimination of Russian speakers as being hyperbolic and out of date. This would therefore potentially point to the fact that media do not possess the kind of influence that we might have expected.

On the other hand, the media analysis of *Chas* revealed the evolution of certain media discourses. The increased levels of optimism and asser-tions that Russian speakers were in an advantageous position appeared to be mirrored in the focus groups. The obvious question here is to what extent these changes are in response to bottom-up changes in atti-tudes, or to what extent media discourses have led Russian speakers to adopt certain positions. The argument could be made either that media discourses have effected this change among Russian speakers, or that the media discourses are reflecting changing attitudes among Russian speakers.

This is perhaps, alas, an impossible question to answer. The Russian speakers who participated in these focus groups did, however, dem-onstrate a relatively high level of uniformity in their assessments of various positions. While there was not necessary unanimity on all issues discussed, the level of homogeneity of opinion was fairly high. This can be explained by the sample bias, comprised as it was of Russian speakers who were undergraduates or postgraduates in Rigan universities. It could also point to the fact that stable positions have been somehow cultivated which are shared by relatively large groups of individuals. In light of the previous discussions of top-down and bottom-up identity pressures, this research holds that the media do have a significant influence over identity formation. Nevertheless, it is most likely a constrained influence.

One important thing to note is that younger Russian speakers reported that they rarely read newspapers at all and were much more likely to access information via television, and more commonly the internet. If the press have any influence over young people then it can be assumed that it is through the mediated interpellation and actions of elites who do pay attention to such discourses. This corresponds to the two-step model of media influence proposed by Katz and Lazarsfeld (1955). Within this model the public are influenced by opinion leaders who pay attention to media discourses and transmit these perceptions to the wider public. Therefore, for a media message to be successful in cultivating an audience and in creating group identities, it is not necessarily essential that these messages are directly consumed by all members of the imagined community. Rather, it is important that these messages become embedded within commonly accepted group consciousness either through direct interaction with a readership, or through the mediated actions of people who consume such discourses and then are able to transmit them to wider audiences.

Additionally, media effects are often brought about through long-term exposure to certain dominant themes and points of view. In line with George Gerbner's cultivation theory (1985: 14), direct contact with a piece of information is not necessarily as important as 'the awareness that a certain item of knowledge is publicly held (that is, not only known to many, *but commonly known that it is known to many*)'. For Gerbner this makes collective action and collective thinking possible. This, of course, is one of the major insights of Benedict Anderson's (2006) work on imagined communities. Anderson notes that the emergence of the printing press enabled the emergence of patterns of identification which were previously impossible on such a large scale. Media effects can therefore be brought about simply by their widespread existence and through their messages being popularly disseminated and embodied by opinion leaders and other influential individuals – notably politicians.

CONCLUSIONS

This chapter has provided a bottom-up perspective on identity formation for Russian speakers in Latvia. The findings of this research help to shed light on a number of the nuances of identity formation which were not apparent from the analysis of political and media discourses which have been discussed in the previous chapters. Of particular note was the fact that the younger two groups of Russian speakers were far more likely to identify themselves as Russian-speakers than the older generation. This indicates that the discursive effects, discussed in Chapter 4, relating to the construction of Russian-speakers by media and political elites are more than plausible. The fact that this signifier was unwaveringly accepted as a valid marker of identity supports the thesis that a form of Russian-speaking identity has been constructed by media and political elites. It also corroborates the thesis put forward in previous chapters that state policies such as those relating to citizenship, language, and education have served to define and demarcate the two largest imagined communities in post-Soviet Latvia.

An interesting insight from this chapter has been the attitudes displayed towards Russia. The focus-group outputs backed up previously conducted research which has shown that Russian speakers in Latvia and the other Baltic states often feel a sense of estrangement from the geographically and politically defined Russian Federation (Vihalemm and Masso 2003; Zepa 2006). This research therefore supports David Laitin's (1995) work which has drawn attention to the nascent emergence of a Russian-speaking nationality in the Baltic states which is distinct from Russian identity.

Adding to this understanding, this research also highlights an important discursive distinction between the culturally and politically conceived ideas of Russia. Whereas the Russian Federation was deemed to be far removed from the experiences of Russian speakers in Latvia, cultural or spiritual Russia was cited as an important element of their identity. Of course, it is often impossible to separate entirely culture from politics. Nevertheless, even if it is not possible to separate these two somewhat abstract concepts, the respondents maintained the distinction between two Russias – the *rossiiskii* world and the *russkii* world. In returning to the discussion of the political influence of the Russian Federation it is possible to surmise that Russia's greatest potential influence over its 'compatriots abroad' lies in the realm of 'soft power' or 'culture'. This reality is one which seems to be reflected in the pragmatic policies adopted by the Russian authorities. (For more discussion on this topic see Chapter 8.)

The other main conclusion to be taken from this chapter is that the young Russian-speaking respondents displayed a great deal of optimism regarding their opportunities in Latvia. It was acknowledged that official state policies have effectively enabled them to attain high levels of bilingualism in Latvian and Russian, and that this has placed them in an advantageous position economically. While there were instances where the respondents relayed their frustrations and difficulties as members of the Russian-speaking community, these were, in fact, far less frequent than had been anticipated.

Naturally it is important to bear in mind the selection bias of this research, which focused on educated people who were linguistically advantaged. More work would need to be carried out on a far more representative sample of Russian speakers in order to extend any extrapolations beyond this sample. Nevertheless, even with this small sample of educated Russian speakers, it was possible to see the possible effects of various discourses on Russian speakers in Latvia.

Of particular interest were the respondents' responses to the media excerpts which were distributed during the discussions. While most of the media excerpts found congruence with the attitudes and assumptions of the respondents, a number of articles did not. Articles which cited overt discrimination against Russian speakers were challenged and contrasted to the actual experiences of Russian speakers. It is possible to see, therefore, a potential shift in the discursive nodal points which underpin Russian-speaking identity. Discrimination and self-marginalisation have been important aspects which have facilitated the formation of Russian-speaking identity in Latvia. The participants of these focus groups, however, displayed a partial desire to move on from these issues, and were willing to accept more positive nodal points linked with economic advantages.

NOTES

1. Large parts of this chapter were earlier published as Cheskin (2013).
2. The English translation used in the *Baltic Times* has been tidied up here. Additionally the words *vobla*, *vodka*, and *chastushki* have been put back into their original Russian in the way that President Vīķe-Freiberga used them while speaking Latvian.
3. In Russia sunflower seeds are a popular snack, sometimes sold by street vendors. The reference here is to the shells of the seeds which are often spat out or thrown away onto the street – a practice often seen as uncouth.
4. For further discussion of this topic see the following chapter which is based on survey data from 9 May in which this question was directly addressed.

CHAPTER 6

The 'Democratisation of History' and Generational Change[1]

Этот День Победы	This Victory Day
Похором пропах,	Thick with the smell of gunpowder,
Это праздник	This is a celebration
С сединою на висках.	With grey hair at our temples,
Это радость	This is joy
Со слезами на глазах.	With tears in our eyes.
День Победы!	Victory Day!
	(Lyrics to the popular song Victory Day)

A TALE OF TWO HISTORIES?

As discussed in Chapter 3, the theme of historical tension and antagonism has been much researched in the Baltic context between the three Baltic states of Estonia, Latvia, and Lithuania on the one hand, and Russia on the other. For the Baltic states it is commonly accepted that between these three countries and Russia 'two narratives of the recent past perennially conflict with one another' (Kattago 2010: 383). According to the official Baltic narrative of the past, the Baltic states are portrayed as victims of merciless Soviet and Nazi occupations, each of which was equally horrific. The Soviet-Russian narrative rejects the label of occupation and instead highlights the heroic efforts of the Soviet Union in liberating Europe from the evils of fascism.

This chapter, however, argues for a more nuanced understanding of actual collective memories of Russian speakers in Latvia. Although existing data point to differing and distinct memory positions of the two constructed 'Latvian' and 'Russian-speaking' communities, it is argued that it is necessary to examine people's perspectives on history in much more detail in order to reveal the complexities inherent in 'learning to remember'. This chapter therefore challenges the commonly accepted view that the majority of Russian speakers in Latvia 'have accepted the vision of history as cultivated by Russia as their own and take it as the basis for their historical vision of Latvia' (Zelče 2009: 54).

While there can be little doubt that Russia plays a very significant role in the creation and perpetuation of collective memories for Latvia's Russian speakers, this assertion needs to be challenged on two counts: firstly, it smoothes out any differences that exist *within* the constructed group of Russian-speakers; secondly, it creates an overly simplified dichotomy between 'Latvian' and 'Russian' history with no democratic space between the two opposing poles. For example, the above quotation from Vita Zelče continues, 'this is a crisis situation for efforts to achieve tolerance in regard to history and memory in Latvia. Its outcome will be determined by the identity values of Latvia's Russians, by their choice of affiliation – Latvia or Russia – and the motivation for this choice.'

This chapter therefore represents an attempt to move away from a strict reliance on elite discourses and the analysis of such discourses. As the previous chapter has highlighted, it is important to examine how Russian speakers engage with the discourses produced in the media and political spaces. In line with the democratisation of history thesis which was discussed in Chapter 2, it is argued that there is a need to move away from the idea of two, and only two, possible histories. Not only is this dichotomy inherently intolerant – demanding as it does that Russian speakers choose between right (Latvian) and wrong (Russian) histories – but it is also unproductive as it manages to ignore the subtle but perceptible moves away from a rigid adherence to Russia's official history that can, it is argued, be increasingly evidenced among Latvia's Russian speakers. These changes in attitudes need to be examined in some depth so that we can come to a fuller understanding of both the impact of political and media discourses, and of the bottom-up and top-down factors which bring about discursive change.

As discussed in Chapter 2, the 'democratisation of memory' occurs when individuals are able to view historical events from a critical and objective viewpoint. Instead of history being used to anchor contemporary identities and political stances, it is seen as a topic which can be examined dispassionately from various viewpoints. In essence it corresponds very closely to Halbwachs' idea of 'formal history' as opposed to 'collective memories' (as summarised by Wertsch in Table 2.1). Within this 'democratisation' there is common acknowledgement that history is complicated and ambiguous, and alternative views of history are tolerated or accepted and are not seen as inherently antagonistic to current identity positions.

Through an examination of data from a survey conducted on 9 May 2011, at the site of the Victory Day celebrations in Riga's Victory Park, it is suggested that a tendency to move towards a democratisation of history is starting to become visible among Russian speakers in Latvia. It is argued that this is most evident when the data is analysed by age groups. Younger Russian speakers generally display views which would suggest increasing openness for constructive debates and the opening up of history within Latvia. This therefore points to temporal changes in the discursive nodal points which anchor Russian speaking identity in Latvia, the implications of which will are discussed below.

OBSERVING VICTORY DAY IN LATVIA

For us, the descendents of those who saved the world from fascism, this is a day of pride for our fathers and grand-fathers.
Harmony Centre Press Release (8 May 2011)

When discussing or analysing questions of national identity in Latvia the issue of Soviet occupation is never far away. This has been demonstrated throughout the course of this study where the issues of education, language, and citizenship are often linked with the history of Latvia's involvement in the Second World War. The occupation question has long been a stumbling block for 'Russian' parties, especially Harmony Centre/The Social Democratic Party 'Harmony' (HC/SDPH), who have tried (to date unsuccessfully) to take their seat within Latvia's numerous governing coalitions. From the focus group discussions, however, it was clear that Russian speakers' attitudes towards this emotive question were not fully universalised. In order to gain a more representative snapshot of Russian-speaking opinion on the issues of history and Latvia's Soviet past it was therefore decided to canvass opinion of people in attendance of the Victory Day celebrations in Riga.

Victory Day is a holiday of great importance within the Russian Federation. Although it was previously a holiday of great significance, Victory Day has become increasingly important in recent years, especially following Putin's rise to power (Schleifman 2001; Forest and Johnson 2002). It is also widely marked in Latvia where each year thousands of people gather for unofficial celebrations in Riga's Victory Park. The sheer scale of the event would seem to confirm the sacredness of the historical myths of Soviet victory over fascism and the liberation of

Europe for those in attendance. In one survey approximately 59 per cent of Latvia's Russian speakers stated that they had celebrated Victory Day in the last five years (Zelče 2009: 21). The celebrations in Riga's Victory Park include fireworks, musical and cultural performances, political speeches, tents selling food and drink, a large screen showing live broadcasts from Russia and other cities in Latvia, and tents with exhibits from political parties and non-governmental organisations (NGOs) relating to the Second World War.

These annual events are organised by the NGO 9may.lv. On their official website 9may.lv refers to itself as a 'social organisation' whose main aims are: 'to help veterans who live in Latvia' and 'to maintain and preserve memories of Victory Day in Latvia' (9may.lv 2011). Nevertheless, the 2011 celebrations had strong ties with the political party HC. Vadims Baranniks, the head of 9may.lv, was also a member of HC and an elected member of the Rigan municipal government. The other main organisational partner for 9may.lv was the youth organisation *Mums pa ceļam/ Nam po puti* (We're going the same way). The organisation claims to be a non-political, youth organisation with the stated aim of 'helping pupils in Russian-language schools to find their place in life and achieve success . . . With our help we want young people to become successful members of Latvian society' (Mums pa ceļam 2011). Nevertheless, again there was a political overlap between the social aims of this organisation and the political participation of HC. For example members of HC (including Vadims Baranniks) were also members of the *Mums pa ceļam* board. Indeed, on their official website there is even a link to the official website of Nils Ušakovs, Riga's HC mayor.

It would therefore be fair to state that 9 May in Latvia has a fairly political character. Within the confines of Victory Park this meant that only sanctioned voices were allowed to be heard during the 2011 Victory Day celebrations. For example, one man was observed being forcibly escorted away from the park by police after he displayed a poster (in Russian) detailing criticism of Russia's Prime Minister Vladimir Putin and President Dmitry Medvedev. I was also asked to leave the park by security staff after initially handing out my surveys, and was forced to stand on the road leading up to the park. Bearing in mind the sensitivities of an event celebrating Soviet 'liberation' in Latvia, the extent of the security presence, and the desire to prevent unsanctioned protests, should perhaps come as no surprise. It is significant, however, that the contents of the celebration would appear to be very much informed by the politics which lie beneath its organisation.

In order to collect meaningful data on Russian speakers' attitudes towards history and toward the 9 May celebrations, a survey was con-

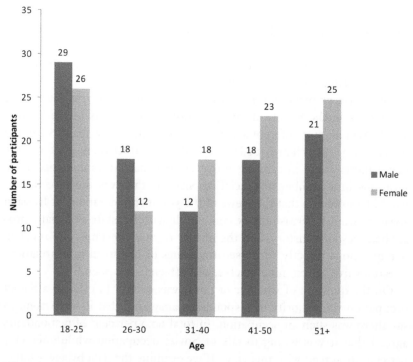

Figure 6.1 Survey respondents (by age group and sex)

ducted on 9 May 2011 during the Victory Day celebrations in Riga. Passers-by were asked to fill out a questionnaire with fifteen questions, marking each question 'agree', 'disagree', 'partly agree', or 'difficult to say' (the questionnaire is included as Appendix 2, along with English translations of the questions). The respondents were divided into five age groups: 18–25 (n=55), 26–30 (n=30), 31–40 (n=30), 41–50 (n=41), 51+ (n=46) bringing the total number of participants to n=202 (see Figure 6.1). Specifically the questions from this questionnaire tackled the issue of history and historical interpretation which were discussed in Chapter 3.

Survey results: occupation and liberation

In the course of the twelve hours that were spent collecting survey data and observing proceedings it was possible to collect a total of 202 completed surveys. The topics broached in the questionnaire ranged from questions of historical interpretation to the issue of why those questioned thought it was so important to attend the celebrations, and also what their views were on alternative historical interpretations. All of the 202 surveys were completed by people who described their first language as

Russian. In fact, in the whole course of the day only four individuals were stopped who said that their first language was not necessarily Russian, although two of these individuals were not sure if they considered Russian as their first language or Latvian. It was decided not to include their completed surveys in the final analysis.

One of the primary aims in constructing the questionnaire was to trace any trends in the historical interpretation of the events of the Second World War among different age groups. Both the media analysis and the focus group research provided some evidence that Russian speakers were being increasingly integrating into 'Latvian' narratives and discursive positions in a number of crucial respects. If this was the case then it would be expected that the views of the younger generations of Russian speakers would increasingly be compatible with the state's officially pro-scribed views on history, and the history of Soviet occupation. As such five questions directly addressed the issues of historical interpretation: questions five, seven, nine, twelve, and fifteen (see Appendix 2).

On the question of whether or not it was correct to refer to a Soviet occupation the majority of respondents answered that it was wrong to say there was such an occupation. In total 60.9 per cent of respondents agreed that it was wrong to talk of Soviet occupation while only 11.4 per cent disagreed with this view. If we examine the data by age groups, however (see Figure 6.2), then it is possible to see that it is within the 41–50 and 51+ age groups that respondents were most likely to say that there was no occupation (75.6 per cent and 87 per cent respectively). Among the three younger age groups the figures were considerably smaller: 36.4 per cent (18–25), 50.3 per cent (26–30), and 56.7 per cent (31–40). Moreover, the percentage of respondents who answered that they 'partly agreed' trends downwards within each age group. So while as many as 49.1 per cent of those surveyed within the youngest age group partly agreed that there was no occupation only 4.3 per cent of those within the oldest age group shared this opinion.

This highlights significant differences in understandings that younger Russian speakers have in comparison with older age groups. The respondents aged 18–25 were over 50 per cent less likely to agree entirely that there was an occupation than respondents aged over 51. This would seem to be compelling evidence that Russian speakers are increasingly being influenced by Latvian narratives and discourses, not least the Latvian memory-myths pertaining to the Second World War. Nevertheless, there were still a large number of young respondents who did think it was wrong to refer to a Soviet occupation. In total 85.5 per cent of respondents in the youngest age group either agreed or partly agreed that it was wrong to talk of Soviet occupation.

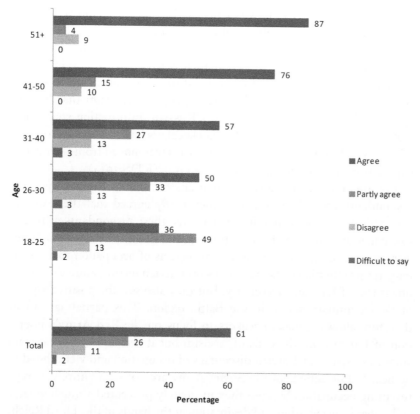

Figure 6.2 It is not right to talk of 'Soviet occupation'. There was no Soviet occupation (by age group and %)

This figure, however, needs to be contextualised within the backdrop of young Russian speakers' attempts to integrate into both Latvian and Russian discourses. As highlighted by the focus groups, it is often very difficult for Russian speakers in Latvia to accept wholesale the idea that the Red Army simply occupied Latvia. Memory-myths passed down from family members, and cultivated within the Russian (especially *rossiiskii*) media have had a significant impact on Russian-speaking perceptions of the Second World War.

At the same time Latvian influences have also increasingly brought to bear on Russian-speaking perceptions, especially within schools. As has been discussed, in 2004, Latvian education reform stipulated that a minimum of 60 per cent of teaching in any state school would have to be conducted in Latvian. Moreover, there have been great efforts to ensure that history is taught from Latvian textbooks and not Russian ones (Culture Ministry of the Republic of Latvia 2011: 21). While there is evidence that teachers in Russian schools (that is, schools which have instruction in Russian) often supplement the official, top-down curriculum with their own bottom-up insights (Golubeva 2010: 322–5; see also Onken 2010: 287–8), it is nonetheless true that these same pupils must have had extensive bottom-up and top-down exposure to various 'Latvian' narratives and myths. Some people may claim that Russian speakers live in an entirely separate, 'Russian' information space. The reality is, however, that many Russian speakers have an increasing sense of loyalty to Latvia, and often see Russia as far removed from their actual experiences (Rodins 2005; Zepa et al. 2005a; SKDS 2014).

For this reason the most common answer among Russian-speaking respondents aged 18–25 was that they *partly* agreed that there was an occupation (49.1 per cent). In other words, these respondents were able to see that the question of occupation was not necessarily clear-cut. They were able to recognise that there were aspects of occupation such as the long-term stationing of Soviet troops on Latvian territory and the consequent loss of Latvian sovereignty. But they also saw the positive aspects of Soviet military action in the Baltic region. This partial agreement therefore allows Russian speakers to focus on the Red Army's liberation of Latvia from the evils of fascism, but it also allows for a certain amount of space for Latvian discourses of occupation and victimhood to be heard. The actions of the Soviet Army are not seen entirely as representing occupation because they ultimately prevented a much greater evil – that is, occupation and decimation at the hands of the Third Reich.

The acceptance of the liberating role of the Soviet Army must be understood as a vitally important nodal point for many Russian speakers in Latvia. In Makarov and Boldāne's survey of Latvian school children (2008) as many as 65.1 per cent of children from schools with Russian as the language of instruction said that in 1944–5 Soviet forces 'liberated Latvia' (see Table 6.1). It would seem therefore that one of the most difficult things for young Russian speakers to accept is that the Soviet Army simply occupied Latvia. If occupation is accepted then it is most commonly accepted in tandem with the understanding that the Red Army *simultaneously liberated* Latvia from a far greater evil. For this reason in Makarov and Boldāne's survey only 4.7 per cent of respondents from Russian schools felt able to answer that the Soviet Army simply occupied Latvia, whereas 25 per cent of surveyed school children answered that the Red Army 'both liberated and occupied Latvia'.

This therefore points to the increasingly visible discursive strategy displayed by Russian speakers in Latvia of integrating into Latvian discourses while maintaining certain Russian/Soviet discourses that are considered ideationally salient to their national identity. To say that the

Table 6.1 School children's assessment of Soviet liberation/occupation by school's language of instruction

School's language of instruction	Liberated Latvia	Occupied Latvia	Both liberated and occupied Latvia	Difficult to say	Total
Latvian (n=207)	12.1	61.7	20.4	5.8	100
Russian (n=193)	65.1	4.7	25	5.2	100
Total	37.7	34.2	22.6	5.5	100

Source: Makarov and Boldāne (2008: 10)

Red Army *both liberated and occupied* Latvia is to embed oneself into both Latvian and Russian discursive positions and narratives. In the survey conducted for this research, within the youngest age group, 49.1 per cent of those questioned answered that they partly agreed that it was not right to talk of Soviet occupation. This is a highly significant finding. This answer allows for individuals to adhere both to the discourse of liberation and to the discourse of occupation. That this figure decreases greatly between age groups (33.3 per cent for 26–30 year-olds, 26.7 per cent for 31–40 year-olds, 14.6 per cent for 41–50 year-olds, and 4.3 per cent for people aged over 51) is also telling. It would appear that this strategy is one which is increasingly gathering momentum and being employed by the younger generations of Russian speakers in Latvia.

The fact that the moment of liberation is widely held onto by Russian speakers was also evident in the survey data. In response to the statement, 'in 1944 Latvia was liberated by Soviet troops', a total of 82.4 per cent of respondents agreed while only 2.5 per cent disagreed and 13.6 per cent partly agreed (see Figure 6.3). There were some differences within age groups (70.9 per cent agreed within the 18–25 age group, as opposed to 90.9 per cent within the 51+ age group). Even among the youngest respondents, however, the memory-myth of Soviet liberation is held onto to a far greater extent than the memory-myth of Soviet occupation is denied. Based on this survey data, it would be fair to say that Soviet liberation is still a prime nodal point in the consolidation of Russian-speaking identity in Latvia.

In the realm of Latvian politics the issue of Soviet occupation constantly looms large over the so-called 'Russian' parties, and it has even been used as a means to exclude HC from joining the ruling coalition in parliament (see Chapter 7). Leading representatives from HC have often expressed the view that it is difficult to say whether there was an occupation from a legal point of view. They have, however, also stated publicly that they accept that Latvia was forcefully *annexed* by the Soviet Union (for example see *Diena* 20 June 2011, 9 September 2011).

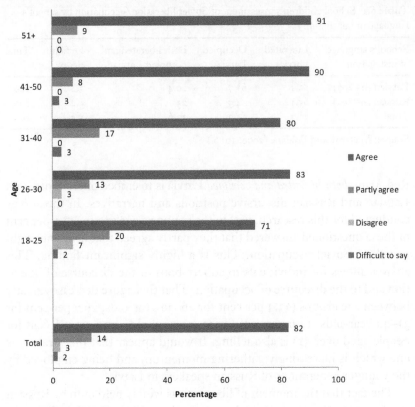

Figure 6.3 In 1944 Latvia was liberated by Soviet troops (by age group and %)

The linguistic signs *occupation* and *annexation* may, on first inspection seem rather similar. However, the discursive meanings and usage that have been built up around these two signifiers varies greatly in the Baltic context. One of the most significant reasons why the word occupation is so unpalatable to HC, and to many Russian speakers, is its immediate connection to the term occupiers. As this research has discussed at some length, Russian speakers have often had to deal with exclusionary discourses which cast them as occupiers in Latvia. HC's decision to start referring to Soviet annexation can therefore be interpreted as a willingness to accept (to a certain extent) official Latvian accounts of the Second World War and its consequences, while not accepting the position that Russian speakers are occupiers and alien to the country. It is therefore a stance which aims partially to depoliticise history (or at least this particular history) and to detach it from contemporary identities.

In order to determine if there was any discernible difference in Russian speakers' attitudes towards the signifiers 'occupation' and

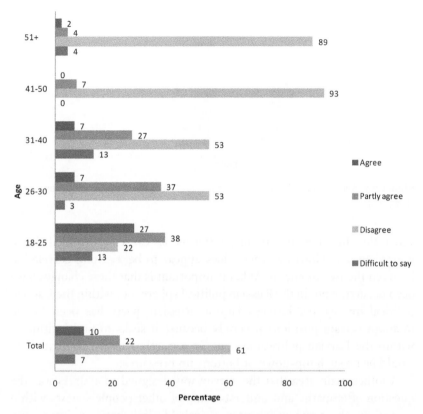

Figure 6.4 Latvia was forcefully annexed by the Soviet Union against the will of a majority of its inhabitants (by age group and %)

'annexation', respondents were asked to respond to the statement: 'Latvia was forcefully annexed by the Soviet Army against the will of a majority of its inhabitants.' The results of this question were striking (see Figure 6.4). Whereas only 0 per cent and 2.2 per cent of the 41–50 and 51+ age groups respectively agreed with this statement as many as 27.3 per cent of respondents from the youngest age group agreed. This would seem to indicate that the idea of forceful annexation is increasingly gaining acceptance among younger Russian speakers in Latvia. Indeed, young people within the 18–25 year-old cohort were over two times more likely to accept fully that Latvia was forcefully annexed than they were to accept fully that Latvia was occupied (see Figure 6.5).

This leads to the conclusion that there is a strong link between the change in political discourse over the last few years and the evolving attitudes of Russian speakers in relation to the question of annexation. Whether politicians have been able to start using the term annexation because attitudes of Russian speakers have been changing, or if vice

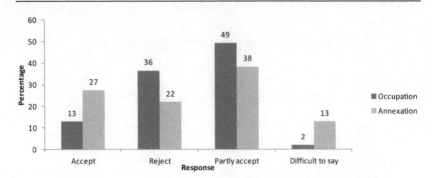

Figure 6.5 Acceptance of Soviet 'occupation' and 'annexation' within age group 18–25 (%)

versa, the changing rhetoric of politicians has caused attitudinal shifts, is hard to say. However, there does appear to be a strong correlation between the two moments. What is important is that these changes have been occurring not in the Russian political sphere, but within the Latvian political mythscape. Latvia's largest 'Russian' party has been forced to adopt certain positions precisely because it seeks to find legitimacy within the Latvian political system. In a purely Russian context there would be no such top-down or bottom-up pressures.

Another main area that the survey was designed to address was the question of empathy and understanding of other people's views within Latvia. In the previous chapter a probable link between intergroup contacts between Russian speakers and Latvians, and increased empathy towards to position of the 'other group' was outlined. If it was possible to find a relatively high level of empathy among Russian speakers towards the historical positions of the Latvian state and 'the Latvians', then this would bode well for increased understanding between Latvia's two largest (imagined) communities, and could tentatively point towards more favourable conditions for a democratisation of history.

Accordingly there were a number of questions within the question-naire which were designed to trace the level of empathy among Russian speakers to various 'Latvian' positions relating to the history of the Second World War.

Two questions were designed to measure indirectly some form of empathy by Russian speakers towards the position of the people who did not agree with their own historical interpretations: 'I can understand why some people do not like to see 9 May being celebrated in Latvia' and 'history is never straightforward. For this reason I can come to terms with the fact that different people have different interpretations of the Second World War and its consequences.' In answer to the first ques-

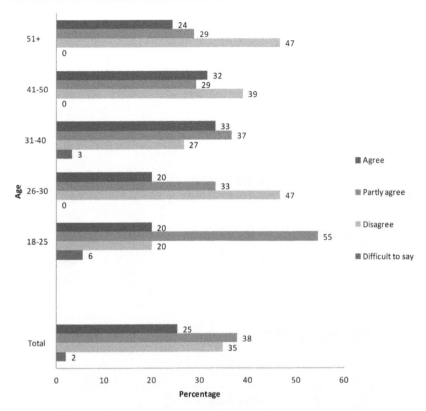

Figure 6.6 I can understand why some people do not like to see 9 May being celebrated in Latvia (by age group and %)

tion, a majority of respondents, across all age cohorts, either agreed or partly agreed that they could understand why some people do not like to see 9 May being celebrated in Latvia (see Figure 6.6). Moreover, for the youngest age group as many as 74.5 per cent of respondents were able to agree or partly agree with this statement. This would indicate that Russian speakers, irrespective of their own views on the importance of 9 May (which, taking into consideration their attendance of the Victory Day celebrations, it would have to be assumed were generally positive), are able to see things from the point of view of other, less positive perspectives.

In answer to the second question the results showed an even higher level of empathy, or at least openness to the possibility of the existence of different versions of history. Unlike for the previous question which was fairly uniform across all age cohorts, the answers to this second question showed a great deal of difference between age groups. Nevertheless, even in the oldest two age groups, a majority of respondents were able to

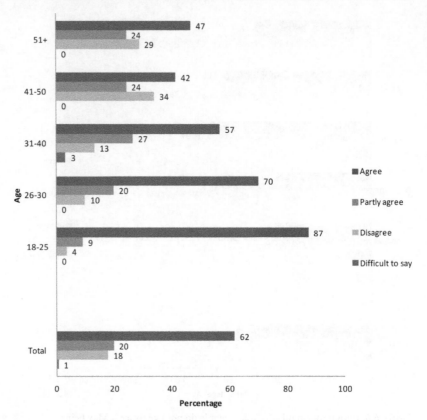

Figure 6.7 History is never straightforward. For this reason I can come to terms with the fact that different people have different interpretations of the Second World War and its consequences (by age group and %)

come to terms with (at least partially) the existence of different historical interpretations (see Figure 6.7). Nevertheless, there is a marked increase in the number of respondents being fully able to come to terms with this difference in the two youngest age cohorts, and especially the youngest. For the youngest cohort the percentage of respondents able to fully or partly accept different historical interpretations stood at 96.4 per cent and the percentage of those questioned able to accept fully such differences was almost two times the corresponding figure for the oldest cohort (87.3 per cent against 46.7 per cent).

This willingness to accept the existence of different histories and historical interpretations was evident in the focus groups, and was also reflected in the pre-election political strategy of HC in 2011, whereby the party called for a three year moratorium on the question of occupation in order to focus on, what they saw as, the more pressing issues of

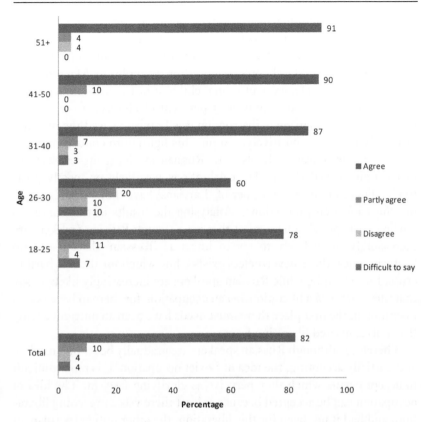

Figure 6.8 The parades of the Latvian legionnaires cover Latvia in shame (by age group and %)

Latvia's economic development and social well-being. In the words of *Saeima* deputy and HC representative Boriss Cilevičs, this strategy was necessary because it would allow people in Latvia 'to agree to disagree' and then move on (personal interview). Again, it is significant that it is within the youngest age groups that the respondents displayed the greatest levels of empathy and openness to different points of view.

A large proportion of respondents therefore expressed their willingness to accept different histories. When presented with the history of the Latvian Waffen SS Legions, however, a significant large majority condemned the 16 March parades as bringing shame to Latvia (Figure 6.8). Although the number of younger Russian speakers who shared this opinion was lower for the two youngest age cohorts, especially for the 26–30 age group, these results were not statistically significant.

The fact that 78.2 per cent of the youngest respondents agreed with this statement was especially surprising given that so many young people had expressed a number of empathetic positions regarding alternative historical interpretations. It is important to bear in mind, however, that a fairly large number of 'Latvians' also have negative opinions regarding the annual 16 March processions. For example, in Makarov and Boldāne's (2008: 11) survey of school children in Latvian-language and Russian-language schools only 67.5 per cent of children from schools where the main language of instruction was Latvian viewed the marches positively or mostly positively. To put this figure into context 94.8 per cent of children from schools with Russian as the main language of instruction viewed the 9 May celebrations positively or mostly positively. Therefore even a number of 'Latvians' have difficulty in accepting the 16 March processions.[2] Analysing the results of this survey as a whole, it is possible to suggest that even though Russian speakers are increasingly more likely to try to integrate 'Russian' discourses into 'Latvian' ones, there nevertheless exists a line which for them is hard to cross. For example, while Russian speakers are increasingly likely to say that there was *both* a liberation *and* an occupation, for there to have been a liberation in the first place there must needs have been an outright enemy that Latvia needed liberating from.

Therefore, although Russian speakers are gradually becoming used to, and partially accepting, the idea of Soviet occupation, it is more difficult to accept events which they perceive as glorifying fascism. The idea of occupation can be accepted because at least there was a preceding liberation, and had it not been for this liberation, the other option (permanent occupation by Nazi Germany) would have been far worse (so the reasoning goes). The understanding that fascism was worse than communism has perhaps therefore become (or is becoming) a new, centrally important, nodal point for Russian speakers in Latvia. Without this it would be almost impossible to celebrate Victory Day in any form.

Another important factor to consider is the role of the Latvian mythscape. Above, it was posited that the Latvian mythscape, and especially the realm of the school, are increasingly influencing Russian-speaking memory-myths. The theme of Soviet occupation has been central within Latvian scholastic curricula. As a result, Russian speakers will have been exposed to the officially approved narratives of the Latvian state. In contrast, the role of Waffen SS veterans is not glorified in official Latvian narratives of the war. While the nationalist National Alliance supports the parades, many other 'Latvian' politicians do not give their open support to the commemorations. In 2014, for example, Einārs Cilinskis (National Alliance) was forced to resign from his post as minister of environmental protection and regional development because of his participation in the commemorative parade. For this reason the top-down and bottom-up processes which influence young Russians speakers' views of the Latvian Legions come primarily from Russian-language media sources and personal transmissions of memory. On this particular question there is little pressure (either top-down or bottom-up) to take account of alternative views.

CONCLUSIONS

There is a tendency when examining the so-called 'memory war' between the Baltic States and Russia to adhere to the idea of two diametrically opposed memory narratives. The results of this survey, however, suggest a far more complex picture. Contrary to the view that Russian speakers simply adhere to the official collective memories of the Russian Federation, the data show that there is an observable shift in attitudes among the younger generation of Russian speakers in Latvia.

Through an analysis of the data by age groups it is clear that on many issues young people express views which do not correspond fully with the official Russian narratives and myths of the Second World War and its consequences. This small-scale survey is perhaps only the first step in investigating this phenomenon in more depth. Nevertheless, it can be posited that young Russian speakers are not only moving away gradually from the views of their parents, and the older generations of Latvia's Russian speakers, but that they are moving away from the views of their contemporaries in Russia on the Soviet history of the Baltic states.

The explanations for this shift in perspective may be complex. We can, however, begin to understand this phenomenon by considering both top-down and bottom-up pressures on the creation and maintenance of collective memories. The fact that Russian speakers live in Latvia and not the Russian Federation means that they are exposed to top-down memory articulations which come from the Latvian state. Perhaps the most obvious example of this top-down pressure can be evidenced in Latvia's education reforms. Efforts by Latvian governments to ensure the 'correct' teaching of history in Latvian schools must, at the very least, lead to a situation where it is almost impossible for young Russian speakers to ignore completely 'Latvian' perspectives of history. Even if Russian speakers decide to disagree with these perspectives, their exposure to them must be significant at some level. Indeed, the evidence from this study suggests that there has been an observable generational shift for people who received their education in an independent, as opposed to Soviet, Latvia.

Additionally, a great deal of research on the identities of Russian speakers outside Russia has demonstrated that these individuals, while maintaining certain elements of cultural 'Russianness', increasingly feel estranged from the Russian political space (Vihalemm and Masso 2003; Zepa 2006) and that they are creating an identity of their own which is neither fully 'Russian' nor that of the titular nationality (Laitin 1995; Kolstø 1999; Pisarenko 2006). It therefore seems logical that the Latvian top-down mythscape is becoming more significant for young Russian speakers in Latvia, even if the Russian cultural mythscape still exerts considerable influence.

Therefore, while there are undoubtedly top-down pressures from Russia which advocate an antagonistic collective memory of the Second World War, their direct political influence is increasingly undermined by this political estrangement, allowing Latvian top-down pressures more leverage. These top-down pressures have also been of growing significance in Latvia's political mythscape. In recent years it has been possible to observe a change in the political rhetoric of the leading 'Russian' political parties, that is, parties whose main electoral base is comprised of Russian speakers (see Chapter 7). Whereas the Interfront movements of the late Soviet period adhered to the Soviet myth that Latvia had experienced its own socialist revolution, the post-independence parties have necessarily softened their rhetoric. Indeed, although, to date, HC/SDPH have been unable to publicly use the 'o' word, they have nevertheless been willing to accept that Latvia was annexed by the Soviet Union and that this led to horrific consequences for many of Latvia's inhabitants. As the party state in their proposal for a parliamentary declaration on inter-ethnic trust:

> an earnest expression of respect for the interests, values, and historical experience of various groups is an essential condition for improving interethnic trust. In particular:
> - An expression of gratitude for the huge sacrifices which have been borne by preceding generations of Latvia's inhabitants during the World Wars in the fight against tyranny and injustice, so that freedom, democracy, and human rights triumphed in Europe;
> - Compassion towards the victims of the Hitlerite and Stalinist regimes which took away thousands of lives, decided the fate of the people, and split the country in two – the consequences of which we are living with to this day. (Harmony Centre 2012)[3]

The stress on empathy for victims of *both* Hitler and Stalin is significant. It is important to note that if these politicians were operating in Russia, that again there would be no top-down pressures on them to modify their views of history. It is because HC/SDPH wish to access political power *in Latvia* that they have adopted more conciliatory positions which find greater accord with the official memory positions of the Latvia state.

While these top-down processes are arguably leading to an increased democratisation of history, there also exist bottom-up processes which prevent Russian speakers from abandoning certain memory positions. As has been discussed, even amidst the top-down pressures of the modern Latvian school curriculum, teachers often supplement the official teaching materials with their own insights and opinions when the two moments are not congruent.

Additionally, the bottom-up views of parents and grandparents should not be underestimated. When memories and myths are transmitted from one generation to another, they necessarily mutate to fit within the changing understandings of different generations. As Halbwachs understood, autobiographical memory is distinct from historical memory. Nevertheless, transmissions of memory most likely persist in relatively consistent forms. As the data from this and other surveys have shown, the Soviet Army's victory over Nazi Germany is widely understood by the older generations of Russian speakers as a positive achievement which liberated Latvia. It is therefore very difficult for the younger generations of Russian speakers to reject this assessment, especially when their grandparents may have fought in the war.

The competing top-down and bottom-up cultural and political influences appear to be leading young Russian speakers increasingly to adopt a position which simultaneously celebrates Soviet liberation, while also begins to acknowledge that the actions of the Soviet Union had severe and negative consequences for the Baltic states. This is a position which allows Russian speakers to maintain the most salient aspects of their parents' and grandparents' memory-myths while also taking into account 'Latvian' collective memories.

For this reason it is still possible to talk of generational changes. Even when nodal points are created from important memories, there is still room for younger generations to alter these myths and adapt them to their contemporary understandings. For example, Maria Golubeva argues that the maintenance of divergent historical narratives by Russian speakers is 'a form of compensation for a sense of deep political disenfranchisement' (2011: 325). Golubeva finds convincing evidence that Russian speakers are disenfranchised by Latvia's state-sponsored political narratives 'that associate their group, however indirectly, with negative moments of history' (2011: 328). The results of this survey data suggest that while young people may indeed be disenfranchised, they are nonetheless potentially *less disenfranchised than their parents*. They are therefore more able to accept, at least partially, certain state narratives. Because young Russian speakers have grown up in an independent Latvia, are more likely to speak Latvian, and are more likely to feel a sense of attachment to Latvia than their parents, it may be posited that these factors temper the bottom-up and top-down pressures which promote an unwaveringly 'Russian' version of history.

We should, however, not get too carried away by the results of this survey. Young Russian speakers do appear to be gradually shifting their commonly accepted collective memory-myths. At the same time there is still a sizeable distance between their newly reconfigured beliefs and those of the Latvian state. On the one hand there is reason to be optimistic about the prospects for Russian speakers to be able to integrate more fully into Latvian discourses and narratives, and for the prospects of a democratisation of history. On the other hand, caution should be applied when analysing these findings. The views of young Russian speakers still diverge greatly from their 'Latvian' counterparts. In order to achieve societal harmony it is necessary for both groups to make concessions, and listen to the other group's point of view. There therefore is need for further research on this topic including the position of the younger generations of ethnic Latvians. If they too are increasingly able to see the complexities of Latvia's twentieth-century history from the complex perspective of the 'other' group, just as Russian-speakers are gradually and increasingly seeing history from a 'Latvian' perspective, then surely it will only be Latvian society that will benefit.

NOTES

1. Large sections of this chapter were originally published as Cheskin (2012a).
2. It is admitted, however, that it is not possible to know what percentage of these children would identify themselves as Latvian or Russian. It is likely that there are a number of pupils in 'Latvian' schools who would identify themselves as Russian-speakers.
3. This quotation was used as the template for question 4, and the sentiment was agreed with by 82 per cent of respondents (see Appendix 2). The full quotation is available as Appendix 1:6.

CHAPTER 7

The Primacy of Politics?
Political Discourse and Identity Formation

The state of Latvia, which was proclaimed on 18 November 1918, has been established by uniting historical Latvian territories based on the unwavering will of the [ethnic][1] Latvian nation for its own state and on the inalienable right to self-determination in order to guarantee the existence and development of the [ethnic] Latvian nation, its language and culture. (The Constitution of the Republic of Latvia 2014)

HEGEMONY AND THE 'PRIMACY OF POLITICS'

Large sections of this research have placed great emphasis on media production. This has been based on the assumption that media discourse plays a centrally important role in the propagation and articulation of social identities. At the same time, however, the analyses of *Chas*, *Vesti Segodnia*, and *Atmoda* have revealed very close links between the realms of politics and the media. The analysis of Latvia's Russian-language press, for example, pointed to a close link between the political imperatives of the country's 'Russian' parties and the discourses that were published within the newspapers in question. While the mass media of communication are essential for widespread dissemination of discourses, here it is also argued that the field of politics is of paramount importance in framing and constituting these discourses in the first instance. This chapter therefore examines political discourses in order to understand their potential impact on both media messages, and individual and group identities in contemporary Latvia.

In seeking to understand why, and how, the realm of politics is so significant in determining popular, discursive production, it is worth revisiting Gramsci's work on hegemonic formations. As discussed in Chapter 3, Gramsci broadly differentiated between two forms of hegemony: political hegemony and cultural hegemony. Gramsci argued for a re-examination of the Marxist conceptions of class, arguing that classes – or groups of individuals under the banner of 'classes' – are not entirely concrete and objective entities. Instead they come into existence not only in the political realm, but also as a result of cultural or ideological (discursive) practices. Even within the cultural realm, however, hegemonies are still formed within a political struggle. That is to say that they are formed when a group is striving to achieve hegemony through political ascendency. Gramsci's insights can be extended to the study of numerous group formations, including groups whose membership coalesces around national and ethnic identities.

For Laclau and Mouffe, Gramsci's work on hegemony is an essential starting point for their 'radical theory of democracy'. Indeed, Ernesto Laclau uses Gramsci's ideas in order to explore the role of politics, and especially antagonistic democracy, in creating social identities. For Laclau (2005: 61) *politics* exists as a process which mediates between the incompatible logics of universality and particularism. In other words it is never possible for any group to constitute fully a hegemonic bloc. This is because group identities are largely formed through the discursive practice of othering. Consolidated group identities are only possible when the in-group is directly contrasted to a rival out-group. The infinite differences that exist within the in-group can only be smoothed over when a universal difference can be established with an external group. This allows two very different individuals to be discursively linked on the basis that they are equally perceived to be different from a member of an external group. In other words, 'we' are all equally different from 'them' and for that reason we are the same.

This leads Laclau to the conclusion that no hegemonic bloc is ever a stable entity. Because the hegemony is not based on actual similarities within a group, there are numerous identities and positions which can challenge this formation and there is always room for competing identities to emerge. As such 'the political' is inherently antagonistic and constantly based on the competing articulations and posturing of opposing groups. In fact it is this antagonism which makes group formations possible at all.

Chantelle Mouffe further distinguishes between 'the political' and 'politics'. For Mouffe (1995: 105) 'the political' is the unavoidable condition of antagonism which is inherent in society and which is therefore evident in all spheres of human relations. 'Politics', on the other hand, is the attempt to organise and regulate this inherent antagonism within formal institutional channels. For this reason the world of politics, that is, what is conventionally understood as politics, (political parties, governments, legislatures, judiciaries, executives and so on) must be seen as the primary realm where 'the political' is organised, regulated, and institutionalised. This is because governments can wield power through recourse to, what Althusser (2008) refers to as, ideological state apparatuses as well as (repressive) state apparatuses. If a government wishes to pass laws and enforce them it will most commonly have a police force and a prison system ready to support the enactment of these laws. Governments will also have authority and oversight over numerous spheres of human life including (but certainly not limited to) education, employment, the regulation of media, financing and the management of museums and archives, and the erection of public monuments.

In modern, democratic states, governments cannot exert their control over these areas without considerable restrictions. The logic of democracy means that governments have a duty to respond to the desires of their electorate at least in some measure. Democratic constraints therefore prevent the exclusive use of repressive state apparatuses. Instead hegemonic positions must also be maintained through the articulation of a form of cultural hegemony, working in tandem with political hegemony.

It is for this reason that governments and political parties also strive to propagate universalised identity discourses. If it is possible to construct an imagined community (which can be based on ideas of class, race, ethnicity, language, ideologies or any other meaningful categorisation), then it becomes easier for that government to claim to be making decisions on behalf of this group. In the case of Latvia this can be seen in the construction of universal notions of Latvianess and Russian-speakerness – that is, what it universally means to be a Latvian or Russian-speaker in contemporary Latvia. These representations have necessarily come at the expense of the particular – the acknowledgement that within each group interests divulge greatly.

In Latvia it is especially apparent how the universalisation of certain groups (Latvians and Russian-speakers) has led to the consolidation of a new Latvian hegemony. Underlying this hegemony is a series of discursive positions and understandings that were documented in Chapter 3. When any elected official assumes political power they will therefore be expected by many people to maintain these discursive positions and to enact laws which adequately reflect the supposed interests of 'Latvians'.

In order to examine these issues, this chapter examines the peculiarities of Latvia's political spectrum and the dilemmas facing political parties whose electoral support comes primarily from the Russian-speaking electorate. It is argued that these discursive practices, which form central elements of Latvia's hegemonic order, also create a series of discursive conditions under which so-called 'Russian' political entities are forced to operate. This chapter therefore examines how these parties have responded to these discursive conditions.

LATVIAN POLITICAL PARTIES AND THEIR DISCOURSES

In this section focus is placed on political parties in Latvia and their various discourses. Methodologically this section is based on a number of interviews with members of the Latvian Parliament. Semi-structured interviews were conducted with six members of the Latvian Parliament: Inese Laizāne (National Alliance), Jānis Dombrava (National Alliance), Visvaldis Lācis (National Alliance),[2] Nikolaijs Kabanovs (Harmony Centre), Aleksandrs Sakovskis (Harmony Centre), and Boriss Cilevičs (Harmony Centre).[3] These individuals were all members of the tenth *Saeima* which sat until President Zatlers successfully called a snap referendum to dissolve parliament – leading to a new parliament being elected in September 2011. All of these deputies, with the exception of Visvaldis Lācis, were re-elected to the eleventh *Saeima*. Boriss Cilevičs, Inese Laizāne, and Jānis Dombrava were also re-elected to the twelfth *Saeima* in 2014.

Latvia's ethnic political spectrum

In Chapter 4 the role of the mass media of communication in creating discursive meanings and identities was explored. In this chapter, following Laclau and Mouffe's work on the role of 'the political' in forming group identities, attention is paid to political discourses. The discursive struggle to form a new hegemony of the Latvian state must be seen as essential for the facilitation of hegemonic groupings and therefore group identities. An examination of political discourse therefore allows us to understand how this struggle is being played out and, consequently, to grasp the effect of such political manoeuvring on identity formation.

As discussed above, the Latvian political spectrum which goes from left to right wing is not the same scale commonly employed in political science to distinguish between left and right wing ideological preferences. Instead the left/right divide often serves to denote ethnic preferences (see Chapter 1). Latvia's left/right ethnic divide is particularly striking when consideration is given to the high levels of support for leftist social ideals in Latvia. Surveys have consistently pointed to leftist social preferences not only among Russian speakers, but also among the Latvian population as a whole (Rose 1997, 2000, 2002, 2005; Makarov 2002). However, the Latvian electorate has never elected a left-leaning government. A major explanation for this discrepancy seems to be that the parties of Latvia's social left are discursively tied to concepts associated with the Soviet past and, by extension, to Russianness. This leads Tālis Tisenkopfs to the conclusion that 'the political superstructure is quite artificially constructed and does not reflect national sentiment' (2002: as quoted and translated in Makarov 2002: 6–7). This 'artificial' political superstructure would suggest that the realm of Latvian politics has been able to create discursive boundaries between 'Russian' and 'Latvian' political perspectives.

For this reason Latvia's left-wing parties (in the conventional, non-ethnicised sense), such as HC, have been unable to shake the notion that they are exclusively Russian parties precisely because they have also adopted leftist values and aims. At the same time, parties that wish to be seen as 'normal', 'Latvian' parties have adopted right-wing policies in order to distance themselves from any association with Russianness and Russia. This is despite the fact that, in an attempt to highlight their left-leaning credentials, HC moderately rebranded themselves for the 2014 parliamentary election campaign, preferring to use the name of the Social Democratic Party 'Harmony' (*Sociāldemokratiskā partija „Saskaņa"*, SDPH).[4]

Of course, the other main discursive barrier HC faces in finding acceptance as a normal, Latvian party is the inevitable stumbling block of historical interpretation. The party have often played a central role in the organisation of Riga's annual 9 May celebrations and their representatives often speak at the events (see Chapter 6), thus reinforcing the image of SDPH as a 'Russian' party, that is, a party that adheres to a 'Russian' reading of history.

When the Latvian political landscape is compared with that of Estonia, it would appear that the presence of large, well-represented 'Russian' parties (that is, parties that are popularly perceived as being 'Russian') in Latvia is therefore largely a result of an explicit ethnicisation of political issues. However, is the field of politics really able to ethnicise and manipulate issues which, on the ground level, are not already moments of contention? In the interviews which were conducted for this research, the ethnicisation of politics was a theme which was widely discussed by the three representatives of HC. All three shared the belief that the biggest differences and conflicts between Latvians and Russians were manifested in the realm of politics and not in the everyday lives of the inhabitants of Latvia. Boriss Cilevičs went as far as claiming that Latvia was unique in having such a mixed ethnic composition without any ethnic violence (a sentiment expressed to me on numerous occasions both by academics and everyday contacts):

> I wouldn't say that the level of intolerance in Latvia is particularly high. Not at all, at the everyday level it's very good. Latvia is one of the few European states where we have never had any ethnically based violence ever. Given this ethnic composition and this very fragmented society it's surprising, it's unique. (Interview with Boriss Cilevičs)

Aleksandrs Sakovskis was also of the opinion that inter-ethnic relations were mostly positive outside of politics, but that within politics they were manipulated:

> If you continue to research this topic you will see that our society is very patient. All parts of our society; both the Latvian and Russian parts. If you analyse the lives of Russian speakers then they have problems. But even having such problems you will not see any real confrontations. No demonstrations, no strikes, not what we see in Europe . . . I think that this is only possible in Latvia and only because the normal, large part of society tries to understand each other. Because all of us, Latvians and Russians, are from the Soviet past . . . the politicians use this in a bad way. They use it for their own interest and their own profit. (Interview with Aleksandrs Sakovskis)

The stark difference in real life experiences and politics was also highlighted in the focus group interviews with groups of Russian speakers. As demonstrated in Chapter 5, the focus group participants generally talked of positive interactions with Latvians in their everyday lives and saw politics as a field which artificially inflated ethnic concerns in order to serve the selfish interests of politicians.

From the 'other', 'Latvian' perspective Inese Laizāne, representative of the National Alliance, talked of how 9 May had been regrettably politicised. Laizāne compared 9 May celebrations that she had personally led, in her home town of Daugavpils, where 'veterans get together by a place of remembrance and are honoured with flowers, songs are sung for them, and the end of the war is emphasised' with those elsewhere in Latvia where: 'unfortunately there are political ambitions, and people fulfil these political ambitions at various celebrations. They turn it into a weapon of hate.'

The ethnicisation of the issue of 9 May, and of the issue of occupation, has been a theme which has largely come to define HC/SDPH and the party's desire to move from the side of opposition to government. Following their strong showing in the eleventh *Saeima* elections, where they became the most represented party in the Latvian Parliament, there was inevitably a great deal of talk about HC forming, or being included in, the governing coalition. In the end, however, HC were excluded from such a coalition and Unity instead formed an alliance with Zatlers' Reform Party (ZRP) and the National Alliance.

Just as was the case in the aftermath of the tenth *Saeima* elections in 2010, the main stumbling blocks for HC's inclusion in government were not their economic programme or their political ideology. Rather it was the question of perceived (lack of) loyalty towards the Latvian state and their reluctance to acknowledge publically the 'fact' of occupation. The constant emphasis on these questions of historical interpretation is all the more strange when we consider that HC's political programme differed greatly from that of Unity and ZRP. HC opposed the scale of Unity's proposed budget cuts and proposed maintaining a much higher budget deficit than Unity or ZRP. In other circumstances these differences would have been centre stage. However, for HC the biggest challenge in coming to power has not been their political or economic programme. Instead it has been the discursive perception that they are pro-Moscow and anti-Latvian.

Following the results of the eleventh *Saeima* elections numerous politicians from ZRP, Unity, and the National Alliance were quoted in *Diena* arguing against forming a coalition with HC:

> V. Liepiņš [*Saiema* deputy for ZRP] said that, in principle, he was not against cooperation with HC in the future. However, he did mention a number of arguments which at present make it impossible to bring them into the governing body. *Primary among these arguments was that he was not convinced of HC's ability to be loyal to the Latvian state* . . . 'the fact of the matter is that they do not acknowledge the occupation. They think that it was a fateful fact which occurred and they do not have a problem with that'. (*Diena* 25 September 2011, emphasis added)

Likewise Krišjānis Kariņš (Member of the European Parliament for Unity) gives his reasons for not allowing HC to join the governing coalition. Again, the primary reasons, at least in the media reporting of Kariņš's comments, are HC's pro-Russianness. Secondary to these concerns are those of policy:

As regards Harmony Centre (HC), the politician points to the fact that this party is oriented not towards Europe, but is manifestly pro-Moscow, and that such political forces do not have a place in the government of Latvia.

. . . Likewise HC, in the opinion of Kariņš, is an economically left-wing party 'who are proposing to increase the budget deficit by 4–4.5% in order to prop up the social sector with borrowed money', which will lead to an economic catastrophe. 'That's like an alcoholic borrowing money in order to continue drinking' added the politician. (*Diena* 27 September 2011)

When asked about this issue of occupation and the difficulty HC has encountered in dealing with it, the members of HC who were interviewed discussed the complexities of this issue for them and for their party. Both Boriss Cilevičs and Nikolaijs Kabanovs explained that is was not a black and white issue:

As for occupation I'm ready to explain. I'm ready to talk about it, but no one has asked me to because my answer will be paradoxical and will make people uncomfortable. People think that either no there was no occupation or yes there was an occupation from 1940 to 1991. But it wasn't like that . . . Let's take the situation, for example, when Germany occupied Denmark. No Danes sat in the Reichstag in Berlin and made the decisions. But for us, Latvians sat in the Supreme Soviet in Moscow, in the Central Committee, even in the Politburo. (Interview with Nikolaijs Kabanovs)

Aleksandrs Sakovskis displayed frustration that Latvian politicians could not drop the issue:

My opinion is that history is history. Someone somewhere has done something. What does this mean? That we, the next generation, always remember when something was done wrong 100 or 200 years ago? . . . But this is moronic. It's moronic. How long do we have to dig up history? (Interview with Aleksandrs Sakovskis)

Boriss Cilevičs noted how Prime Minister Dombrovskis simply used the issue of occupation 'to cope with the problems within his own bloc', adding that: 'We've never defended the view that events here in 1940 were something like Socialist revolution or whatever. We never said that it was just. We said it was a historical fact – how to describe it is not essential.'

It was this desire to move beyond history that motivated HC's call for a three year moratorium on the occupation question which was outlined in the party's eleventh *Saeima* pre-election campaign. The rationale behind this moratorium was that it would allow Latvian politicians to stop focusing on history, and instead focus on the more pressing issues of Latvia's economic and social well-being.

Predictably, the call for such a moratorium went largely unheeded in the debates in the run-up to the 2011 elections. To a great extent this was because a number of prominent 'Latvian' politicians publicly voiced their mistrust of HC and doubted their sincerity when trying to sound a reconciliatory note. Jānis Dombrava, in his interview, stated:

> In principle [Harmony Centre] are a hateful force for Latvians. Harmony Centre try to, let's say, join the mainstream by talking about social integration in the pre-election period, and about how we are all for national friendship. At the same time the rhetoric which is used for a Russian audience is fundamentally different.

For Visvaldis Lācis, it was unacceptable for Russian speakers to expect to be able to move beyond history and agree to disagree. Instead, the onus was on them to prove their loyalty to the Latvian state. Pressed on whether it was appropriate to confer citizenship to people who have lived all their lives in Latvia and who spoke Latvian fluently, the politician answered:

> VL: Under no circumstances. In my opinion, we can give citizenship to someone once they have assimilated. We are 58.5 per cent [of the population of Latvia] and cannot assimilate 40 per cent. whose TV and radio all comes from Russia.
> AC: Even if that person knew all about Latvian history and Latvian culture?
> VL: Yes, but they are hateful. Kabanovs[5] also knows Latvian culture.
> AC: But what if he shared the exact same opinions as you?
> VL: Then we could. *But firstly he has to prove it publicly!*

Here it is obvious that Russian speakers are presumed hateful until proved loyal to the Latvian state. They are, first and foremost, Russians, whose inherent interests naturally go against the interests of the Latvian nation. As Visvaldis Lācis stated, 'Latvia's Russians who are here are also Russians because they belong to the Russian nation. They vote for their own privileges.'

It would seem therefore that overt ethnicisation is a feature of Latvian politics which is very difficult to now avoid. For HC/SDPH this has been both their strength and weakness. It is their strength insomuch as it allows them to draw great support from the Russian-speaking electorate but at the same time they are unable to 'join the mainstream' of Latvian politics. The demand to acknowledge Latvia's occupation is therefore one which is unpalatable to HC/SDPH as it would most likely divert a significant amount of support away from their party.

Accordingly, the party are often left trying to balance the need to appeal to a demarcated political electorate who have certain, assumed values and collective memories, with the need to gain legitimacy and acceptance in the eyes of the other political parties in Latvia. One of their strategies has therefore been to use the word 'annexation' (see also Chapter 6) in place of occupation. Boriss Cilevičs, in an article on the HC website states:

> Of course, in 1940 the independence of Latvia was forcefully liquidated as a result of the agreement between two superpowers . . . Never have I, in any way, tried to defend the desire of the USSR to incorporate and *annex* Latvia. However, it is doubtful that we can assess these events using contemporary standards. For this reason it is not entirely correct to talk of fifty years of occupation.
> (Harmony Centre 2011, emphasis added)

This is seen as a compromise whereby Russian speakers are able to acknowledge the harm done under Soviet rule by Stalinisation and Soviet Communism, while also distancing themselves from an outright condemnation of the role of the Soviet army in the Second World War. This can be seen as an integrational discursive strategy that aims at overcoming the existing discursive contradictions in 'Latvian' and 'Russian' memory discourses. Indeed, this was a strategy evident in the positions taken by many Russian speakers in relation to the question of occupation in this research (see Chapter 6).

The fact, however, that HC/SDPH are perceived as a 'Russian' party further facilitates the desires of a number of politicians to highlight the ethnic divide in Latvia. For example, numerous politicians often manifest a belief that Moscow is attempting to create a 'fifth column' comprised of Russian-speakers who are loyal to Russia and not to Latvia (see Golubeva 2010: 167). As has been seen, in the political rhetoric of Latvia's nationalistic parties, Russian speakers are often closely connected with Russia and Russian influences. Latvian politicians from the nationalistic blocs For Fatherland and for Freedom/LNNK (FF/

LNNK) and All for Latvia! (who in 2011 merged into a single political bloc: the National Alliance) refer to parties that claim to represent Russian speakers as 'anti-Latvian' and 'pro-Russian'. For example, Mārtiņš Kālis, an All for Latvia! candidate for the 2009 elections to the European Parliament, writes in his blog at *Diena*'s internet portal: 'Parties who represent Russian-speaking interests could find significant success in the elections . . . this time when we will elect only 8 members of parliament as many as 3 representatives could be from *pro-Russian* parties – FHRUL, Harmony Centre, and LFP/LW' (*Diena* 4 June 2009, emphasis added).

This 'pro-Russianess' is also extended to all Russian speakers in Latvia. Kālis goes on to reassure the reader that 'a Latvian would not want to think anything bad about his Russian-speaking colleague or fellow student', but then goes on to justify why in fact Latvians *should* be wary of them:

> For the Latvian who doubts the relevance of the Latvian national standpoint, he should put himself in the skin of a Russian-speaker to understand what motives will influence Russian-speakers in these elections . . . For exactly this reason we must elect at least one Latvian nationalist representative to the European Parliament. *There is no other way to stop Latvia's gradual Russification.* (Emphasis added)

Here it is clear that Russian-speakers will solely be interested in securing their own, Russian-speaking interests, which Kālis defines synonymously with Russification. Indeed, in the political rhetoric of the more vocal and nationalistic 'Latvian' parties there is an unmistakable, underlying belief that Russian speakers are more loyal to Moscow than to Latvia. Just as in the media discourses which were analysed above, a number of Latvian politicians are equally keen to create a polemic, discursive divide between 'Latvians' and 'Russians', with each group being defined by supposedly inherent characteristics.

For example, this was seen in a series of controversial adverts produced by FF/LNNK which attracted much attention in the Russian-language media. The adverts first depicted a sinister-looking Russian-speaking couple who (in Russian) refuse to buy a Latvian Christmas tree from a kindly Latvian market tradesman. The advert concludes with the slogan 'support your own'.[6] HC produced their own response to this advert in which the FF/LNNK advert is depicted through a series of animated frames. In this response, instead of the Russian-speaking couple refusing to buy the Christmas tree because it was Latvian, both they and a Latvian mother and daughter decide that at 20 lats it is too expensive.[7] FF/LNNK responded to this with another advert that asked, 'what is Harmony Centre targeting?' and a sniper viewfinder being focused on Riga's Freedom Monument. The narrator announces, 'Now Harmony Centre is redrawing our video clips, laying scorn to our desire to support Latvian producers. Tomorrow they will rewrite our language law, change the electoral procedure, and redraw the map of Latvia' – at which point a map of Latvia is shown being engulfed in a red wave emanating from Russia.[8]

The adverts, which *Vesti Segodnia* compared to German propaganda in the 1930s (26 February 2009), clearly propagated the notion that, if not all Russian speakers, then at least the 'Russian' party HC, is inherently disloyal to Latvia and loyal to Russia. This is naturally a strategy that allows Latvian nationalists to gain legitimacy for their harsh stances against non-Latvians in Latvia; as the external 'other' this portrayal is centrally important to the discursive placement and unification of Latvian nationalists and as such must be seen to form a central element in their hegemonising project.

This distrust of Russian speakers, however, is not limited to relatively small parliamentary parties. As alluded to earlier, at the official, governmental level Estonia, Latvia, and Lithuania have often securitised their non-titular populations, viewing them as potential threats to the political integrity of the Baltic states and as a potential foreign policy tool in the hands of Moscow (Jaeger 2000). To this day, Baltic intelligence services are very concerned with the potential for Russia to interfere in the domestic affairs of their countries by manipulating and cajoling Russian speakers into political and social action. In its 2013 annual report, Latvia's Constitutional Protection Bureau (CPS) states that,

> Russia's long-term aim is to restore its great power status and increase its influence abroad, including in Latvia. At the same time, Russia's goal is to weaken Latvia's position in NATO [North Atlantic Treaty Organization] and the EU. *One of Russia's mechanisms for achieving its foreign policy objectives is its compatriot policy.* (Constitutional Protection Bureau of the Latvian Republic 2013: 6, emphasis added).

While the CPS notes that Russia will not be able to influence all of Latvia's Russian speakers, this nonetheless demonstrates the ongoing securitisation of Russian speakers in Latvia, and this is especially true in light of the Ukrainian crises of 2013–14 (see below).

In summary, overt ethnicisation has been a central characteristic of Latvian politics since the country gained independence from the Soviet

Union. Without doubt certain Latvian politicians and political parties use and inflate ethnic issues in order to further their own political aims. It is possible to see how this ethnicisation is an integral aspect of Latvian politics and how it has been used in order to reinforce discursive boundaries between competing political movements and groupings. It is clear that the strategy of overt ethnicisation is one which has allowed certain politicians to create and maintain some form of cultural hegemony. For this reason, from the perspective of Russian speakers and their identity formation, this ethnicisation is not simply a matter of symbolic concern. As discussed above, perceptions and narratives of Latvian statehood have played a major role in determining many concrete policies including those relating to education, citizenship, and language.

In assessing the impact of these state policies on language and education there is strong evidence, for example, that the political sphere directly influences people's opinions and attitudes towards the state language. A report by the Baltic Institute of Social Sciences concludes that in times of political tension surrounding the issues of education and language, Russian speakers are most likely to have negative attitudes towards the Latvian language (Zepa et al. 2008b: 5). The media analysis of Chapter 4 likewise demonstrated that these issues still provide opportunities for the Russian-language press to pursue self-marginalising and anti-discursive strategies, portraying Russian speakers as an oppressed political class in opposition to the Latvian state.

Official Latvian state policies, however, have not always been negative in the sense of fostering non-porous boundaries between Latvians and Russian speakers. In Chapter 4 the media analysis also revealed an increasing attachment and co-option of Latvian symbols within media discourses. One aspect of state policy which has arguably facilitated this attachment relates to national holidays and celebrations. For example, *Līgo svētki*, the annual summer solstice event which is based on a combination of ancient pagan rituals and more modern Latvian traditions, is an event which has been able to bring together Latvians and Russian speakers both symbolically and literally. In Chapter 4 it was noted that the media depictions of this holiday are positive in the Russian-language press. The organisation of events in Latvia's major cities has often been seen as a positive way to allow the country's Russian-speaking inhabitants to celebrate a festival that is traditionally marked in the countryside. Folklorist Ilga Reizniece, commenting on the urbanisation of these festivities, notes

> It doesn't feel the same on concrete; you need to celebrate these festivals in nature. But there are a lot of people in Riga who don't

have a place in the country, or who can't get to the country, so it's designed for them . . . and also for Russians who definitely have nowhere to stay [in the country]. (*Diena* 23 June 20.11)

The celebrations of *Līgo svētki* should therefore be seen as a positive means whereby the state and local governments can create a sense of collective identity among Russian speakers and Latvians. The fact that Russian speakers are able to participate in an event which is uniquely 'Latvian' must be seen as important in allowing them to feel a sense of attachment to Latvia. Inese Laizāne, Member of Parliament for the National Alliance, talked of how important it was that Russians attend 'Latvian' festivals. In answer to the question of what Russian speakers would need to do in order to integrate into Latvian society, she stated:

> You speak Latvian, that's the first step. The second step, if you want to integrate, then you'll go to the song festivals, you'll celebrate our festivals, you'll want to find out about our culture and history . . . I think that in this area there is progress. Where we see regression is in the use of language in everyday life. For example, I know a lot of Russian people who celebrate Latvian festivals, participate in them and support them, but at the same time, in shops and on the street they speak Russian.

While Inese Laizāne perpetuates the dichotomous notion of 'our' festivals, 'our' culture, and 'our' history, there is at least an opportunity for Russian speakers to participate in a cultural space that is unique to Latvia. It is, of course, important to bear in mind that the organisation of large-scale, inner-city celebrations of *Līgo svētki* is a relatively new phenomenon. Moreover it has coincided with the emergence of HC as the controlling party within Riga's municipal government. Therefore, the specific policy of organising such large-scale celebrations can perhaps be attributed more to the regional success of HC than to state policies per se.[9]

A report by the Baltic Institute of Social Sciences (Zepa et al. 2008a: 85) found that non-Latvians are often less likely than their Latvian counterparts to celebrate many of the country's official holidays such as the Proclamation of the Republic of Latvia (18 November) and Restoration of Independence Day (4 May). For example, 64 per cent of non-Latvians who were surveyed stated that they never or almost never attended concerts on 18 November compared to 44 per cent of Latvians (2008a: 93). One reason cited for the lack of participation among Russian speakers was that these dates are intrinsically linked with historical interpretations of the past, and that Russian speakers often lacked a full knowledge of what was being celebrated (2008a: 80–2). Nevertheless, even with fewer Russian speakers participating in various Latvian holidays, these celebrations should still be seen as a potential source of collective identity creation that has the power to draw Russian speakers closer to the Latvian state and to help them associate themselves more with Latvia (2008a: 16). Such positive experiences also potentially enable Russian speakers to pursue integrational discursive strategies as they are able to find common ground with official Latvian discourses and experiences.

RISING POLITICAL TENSIONS 2010–14

In Chapter 4, the media analysis from 2008 to 2010 pointed towards a relative easing of ethnic tensions in Latvia. The analysis from the Russian-language press showed signs of increasing optimism concerning the place of Russian speakers in contemporary Latvia. A focus on discursive articulations allowed us to see how Russian-speaking discourses were able to combine elements of both Russian and Latvian discourses in order to create positive positions that fostered improved discursive ties with Latvia.

Potential drops in ethnic tensions, however, can present serious problems for certain political groups. As has been noted earlier, according to the theory of Laclau and Mouffe, the solidity of any group identity is necessarily fixed on an 'equivalence of difference'. That is to say, members of the in-group are all portrayed as equally dissimilar to members of the out-group and therefore similar to one another. In periods when discursively attributed differences become porous, it follows that it becomes more difficult to maintain clear group boundaries. Politicians and political parties who rely on strictly demarcated ethnic borders therefore have a vested interest in constantly highlighting ethnic difference. Without this, internal group identities can be weakened. This can be seen in 2010 when FF/LNNK announced plans for a new referendum, seeking to ensure the status of Latvian as the sole language of instruction in all publically funded schools from 2012 (see Auers 2012: 63). A number of the focus group respondents in Chapter 5 expressed their relative acceptance of the compromise of having 60 per cent of instruction in Latvia. However, from the perspective of nationalist politicians, there is a constant need to reinforce ethnic boundaries.

Although FF/LNNK (in collaboration with All for Latvia!, and later merged as the National Alliance) did not succeed in gathering the constitutionally required number of signatures for a nationwide referendum

(10 per cent of the registered electorate), their actions inevitably stoked ethnic tensions.[10] Perhaps inevitably, the failed attempt to initiate a referendum led to a counter-reaction by Russian minority organisations and representatives. The previously fringe 'Russian' organisations United Latvia and Mother Tongue, for example, were able to galvanise support for a counter-referendum that would make constitutional changes to give Russian the status of the second state language of Latvia. They were successful in gaining the public backing of HC and then were able to secure 187,378 signatures (from a required 154,379) in favour of staging a referendum (Lublin 2012: 386).

There was, however, little chance that the referendum would ever be successful. In the end, 75 per cent of voters opposed the introduction of Russian as a second language from a turnout of 71 per cent of eligible voters (2012: 387). Nevertheless, this was a prime example of the 'primacy of politics' in setting identity agendas and demarcating group boundaries. Without the increase in perceived hostilities towards the Russian language, it would have been much more difficult for the radical leaders of Mother Tongue, Vladimirs Lindermans and Yevgēņijs Osipovs, to have gained notoriety. Mainstream political parties were forced to side with a yes (in favour of Russian as a second state language) or no vote (in favour of the status quo). For David Lublin (2012: 386), this 'serves as an example of how pressure from more extreme parties can help polarize more moderate ethnic parties and leaders, among both the majority and the minority'. Inese Šūpule (2011: 135) sums the situation up very well. Following her analysis of online discussions of referenda initiatives in 2011, she concludes that 'in the context of ethnic peace such initiatives as these . . . might be regarded as provocations and definitely not as instruments for solving ethnic cleavages as they cause ethnic mobilization and radicalization at the same time'.

For HC, this is illustrative of the ethnic dilemma facing the party. Because prominent HC politicians eventually backed the language initiative, they reinforced 'Latvian' portrayals of their party as pro-Russian and anti-Latvian. At the same time, ignoring the referendum had the potential to weaken their support among Russian speakers. As the results of the referendum show, there was an almost exact match between ethnicity and support or opposition to the language referendum. Lublin (2012: 387) estimates that only 2.3 per cent of ethnic Latvians voted in favour of the constitutional amendments, while only 4 per cent of ethnically non-Latvians voted against it.

Although the constitutional referendum of 2012 ultimately failed, it also exacerbated ethnic divisions at the political level in Latvia. The Presidential Commission of Constitutional Rights, for example, soon published a paper 'On the constitutional foundations of the Latvian state and the inviolable core of the Constitution' (President.lv 2012). This document set out to establish a clear agenda for a discussion on what constitutes the founding principles and values of the Latvian state: 'we need to be able to answer the questions: why was the Latvian state founded? What is the identity and purpose of the Latvian state?' (2012: 56). The paper notes that the 2012 constitutional referendum had made this a matter of high importance (2012: 43).

From a legal perspective, the paper asks if there is an inviolable core to the constitution that should not be changeable and if there are core features, identities, and functions of the Latvian state. The paper concludes that there are a number of such principles. Specifically four inviolable aspects of state identities are identified (2012: 104–9): (1) the national character of the Latvian state (*Latvijas valsts nacionālais raksturs*); (2) the territory of the Latvian state; (3) the Latvian nation (*Latvijas tauta*); and (4) the sovereignty of Latvia's state power. The paper also discusses the possibility of introducing a preamble to the constitution setting out and codifying these principles. Shortly thereafter, Egils Levits, judge at the Court of Justice of the European Union, drafted and proposed a new preamble. The final version, following months of intense debate, was passed by the *Saeima* on 19 June 2014 (see Appendix 3). While many people, including representatives of HC, questioned the need for a preamble, the most controversial aspects of the initial drafts were the description of Latvia as a 'nation-sate' (*valstsnācija*), and the use of the ethnicised concept of the Latvian nation (*latviešu tauta / latviešu nācija*).

The use of the term nation-state in the original proposal makes a clear connection between the purpose of the Latvian state and the interests of the ethnically defined Latvian nation. As Levits (2013: 28) himself explains in a commentary to his proposal:

> Because the Latvian state has been established by the ethnic Latvian nation with a specific goal – to make it possible to secure the long-term survival of its culture and language in an effective manner, it follows that in Latvia it is precisely the ethnic Latvians who constitute the state nation.

The final version of the preamble rejects the term nation-state and also opts for the more neutral (*latvijas tauta*) in certain places. This can be translated as 'the people of Latvia' (literally: 'the nation of Latvia') rather than 'the (ethnic) Latvian nation' (*Latviešu tauta*). But even with these changes, the meaning of the preamble is still clear. Corresponding with the discourses of the *Atmoda* period, the preamble establishes and codifies the idea that the Latvian state is a political entity which is designed to cater to the needs of the ethnically Latvian nation. It does so by referring to the ethnic Latvian nation (*latviešu nācija*) on two occasions. The preamble's first paragraph establishes that the Latvian state,

> has been established by uniting historical Latvian lands and on the basis of the unwavering will of the [ethnic] Latvian nation (*latviešu nācijas*) to have its own state and its inalienable right of self-determination in order to guarantee the existence of and development of the [ethnic] Latvian nation (*latviešu nācijas*), its language and culture throughout the centuries.[11]

Mirroring the discourses found within the pages of *Atmoda*, the rights of national minorities are protected and respected, but minorities appear as an appendage to the Latvian state and not an integral part of it: 'Latvia as democratic [sic], socially responsible and national state (*nacionāla valsts*) is based on the rule of law and on respect for human dignity and freedom; it recognises and protects fundamental human rights and respects ethnic minorities.'

Additionally, while the term nation-state is absent from the preamble, it remains in use in the country's Citizenship Law. The law establishes a number of criteria for eligibility. At one point the Citizenship Law (Section 2) notes that Latvians or Livs can submit documentary confirmation of 'belonging to the nation-state (ethnic Latvians) or autochthon population (Livs)' (*valstsnācijas (latviešiem) vai autohtoniem (līviem)*).

These legal documents therefore provide rigid demarcations between the 'true' representatives of the Latvian state (ethnic Latvians) and individuals who, although respected, are not members of the core nation. In terms of the discursive identity strategies of Latvia's Russian speakers, this re-emphasis on Latvians as the ethnic core of the Latvian state has a number of possible consequences. Notably, it reduces the possible discursive space for Russian speakers to argue that they belong to the contemporary Latvian state. In the media analysis of Chapter 4, it was observed that Russian-speaking discourse often results from a synthesis between 'Latvian' and 'Russian' discourses. With the hardening of group boundaries it inevitably becomes more difficult to adopt 'Latvian' positions, and therefore for non-Latvians to lay symbolic claim to discursive positions associated with the Latvian state and ethnic Latvians.

CONCLUSIONS

An examination of politics, understood as the realm where antagonisms are organised and institutionalised, is very important for our understanding of the contemporary identity formation of Latvia's Russian speakers. Political designs have been at the core of Latvian nation and state building. This chapter has therefore explored how political decision making can affect discursive understandings and realities for group relations. In the case of Latvia, politics continues to be deeply divided along ethnic lines. This creates incentives for certain political actors to use ethnicity as a political tool.

Fluid and overlapping political and cultural identities can be seen as a threat to a hegemonic order that has been, in no small part, legitimised in ethnic terms. The analysis of previous chapters has shown how discourses (either as articulations or as interpretations – encoding/decoding) can change over time. Many Russian speakers have therefore been able to adapt to the mythscape and discourses associated with the contemporary Latvian space. This has meant that clear demarcations between Latvians and non-Latvians can be challenged by discursive change. In response to this development of porous boundaries (even if it was in a relatively nascent form), a number of political actors have taken measures to reinforce and re-emphasise group boundaries.

In the early to mid-1990s Latvia was often described as a 'nationalising state', that is, an ethnically heterogeneous state that is seeking to become a nation-state 'by promoting the language, culture, demographic position, economic flourishing, or political hegemony of the nominally state-bearing nation' (Brubaker 1996: 63). In recent years Latvia can be considered as a state undertaking renewed nationalisation as a number of political elites have again attempted to turn a heterogeneous state into a 'Latvian' nation-state.

The imperatives for this renationalisation (or re-emphasised nationalisation) appear to have come largely from the political rather than the social realm as has been evidenced by the political initiatives discussed above. It is perhaps too early to examine the effects of this nationalisation. In the short term it has led to countermeasures that are designed to defend the interests of Russian speakers against the nationalisation of the Latvian state. This, in turn, further encourages nationalising measures in response to the perceived threat of 'Russian' mobilisation, and encourages calls for further Latvianisation and derusification of the Latvian state.

A further consequence of these increased (political) ethnic tensions is that the relationship between Russia and Russian speakers can be radically altered. Earlier it was argued that the discursive position of Latvia's Russian speakers is a synthesised position of Russian and Latvian discourses. It therefore follows that shifts in perceptions of Latvian discourses can lead to shifts in minority identities and also relations with Russia and its associated discourses.

NOTES

1. The official English translation of the Preamble to the *Satversme* translates '*latviešu nācijas*' as 'the Latvian nation' (see Appendix 3). In this translation, however, the word 'ethnic' has been included in brackets. This more accurately reflects the meaning of the word *latviešu* which has clear ethnic connotations. The main text of the *Satversme* uses the word *latviešu* solely to refer to the Latvian language. Instead, the constitution refers to the more neutral 'people of Latvia' (*Latvijas tauta*).

2. Although Visvaldis Lācis was a member of the National Alliance on the day he was interviewed, the following day he was expelled from the alliance as a result of a scandal involving certain discrepancies with his expenses claims. He then became an independent Member of Parliament. He did not stand for re-election to the eleventh *Saeima*.

3. Interviews were conducted in English, Russian, and Latvian, according to the preference of the interviewee.

4. In this chapter the party is referred to as HC, reflecting the fact that this was the party's name at the time of the interviews with HC representatives. In Chapter 8 the party is referred to by its current title, SDPH.

5. Reference to HC politician Nikolaijs Kabanovs, who was also interviewed.

6. The advert can be viewed on FF/LNNK's YouTube channel, available at <http://www.youtube.com/watch?v=YYynwubZwKc> (last accessed 4 September 2011).

7. This response can be viewed at Nils Ušakovs' (Mayor of Riga and HC representative) YouTube channel, available at <http://www.youtube.com/watch?v=mQ5ew6uslfAandfeature=related> (last accessed 4 September 2011).

8. This final advert can also be viewed on FF/LNNK's YouTube channel, available at <http://www.youtube.com/watch?v=ox-IoiUK8GA> (last accessed 4 September 2011).

9. For an assessment of the impact of the HC-controlled Riga government on minority policy in Latvia (and a comparison with Estonia) see Cianetti 2014.

10. 120,433 signatures were gathered out of a necessary 153,232 (Šupule 2011: 124)

11. The official English translation of the preamble to the *Satversme* does not include the word ethnic and prefers 'Latvian nation'. However, not least because of the social context and political debates surrounding the preamble, it is argued here that a more accurate translation is 'ethnic Latvian nation'. The official English translation can be found at http://www.saeima.lv/en/legislation/constitution (last accessed 27 March 2015).

CHAPTER 8

The Russian Federation and Russian-Speaking Identity in Latvia

Хотя враждебною судьбиной	Although we've been split apart
И были мы разлучены,	by inimical fate,
Но все же мы народ единый,	we're still one race,
Единой матери сыны;	the scions of a single mother!
Но все же братья мы родные!	That's why they hate us!
Вот, вот что ненавидят в нас!	You'll not be forgiven for Russia
Вам не прощается Россия,	nor Russia forgiven for you!
России – не прощают вас!	

(Fyodor Tyutchev, To the Slavs)[1]

Rogers Brubaker notes that Russia, as the 'natural external homeland' for many of Latvia's Russian speakers and Soviet migrants, inevitably plays a significant role in the formation of their national identity. Brubaker cites the example of interwar Europe to illustrate how 'fault lines' of tension emerge between nationalising states such as Poland, where there were sizable German, Belarusian, and Ukrainian populations, and the homeland nationalism of Germany and the Soviet Union. Here, the Soviet Union and Germany attempted to exert their influence on peoples that they considered as 'their own'. Germans living in Poland consequently had to contend with and manage competing national identities. According to Brubaker this phenomenon is all the more apparent in 'nationalising states' that are attempting to define and consolidate their statehood such as Latvia and Estonia, where 'their restrictive citizenship policies toward their large Russian minorities, have met with harsh Russian condemnations of "apartheid" and "ethnic cleansing" and repeated assertions of Russia's right to protect Russians against allegedly massive human rights violations' (1996: 108).

It is perhaps not surprising therefore, that Russia should be able to hold some cultural, political, social, or economic influence over Russian speakers in the Baltic states. In the chapter that follows, consideration is given to how the Russian Federation has discursively conceptualised its 'diaspora' in Latvia, and how this has evolved into observable policies and discursive expectations. Following on from the previous chapter, this chapter also investigates the impact of the renewed nationalisation of the Latvian state as well as the political crises that tragically engulfed Ukraine in 2014.

Methodologically this chapter is based primarily on analysis of the 'Russian Century' (*Russkii vek*) website.[2] *Ruvek* is a self-described 'portal for Russian compatriots' organised by decree of the Russian Ministry of Foreign Affairs, whose main aim is to 'provide information to a wide public, to compatriot organisations, and to the state organs of Russia and foreign countries, about the activities of the Russian Federation in support of compatriots living abroad' (Ruvek.ru 2014). All articles in the section of the website entitled 'Russia and compatriots' were analysed from February to May 2014 (a total of 144 articles). Materials were analysed using CDA in a similar manner to that which newspaper articles were scrutinised in Chapter 4. Macro-level discourses were mapped that related to the perceived group identities of 'Russian compatriots'. Special attention was given to referential strategies that sought to name, categorise, and consolidate this group. Additionally, focus was placed on predicational strategies that sought to define the features of this group (see Reisigl and Wodak 2001: 8). Materials were also widely consulted from the official website of the Russian Ministry of Foreign Affairs (MFA). Of specific interest were the articles in the section of the website entitled 'Articles, speeches and interviews on the topic of compatriots by the Minister of Foreign Affairs of the Russian Federation, his deputy, and leaders of the subdivisions of the MFA'.[3]

RUSSIA'S COMPATRIOT POLICIES AND DISCOURSES

In the post-Soviet era, the Kremlin has had a complicated relationship with the group of individuals that it has come to refer to as its 'compatriots abroad'. After the demise of the Soviet Union, approximately twenty-five million ethnic Russians found themselves living in territories outside the newly reconfigured space of the Russian Federation.[4] These individuals have, at various times, been referred to as the 'Russian diaspora' (*rossiiskaia diaspora*), 'compatriots abroad' (*sootechestvenniki za rubezhom/zarubezhnye sootechestvenniki*), and 'Russian compatriots' (*rossiiskie sootechestvenniki*).

In the 1990s it became increasingly common to refer to a Russian diaspora. However, as Smith and Wilson (1997: 854) note, the attempt to create a discursively meaningful group based on the linguistic sign 'Russian diaspora' was never going to be easy. In large part this was due to the relatively fragmented identities of the individuals who made up this discursively portrayed group. At the same time, the conscious decision to label these people as a well-defined entity must be seen as significant for the formation of Russian-speaking identity in Latvia. Such a move helped to establish (or preserve) discursive ties between these people and the Russian Federation. Graham Smith notes that the recodification of Russians abroad as a diaspora community therefore signifies two things:

> On the one hand . . . that Russia has abandoned its claim to a larger homeland and no longer seeks sovereignty beyond *Rossiia*. On the other hand, such a change in policy emphasis also signals that Russia has a clear part to play as the historic homeland (*rodina*) of the Russians. (1999b: 508)

By claiming that Russia has strong links with its diaspora, Russian policymakers were attempting to ensure that Russia continued to be an important nodal point in the identities of Russian speakers. This is another example of a disparate group of individuals who are being discursively conceptualised as a single, imagined community. In this instance, instead of politicians and journalists from Latvia, it is politicians from Russia who have been keen to create and cement a meaningful group (diaspora) for their own political ends.

A significant feature of President Putin's presidencies has been the renewed attention and increased financial resources paid to the compatriot issue compared to that of his predecessor President El'tsin. As Maria Nozhenko (2006) notes, there was a noticeable change in Moscow's official attitude towards Russian compatriots abroad from 2002 onwards, when the diaspora was increasingly seen as a resource the Kremlin could utilise in order to achieve a number of specific aims. If El'tsin's policy was to abandon Russian claims to a larger homeland, then under President Putin we have witnessed the increasing politicisation of the compatriot issue (something referred to below as the *Rossiisification* of Russian compatriots). 'Compatriots', for example, figure prominently in the 2013 Foreign Policy Concept of the Russian Federation, where they are named as an important element in the implementation of Russia's foreign policy objectives.

The increased emphasis on the compatriot issue has arguably been motivated by domestic factors such as the desire to strengthen Russian identity (Cheskin 2010b), or to deflect criticism away from Russia's own human-rights abuses by drawing attention to the discrimination of Russian speakers in Latvia, Estonia, and Ukraine (Fawn 2009). This notwithstanding, Russia's impact on Latvian Russian speakers cannot be dismissed out of hand. Russian state funding has increased in recent years to facilitate and cultivate links with Russian compatriots living abroad. Consequently there has been a noticeable expansion of Russian-funded NGOs, cultural organisations, and think tanks which all aim at promoting a positive image of Russia abroad (Popescu 2006: 2). These cultural initiatives have the potential to weaken the influence of Latvia's domestic cultural spaces. One study of Russian cultural influence in Latvia, for example, found that within Latvia's locally based Russian-language media, there was a much higher level of interest in Russian cultural institutions operating in Latvia than in Latvian ones (Tabuns 2006). This, Tabuns notes, is especially true for the influential House of Moscow (*Dom Moskvy*), a cultural centre largely funded by Moscow's municipal government.

Internationally, the compatriot issue became a matter of world focus in 2014 following Russia's de facto incorporation of the Crimean Peninsula into the Russian Federation, and during the subsequent armed conflict in the Donbas region of Ukraine. President Putin justified Russia's actions in Crimea by noting Russia's historical ties with the peninsula and citing the need to defend the rights and lives of Russian speakers (President of Russia 2014). The shocks of the political crises in Ukraine were also evident in the Baltic states. Following the disputed Crimean referendum, international journalists were keen to ask if Russia would try to intervene in Estonia and Latvia (BBC 2014; The Spectator 2014).[5] A major concern for many was that Russia would extend its assertive compatriot discourses and policies to Russian speakers in Latvia.

In order to understand, therefore, the potential impact of the events in Ukraine, analysis was conducted of the discourses surrounding Russia's compatriot policies during the Ukrainian crises of 2014. The following section carefully examines how Russia has been attempting to reach out to its so-called 'compatriots abroad' through an analysis of the *Ruvek* web portal. This analysis is later used to assess the extent by which these discourses have potential influence over the identities of Russian speakers in Latvia.

It is acknowledged that numerous compatriot discourses may coexist, and that they can be articulated by a number of different actors. In many instances these discourses are likely to be contradictory. This research, however, focuses on the compatriot discourses produced by, and within, the state structures of the Russian Federation. For this reason, *Ruvek*'s position as a state-sponsored news outlet makes it very useful as a means to study Russia's publicly disseminated discourses towards its compatriots abroad.

'Consolidation' of the 'compatriot movement'

As has been noted, Russians and Russian speakers were actually relatively fragmented at the start of Latvia's post-Soviet independence. This point that has not been lost on Russia's Foreign Ministry and the bodies now charged with formulating and implementing compatriot policies. The materials from the Russian Ministry of Foreign Affairs often talked of the need for the 'consolidation of the Russian (*rossiiskoi*) community' outside of Russia (for example Ministry of Foreign Affairs of the Russian Federation 2013a, 2013b). The discourses within *Ruvek* mirrored these sentiments and it was clear that 'consolidation' and 'unification' of Russian compatriots were major priorities. It was common, for example, to emphasise the potential power of a unified, international community: 'We are strong not as individuals, but in unity, in cooperation, and in mutual assistance' (*Ruvek* 8 May 2014).

As part of Russia's attempts to unify its diaspora, in 2007 the Foreign Ministry established a Coordinating Council for Russian Compatriots Living Abroad, which, in 2009, became the International Coordinating Council of Russian Compatriots Living Abroad (hereafter ICC). During the period of analysis numerous articles were devoted to the activities of individuals who worked at the national level of Coordinating Councils in various parts of the world. In February and March there were eight such articles, each with the same opening paragraph:

> The movement for Russian compatriots develops with each passing day. Its leaders – representatives of national Coordination Councils in various countries of the world, are extremely interesting people. We would like to know more about the people who give their energy, time, spirit, and soul *for the consolidation of Russian compatriots* in their countries of residence, and *for the development and strengthening of the Russian World*. (For example, *Ruvek* 25 February 2014, emphasis added)

In these articles, which take the form of informal interviews, the representatives are often asked questions such as 'How successful have you been at unifying compatriots?' In almost all cases the representatives stress the central goal of helping to consolidate the compatriot movement, often citing their efforts to bring together otherwise atomised cultural organisations under the single rubric of the ICC. There are a number of important points to be made here. Firstly, the persistent use of the word 'movement' to describe the activities of the ICC, presents an image of real purpose that requires a unified, well-organised, and mobilised community behind it. In one article entitled 'On the path to consolidation' (*Ruvek* 11 March 2014), the author notes that funding opportunities from Moscow have 'breathed new life' into the compatriot movement, noting that: 'The most important thing here is the mobilisation of our personal, creative, and intellectual powers and possibilities so that all of our units can work clearly, efficiently, and harmoniously.'

The message here, and throughout the entire monitoring period, was clear – 'a badly tuned instrument . . . makes it harder to create an effective sound' (*Ruvek* 11 March 2014). In other words, the compatriot discourse aims to create strict understandings of how Russian compatriots should think and act. This is, of course, primarily achieved by claiming to be the legitimate representatives of Russian speakers the world over: 'We, the representatives of Russian compatriots . . .' (*Ruvek* 8 May 2014).

The discursive consolidation of the imagined community of Russian compatriots is further enhanced by recourse to discourses of shared discrimination and threat. Russian speakers can be united as a 'movement' because they are united by their need to fight mutually experienced discrimination, Russophobia, and humiliation. The Ukraine crisis provided a clear grounding for such discourses, with a constant stream of depictions of 'mini-fuehrers' (*Ruvek* 24 April 2014), 'Banderites'[6] (*Ruvek* 10 April 2014), and 'neo-Nazis' (*Ruvek* 10 April 2014). Although the focus of this discourse inevitably centres on Ukraine, the position of compatriots in other parts of the world is not ignored and clear links are drawn between the Baltic authorities and those of Ukraine (*Ruvek* 25 April 2014). For example, one article notes that,

> The Latvian army is gearing up to perform the same function as those of the armed groups of Kyiv's self-proclaimed authorities in the Donetsk Republic. We know what these groups of bandits are doing there – opening fire on the civilian population. (*Ruvek* 24. April 2014)

The 'Rossiisification' of Russian compatriots

Analysis of the *Ruvek* articles reveals a series of complex strategies that are used to disassociate Russian compatriots from their country of residence. This is achieved in the manner discussed above, by depicting Russophobic elites and comprehensive discrimination. But it is also forged through the articulation that Russia is the real homeland for compatriots. As a result, even when it is asserted that 'we remain patriots of the country in which we live', this sentiment is accompanied by the caveat 'but the fatherland is the same for all of us – Russia' (*Ruvek* 20 May 2014).

A number of articles warned of the dangers of becoming assimilated into non-Russian cultures. As one author notes,

> Look at the delight with which they try to implant . . . their culture – in the main *a foreign culture*, which was meant to crush our identity, our individuality, and that self-same Russian soul that is incomprehensible, frightening, and at the same time, of interest to many foreigners. (*Ruvek* 8 May 2014. emphasis added)

Other articles pointed out that living abroad should not take away identification with Russia (*Ruvek* 13 March 2014), or stressed that Russians are only 'guests' in their countries of residence (*Ruvek* 7 April 2014).

The compatriot discourse therefore attempts to remove a number of discursive ties between Russian compatriots and their countries of residence. It can be seen as part of a broader strategy of what is here termed *Rossiisification*. The term Rossiisification is deliberately used in this work as a phenomenon distinct from Russification. Russification has historically been used to describe attempts to introduce and bolster Russian cultural, linguistic, and spiritual values and practices, based on a strictly ethnic (*russkii*) understandings of Russianness. Rossiisification, on the other hand, refers to an attempt to forge ties with Russia on a more civic (*rossiiskii*), state-based level. In other words, ties are not meant to be abstract cultural ones, but concrete attachments to the Russian Federation. This position is summed up well by one article entitled 'Being Russian is not just an attachment to ethnicity (*natsional'nosti*)' (*Ruvek* 8 May 2014). Instead, the article argues, 'being Russian . . . is first and foremost attachment to a state – to Rus', Russia, the USSR, and Russia'.

This is also reflected in the increased use of the appellation (civic) Russian (*rossiiskie*) to describe compatriots. Whereas it was common before 2007 to refer to 'compatriots abroad' (*sootechestvenniki za rubezhom/zarubezhnye sootechestvenniki*), it has now become increasingly common to speak of 'Russian compatriots' (*rossiiskie sootechestvenniki*). This has become codified through the adoption of the collocation 'Russian compatriots' in the official name of the ICC. There are two Russian adjectives that can be translated into English as Russian: *russkii* and *rossiiskii*. The former signifies ethnic qualities of Russianness, for example the Russian language (*russkii iazyk*) and ethnic Russians (*russkie*). The later refers to civic qualities and institutions related to the territorial and political entity of the Russian Federation, for example the Russian Football Union (*Rossiiskii futbol'nyi soiuz*) and Russian citizenship (*rossiiskoe grazhdanstvo*). It is therefore highly significant that Russian compatriots are referred to as *rossiiskie* and this subtle discursive shift is indicative of Russia's increased focus on strengthening political loyalties among its so-called diaspora.

Reference to Russian compatriots as *rossiiane* (Russians, implying a civic description) and not *russkie* (Russians, but implying an ethnic categorisation) is particularly interesting. Previously *rossiiane* has been used to describe people with Russian citizenship irrespective of ethnic backgrounds. *Russkie* has instead been the term used to refer to ethnic Russians irrespective of their citizenship. In the *Ruvek* articles, however, compatriots are commonly referred to as *rossiiane* and are ascribed ethnic, and even genetic, characteristics:

> Collectivism as a trait is an internal characteristic of the Russians (*rossiianam*) ... and today it remains an unavoidable tradition of our people irrespective of their place of residence. In truth 'Russianness' (*russkost'*) can be considered as a genetically born feature of their character. (*Ruvek* 5 March 2014)

In other articles reference is made to the seemingly contradictory constructions 'ethnic Russian' (*etnicheskii rossiianin*) (*Ruvek* 20 March 2014), 'Russian ethnos' (*rossiiskii etnos*) (*Ruvek* 4 April 2014), and a 'Russian ethnocultural space' (*rossiiskogo etnokul'tornogo postranstva*) that go beyond the borders of the Russian Federation (*Ruvek* 24 March 2014). Natalya Kosmarskaya (2011: 54) has also noted the tension between Russia's 'ethno-selective' conception of its diaspora, and the practical, political considerations that have required a looser, more civically defined notion of compatriots. For Kosmarskaya (2011: 59), the term 'ethno-Russians' (*etnorossiiane*) allows compatriot policies to be configured towards ethnic Russians, but also widens the category to encompass non-Russians who have spiritual and historical links with Russia.

The strategy of Rossiisification, however, also should be understood as a discursive and institutional attempt to tether compatriots with the state structures of the Russian Federation. Russia's federal law 'On the State Policy of the Russian Federation in Relation to Compatriots Aboard', initially signed by President El'tsin in 1999, but amended most recently in 2010, establishes clear links between state structures and compatriot organisations. Article 26 describes the Worldwide Congress of Compatriots as 'the highest representative organ, providing mutual interaction between compatriots and the state organs of the Russian Federation' (Ministry of Foreign Affairs of the Russian Federation 2010a). Additionally, the ICC, as 'an organ of the Worldwide Congress of Compatriots', is charged with a supreme representative role in the periods between congresses (Article 26, Section 3).

It is hardly surprising, therefore, that in the *Ruvek* articles the role of the Russian state, its political organs, and the politicians who represent the Russian Federation are highlighted as essential components in the consolidation of the Russian diaspora, and as guarantors of the rights of Russian speakers abroad. In all 144 articles from the monitoring period, there was only a single article that belied even a hint of deviation from the officially held positions of the Russian Federation.[7] In all other cases, the discourses mirrored those of the political establishment, and were entirely positive in their assessments of Russia's political decision making at both the domestic and international level. In fact, the official political discourses were repeated in some detail. *Ruvek* reproduced a number of interviews and speeches from top politicians including Foreign Minister Sergei Lavrov, Prime Minister Dmitry Medvedev, and President Vladimir Putin. Although appearing under the rubric 'Russia and Compatriots', in many instances there was no clear link between the content of these materials and compatriot issues. Interviews with Medvedev and Putin, for example, talked at length about Russia's trade deals with China without mentioning the compatriot issue in any detail (*Ruvek* 19 May 2014, 20 May 2014).

The process of Rossiisification links concrete state structures and positions with the Russian diaspora. This does not preclude, however, the use of cultural discourses which aim at strengthening ties with 'the historical motherland' (a phrase often repeated both in the *Ruvek* articles and in the materials from the MFA website). This can be seen clearly with frequent references to 'the Russian World'. The Russian World is conceptualised as a supranational, spiritual, ethnic, and linguistic space, transcending political and territorial borders. It is, nonetheless, a concept that is explicitly tied to the Russian Federation:

A direct link with the motherland internally strengthens Russian (*rossiiskie*) compatriot organisations and attaches the characteristics of community to the spiritual space of Russians (*rossiiane*) living abroad. In truth, this allows us to refer to the community of Russians (*rossiian*) living abroad as the Russian World. (*Ruvek* 5 March 2014)

In order to meet its main objectives, the multidimensional Russian World beyond Russia is based firmly on compatriots. The main goals are, first and foremost, strengthening ties with the historical homeland and the preservation of the Russian (*rossiiskogo*) civilisational space (language, culture, national customs and traditions). (Ministry of Foreign Affairs of the Russian Federation 2013c)

History and culture

The compatriot discourse articulates an image of a global Russian space that is not only Russian (*russkii*) but also Russian (*rossisskii*). The historic Russian world that used to exist on the map, demarked either as the USSR or the Russian Empire, is used to invoke deep emotional ties between Russian speakers and a contemporary, spiritual space. It is a space, moreover, that the compatriot discourse constantly emphasises as Russian speakers' 'historic homeland'.

Russia . . . gathered under its wings tens and hundreds of nations and ethnic groups (*narodnostei*) and became not a stepmother for them, but a loving mother, which, it is sad to say, exists in the present time only in people's hearts and not on the map. (*Ruvek* 8 May 2014)

In Chapter 6, the contemporary complexities of memory and memorialisation were explored among Latvia's Russian speakers. From the perspective of Russia's compatriot discourse there is no ambiguity in terms of historical interpretations. As one article puts it, '*Real Russians (rossiiane)*, wherever they live, remember the heroes of the Great Patriotic War as a mark of profound acknowledgement of their eternal achievement, carried out so that we could live in peace' (*Ruvek* 8 May 2014, emphasis added).

This strategy exerts genuine pressure on Russian speakers to avoid defiling the memory of their heroic ancestors and to be 'real Russians'. This is, or course, contrasted to the position of 'homo Latviensis', who is expected to condemn the role of the Soviet Union in occupying Latvia following Soviet 'Victory' (in inverted commas) in the Second World War (see Chapter 3). Indeed, the Latvian government is singled out in one article for failing to honour the memory of the people who suffered in the Nazi concentration camp in Salaspils: 'instead, immediately after the Victory Day celebrations, the *Saeima* hurriedly passed a law on criminal convictions for . . . denial of "Soviet occupation"' (*Ruvek* 20 May 2014).

Predictably, in this respect, the compatriot discourse offers an inverted image of the discourses of the Latvian state. A clear dichotomy is maintained between 'the achievement and glory of our nation' (*Ruvek* 18 April 2014) (a nation that is celebrated for conquering fascism), and the neo-Nazis who persecute Russians and fail to acknowledge this heroic history. Ukraine is singled out as the best example of a fascist state, but an image is also created of Russia as an island of morality surrounded by fascism: 'It seems that the world is going back seventy years in time and around us Nazis are committing acts of brutality' (*Ruvek* 20 March 2014).

Historical orientations are therefore constructed as essential values for all 'real' Russians. In fact, historical traditions are used as the basis to argue that Russians have developed a series of intrinsic values that mark them out as representatives of a distinct national group. For example, *Ruvek* reproduces the Resolution of the VIII Regional Conference of Russian Compatriots Living in the Countries of Europe (organised under the auspices of the ICC). The authors of the resolution conclude by pledging their support for the Russian (*rossiiskuiu*) community against nationalists 'for the defence of the Russian language, the values of Russian culture, its centuries-old traditions, customs, and way of life' (*Ruvek* 27 March 2014).

Specific values and traits are thus assigned to the imagined community of historical Russians (that is, not just people living in Russia) including collectivism (*sobornost'*) (*Ruvek* 5 March 2014), a disdain for individualism and liberalism (*Ruvek* 23 May 2014), Orthodox faith (*Ruvek* 7 April 2014), and 'charity, empathy for one another, and mutual assistance' (*Ruvek* 28 April 2014). According to one author, these shared characteristics and values represent spiritual bonds which are 'born in the historical path of the nation, creating invisible links between us' (*Ruvek* 28 April 2014).

These discursive, predicational strategies (Reisigl and Wodak 2001: 8) aim to attribute traits and features to Russians by providing a set of positive characteristics. Inevitably though, the process is also accompanied by a negative process of othering. The positively portrayed values of collectivism and mutual concern are held in sharp contrast to those of a spiritually and morally corrupt West with its (in ironic, inverted commas) 'victorious European values' (*Ruvek* 14 April 2014). This strategy aims to delegitimise any ties Russian speakers might have with 'the West' in favour of strengthening ties with their 'historic homeland'. The West, after all, is portrayed as an entity that is intent on debasing the honour of Russian speakers and their predecessors: 'The information machine, actively supported by the USA and the West, released a frenzied propaganda against everything that was sacred for generations of people. In Ukraine the heroic deeds of our fathers, grandfathers and great-grandfathers were levelled pedantically and systematically' (*Ruvek* 13 May 2014).

European values are therefore presented as alien and 'fake' to Russians. Andrei Leonidov, director of the Institute of Russia's Near Abroad, introduces the dual concepts of postmodernism and tradition to illustrate this point:

> Postmodernism and traditions are conceptually distinct and entirely opposed to one another . . . The South-East [of Ukraine] and the Russian nation are real, but . . . Avakov [Ukrainian Minister of Internal Affairs] is a fake, along with the current Ukrainian government that only exists thanks to the postmodern support of the West and their fake ideology, which is based exclusively on lies and fuzzing the minds (*zapudrivanii mozgov*) of its citizens. (*Ruvek* 30 May 2014)

The discursive othering of the West and supposed Western values fits the domestic, neo-traditional strategy of President Putin whereby Western-financed NGOs have come under closer scrutiny and control (Lavinski 2013) and legislation has been passed against support for same-sex marriages, an issue discursively tied to the West (Wilkinson 2012). In an extensive interview with Aleksandr Zinchenko, described as 'the leader of the anti-Maidan', this anti-Westernism is set out in clear terms. Using the example of transgender icon Conchita Wurst, the winner of the 2014 Eurovision Song Contest, Zinchenko laments the 'decline of Europe':

> Conchita Wurst, I say with deep regret, is the epitome of modern Europe: freedom taken to absurd levels, even to the point that it no longer looks human. These are the standards that Europeans are bringing to the world. They are the very same standards that Euromaidan wanted to force on our country. (*Ruvek* 23 May 2014)

These articulations of Russianness and Russian values aim to consolidate the Russian diaspora behind cultural and civilisational values. They are also used in defence of the Russian state, 'the bastion of traditional values' (*Ruvek* 23 May 2014). In this context Russia's takeover of Crimea is depicted as a spiritual event that resulted from the spirituality of President Putin himself:

> Earlier the political class was not ready to comprehend the words of Putin [his calls for greater spiritual bonds]. But in March 2014,

not just the political class, but the majority of the Russian nation and our compatriots listened to the Russian President's speech to the Federal Assembly with tears in our eyes, as he spoke about the reunification of the separated nations of Crimea and Russia, and we felt the bonds in our hearts. (*Ruvek* 28 April 2014)

POLITICAL DISCOURSE AND RUSSIAN-SPEAKING IDENTITIES IN LATVIA

Chapter 2 introduced the notion that Latvia's Russian speakers inhabit dual, often contradictory mythscapes. On the one hand they live, work, and study in contemporary Latvia and are exposed to the national discourses of the Latvian state that have been examined in the course of this study. On the other hand, many of these individuals also inhabit a media and cultural space that exposes them to the narratives and discourses of the Russian state.

A central argument of this research is that the political realms that create these discourses, in both Latvia and Russia, are hugely influential in determining group identities. Within Latvia, politicians have found that ethnicisation is an effective strategy to garner votes and to sculpt willing electorates (see Chapter 7). The fact that 'Russian' parties have, to date, been largely marginalised by 'Latvian' parties testifies to the boundaries which have been erected in Latvian politics. Of course, this ethnicisation is itself a consequence of Latvian state policies which have often served to demarcate the county's two main communities. The citizenship law, along with policies on education and language, have aided a relative consolidation of Russian speaking group identity (see Chapter 3). This group identity could not have been so easily imagined without the shared sense of marginalisation and discrimination that has been fostered by these policies. If, for example, citizenship had been granted to all Russian speakers, then it is likely that large numbers of Russian speakers would have been more willing to vote for what are now perceived as 'Latvian' parties. As discussed above, a substantial proportion of Russian speakers supported Latvian independence and participated in the activities of the Popular Front. The policies which denied these people a legitimate place within Latvian political life must therefore be seen as highly significant in terms of removing discursive ties between Russian speakers and the Latvian state.

It is also important, however, to examine Russia's influence on group identities. In this work, Russian speaking identity has been conceptualised as a synthesised position between competing Russian and Latvian discursive positions. This model corresponds with Brubaker's triadic nexus, and helps us to understand that changes in Russian speakers' relationship with Latvia ('the nationalising state') will also facilitate changes in their relationship with Russia ('the external homeland'). The analysis of Russia's compatriot discourse demonstrates that Russia has been pushing for improved ties between its 'compatriots' and Russia. Indeed, calls for greater ties with the 'historic homeland' have often been grounded on depictions of Latvia and other 'host' countries as discriminatory, fascistic, and humiliating for Russians and their great history. As such, Russia has a lot to gain when 'nationalising states' provide ammunition for these claims.

This does not mean that the Latvian state *is* fascistic or discriminatory to the degree depicted in the compatriot discourse. Instead it is more important to understand how Russian speakers *perceive* the Latvian state. It was with this understanding that Rogers Brubaker depicted his triadic nexus in terms of *stances* and *representations* (Brubaker 1996: 68–69; see also Pettai 2006: 133; Cheskin 2015). Stances are the policies and discourses that are produced by the respective nodes of Brubaker's nexus. Representations are the ways that these policies and discourses are interpreted. This has some similarity to Stuart Hall's (1980) work on encoding/decoding, referred to above.

As this author has previously argued (Cheskin 2015), it is appropriate to subdivide Brubaker's fields into their cultural, political, and economic components (see Figure 8.1). This differentiation helps to understand the complex push/pull factors that orient Russian speakers towards or against their 'nationalising state' of residence (Latvia) and their 'external homeland' (Russia). As this research has shown, a number of Russian speakers make a distinction between their cultural understanding of Russia and the 'actual' (political) Russia – the Russian Federation. For many Russian speakers, Russia appears to be an abstract entity that is important for its literature, culture, language, and history. On the other hand many of Latvia's Russian speakers have never lived in Russia and therefore do not necessarily feel strong political attachments to the Russian Federation and its attendant political structures (Cheskin 2015).

At the same time, the analysis of Russia's compatriot discourse shows that Russia has been attempting to Rossiisify its 'compatriots' by strengthening not only cultural ties with Russia, but also linking these with political preferences. Where Latvia has been unable to provide political forms of identification for its Russian speaking population, Russia has increasingly been willing to step in as a political sponsor of Russian-speaking identities. The Russian state has therefore increased its potential political attractiveness (for some individuals at least) by

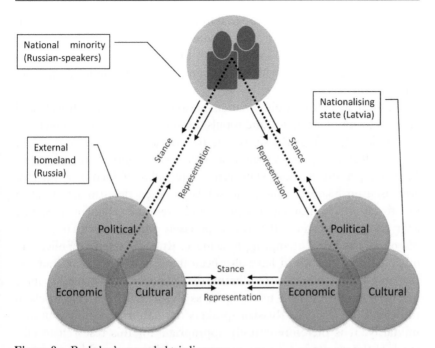

Figure 8.1 Brubaker's expanded triadic nexus

Source: Adapted from Cheskin (2015: 82). The original article uses an expanded quadratic nexus that includes 'international organisations' (primarily the EU). For the sake of parsimony this model reverts back to the original triadic nexus.

outlining a state that is true to certain 'Russian' values. The compatriot discourse, for example, highlights 'fascistic' countries such as Latvia and contrasts them to Russia's enlightened policies and achievements.

This strategy is aided by relatively low levels of cultural attraction towards Latvia among Russian speakers (Cheskin 2015). As demonstrated in the focus group interviews, Latvia's Russian speakers often feel that Latvian culture is not 'their' culture. In fact, the newly adopted preamble to the constitution attests to recent efforts to re-emphasise and codify the centrality of Latvian culture for the (political) Latvian state. According to the preamble, the 'ethnic Latvian nation' is the state's central focus while national minorities are not part of the core nation, but only an appendage to it (see Chapter 7). The possible result of this is that, for many people, the Latvian state further forgoes its cultural attractiveness, and that this will be accompanied by a loss in political attraction.

In contrast there is evidence that economically Latvia, along with the other Baltic states, has much greater appeal than Russia (Haas 1996: 70; Solska 2011; Cheskin 2015: 77–9). This is a result of generally higher living standards in Latvia compared to Russia. This economic attraction therefore has potential to reduce political association with the 'real' external homeland of Russia. Although the Russian discourse attempts to tie Russian statehood with civilisational values, it is more difficult to do this with economics.

Nevertheless, this differentiation between economic, political, and cultural forms of attraction and repulsion shows how Russia can increase its political appeal. If Russia is able to offer a credible defence of the rights of Russian speakers then it can increase its political attractiveness. Moreover, if the Russian state can create poles of identification that are based on history, values, and solidarity, then this can also weaken identification with Latvian discourses and strengthen Russian ones. The analysis of *Ruvek* shows that this is precisely what Russia's compatriot discourse has been attempting to achieve. Russia's assertive policies in other parts of the world have also been important – nowhere more so than in Ukraine. It is towards Ukraine that Russia's compatriot discourse has been employed with most rigour as Russia has been able to claim to defend the rights of Russian speakers not only rhetorically, but also militarily. It is therefore entirely appropriate for this research to take stock of the events in Ukraine in 2013–14 and their possible impact on Russian-speaking identities in Latvia.

AFTER UKRAINE

The political crises that erupted in Ukraine in late 2013 and 2014 took most analysts completely by surprise. Following the spread of the initially peaceful 'Euromaidan' protests in Kyiv, the country was shocked by the shooting of hundreds of protesters at Independence Square. Not long afterwards, following President Yanukovych's flight to Russia, the Crimean peninsula was incorporated de facto into the Russian Federation following a legally dubious referendum. The following month the country was again stunned by the deaths of forty-two pro-Russian activists in Odessa's House of Trade Unions. Most tragically, Ukraine witnessed (and at the time of writing, is still witnessing) the loss of thousands of civilian and combatants' lives in the Donbas region of the country. President Putin justified Russia's actions in Crimea by citing the need to protect the peninsula's Russian speakers against the 'nationalists, neo-Nazis, Russophobes and anti-Semites' (President of Russia 2014) who had, he argued, seized power in Kyiv. As Putin explained in the address that heralded Russia's official recognition of Crimea and Sevastopol as constituent entities within the Russian Federation, 'we could not abandon Crimea and its residents in distress. This would have been a betrayal on our part' (President of Russia 2014).

These events were inevitably accompanied by a sharp increase in Russia's propaganda efforts to portray the Ukrainian authorities as illegitimate and fascistic. This was clearly seen in the analysis of *Ruvek* articles above. A major focus of Russia's media has been to highlight discrimination of Russian speakers and the threats they face, not only to their culture, but also to their lives. For Russian speakers in Latvia this has a number of potential implications. The first, and perhaps most important, consideration is that Russia has provided clear proof of its willingness to act in defence of the interests of Russian speakers. As one *Ruvek* article (7 March 2014) states,

> For Russia nothing has been, or is, more important than the inter-ests of the nations who inhabit Ukraine, including our numerous compatriots. Ensuring and protecting their rights and freedoms, first and foremost their right to life, is a responsibility of the Russian state.

The sight of thousands of Crimean inhabitants celebrating Victory Day on 9 May 2014, triumphantly broadcast on Russian television, therefore sends out potentially powerful messages to Russian speakers in Latvia. It also poses a difficult question for Latvia's 'Russian' parties, that is, parties whose main support comes from Russian speakers.

Latvia's 'Russian' political parties at a crossroads?

As detailed above, a major strategy of Russia's compatriot discourse has been to mobilise Russian speakers. A number of the *Ruvek* articles called for Russians to stop their passivity in the face of outright discrimina-tion and hostility. Compatriots were encouraged to speak out against prejudice, and to voice their concerns loudly: 'We are not talking about a passive information tactic, but an offensive, attacking one' (*Ruvek* 5 March 2014). For one author, the problem with Ukraine was that Russians failed to take action earlier. Instead of talking, Russians should have 'worked everything out, planned activities, started to implement them, and only then talk' (*Ruvek* 25 February 2014).

This increased emphasis on mobilisation, coupled with the assertive pol-icies and rhetoric of the Russian state has a number of potentially significant implications for Latvia's 'Russian' political parties. This section focuses on the two main parties in Latvia which are often seen as representatives of the Russian-speaking community, the Social Democratic Party 'Harmony'

(SDPH) – formerly Harmony Centre (HC) – and the Russian Union of Latvia (RUL) – formerly For Human Rights in a United Latvia (FHRUL). If Russian-speaking discourse in Latvia is a synthesised position between Russian and Latvian discourses, a salient question is how these parties have reacted, and will react, to changes in the discursive strategies of the Latvian and Russian states. To search for answers to this question the respective websites of SDPH and RUL[8] were examined for a period of four months from February to May 2014. All news articles published in Russian were analysed. SDPH published most articles in both Latvian and Russian – during the monitoring period forty-seven news articles were published in Russian and forty in Latvian. The bulk of articles from the RUL website were in Russian – only eight articles were published in Latvian, compared to ninety-three in Russian over the monitoring period.

Harmony is currently the most successful of Latvia's 'Russian' parties. In the 2010 parliamentary elections HC obtained twenty-nine out of 100 seats, and in the snap-elections of 2011 it increased this number to thirty-one, making HC the most represented party in the *Saeima*. In 2014 the party lost seven seats but was still the most repre-sented party in parliament. The party has, however, not been included in any government coalitions to date. SDPH positions itself as left wing (in the ideological sense and not in the ethnicised sense that the term is often understood in Latvia). This is reflected in its name change for the 2014 election campaign, whereby 'social democratic' is now included in the party's official title. As discussed in Chapter 7, the party often has to tread a fine line between keeping its mainly Russian-speaking electorate happy, and trying to adopt a moderate position that focuses on non-ethnicised issues. Of the forty-seven articles that were examined, a majority focused on concrete policies that were not related to questions of identity or ethnicity (economic issues, taxes, government spending, land reform, legalisation of drugs and so on).

The events in Ukraine, however, forced the party to draft a formal response to the crises, setting out its official position (SDPH 5 March 2014). In this document SDPH demonstrates a keenness to avoid taking sides and lists nine points including 'support for the unconditional ter-ritorial integrity of Ukraine', a call for 'immediate, constructive dialogue between the EU, Russia, and Ukraine', support for 'the observance of wide-ranging rights of national and linguistic minorities of Ukraine', and a 'categorical repudiation of the efforts of certain Latvian politicians to escalate the situation in Latvia by using rhetoric aimed against represent-atives of national minorities'. SDPH therefore attempted to approach the issue from a relatively neutral stance and avoided references to Russian speakers or Russians in Ukraine.

Indeed, in almost all of their articles there was a noticeable absence of references to Russian speakers. Even in cases where the issues were potentially highly ethnicised, such as legislation to introduce a preamble to the constitution (see Chapter 7), the discourse of SDPH remained relatively non-ethnicised. Instead, rebuttals to these policies were framed in terms of human rights and legal norms. In response to legislative efforts to criminalise denial and trivialisation of Soviet and Nazi aggression against Latvia, SDPH Member of Parliament Valērijs Agešins (SDPH 19 March 2014) states, 'In reality we are talking about the contravention of a fundamental human right – the right to freedom of speech that is fixed in the hundredth article of the Constitution. This article clearly forbids censorship.' Agešins also notes that this legislation is not consistent with the European Convention of Human Rights.

This is also evident in SDPH's response to the proposals for a constitutional preamble. While the term 'ethnic Latvian nation' (*latishskaia natsiia – latviešu nācija* in the original Latvian) is criticised, SDPH again refrain from referring to Russians or Russian speakers. While the author notes that the founding fathers of the 1922 constitution 'acknowledged the multinational character of the people of our country', there is no attempt to list any particular ethnic or national group. Instead the article emphasises the fact that 'the letter and spirit of the constitution is based on the idea that it is precisely the people of Latvia who are the proprietors of supreme authority' (SDPH 27 March 2014). In fact, Harmony goes to some lengths to distance the party from any discursive portrayals of being a pro-Kremlin party. Following *Saeima* speaker Solvita Āboltiņa's reference to SDPH as 'a pro-Putin party', Harmony MP Irina Cvetkova laments the Ethics Commission's refusal to uphold her complaint. In the news article, the author deliberately refers to the party by its full title: 'the social democratic party "Harmony"' rather than a Russian or pro-Putin one (SDPH 2 April 2014).

In terms of the three main discursive strategies outlined in earlier chapters – anti-discourse, integrational discourse and constructive discourse – SDPH pursues elements of all three strategies. However, of the three approaches, anti-discursive strategies are used relatively sparingly. When employed, this strategy was exclusively directed towards the incumbent Latvian authorities and structures whose European and democratic credentials were often questioned: 'The battle against people who think differently fits with the traditions of the middle ages and is a step towards totalitarianism' (SDPH 19 March 2014). In these instances, Harmony is able to attack nodal points that have been central to Latvian state and nation-building. Just as with the media discourse, Latvian discourses of Europeanness are questioned and European legal norms and democratic traditions are used as the basis for this criticism.

The party is careful, however, not to overplay negative discursive strategies. They are also keen to integrate their discourses within popularised Latvian discourses. Discussing the situation in Ukraine, one article notes that,

> in [the Cold War] . . . fate placed Latvia under the flag of the USSR. But now, sixty years after the start of this war, we are again facing calls to choose our flag. *But I want us to have only one flag – the flag of Latvia and the interests of Latvia.* (SDPH 16 April 2014, emphasis added)

Additionally, Mayor of Riga Nils Ušakovs adopts a position that goes entirely against the discourses of the Russian Federation when he speaks encouragingly of the presence of NATO troops in Latvia: 'Let them spend their money here. They have good wages. Latvia is a NATO country. This means that NATO soldiers regularly appear here' (SDPH 19 May 2014).

Even commenting on the Victory Day celebrations in Riga, SDPH attempts to adopt an integrational tone. The single article devoted to the events is entitled 'Ušakovs asks for people to protect and love Latvia regardless of nationality' (SDPH 10 May 2014). In this article the party refers to the sacred memory of the people who fought against Nazism, but the discourse is framed in terms of loyalty to Latvia: 'the children of the soldiers and veterans need to be worthy of their memory. They need to respect their state, Latvia, and trust in it.'

Harmony also attempts to create constructive discursive positions by stressing the value of Latvia's multi-ethnic and multinational character. Echoing discourses seen in the Russian-language press, the party states, 'Latvia is a natural, historical, and geographic 'bridge' between Russia and Europe' (SDPH 18 March 2014). In fact, the constructive position of SDPH is largely based on a de-emphasis of ethnic issues and an emphasis on economic ones: 'our home is Latvia, and inhabitants of this land need to be united in loving and protecting their home, ignoring questions of history, language and the such like. Only under these conditions will Latvia become a "prosperous home"' (SDPH 10 May 2014).

This analysis therefore suggests that Harmony has generally attempted to position itself as constructive and integrational in terms of its relations to the discourses of the Latvian state. However, pressures to adopt a more ethnicised and anti-discursive tone were also visible. This was especially clear after the party's relatively poor showing at the

2014 European parliamentary elections. Notwithstanding their previous domestic popularity, the party only managed to secure 13 per cent of the vote and one seat in the European Parliament (down from two seats in the previous elections). The Russian Union of Latvia also won one seat with 6.4 per cent of the vote. It was notable that these elections occurred under the backdrop of Russia's annexation of Crimea and the ongoing armed conflict in the south-east of Ukraine. The day after the elections the Harmony website, referring to RUL, warned that 'Radical Russian forces will enter the next *Saeima*' (SDPH 26 May 2014). However, only two days later, the website adopts it own more radical tone:

> Ethnic Latvians (*latyshy*) are scared because they've started to think what they would do if they were in the position of ethnic Russians (*russkikh*) in the circumstances that have developed. After twenty-five years of persecution and insult they would also have turned to 'radical leaders' (*buinymi vozhakami*) or 'little green men'[9] for help. When there is a defender of the oppressed (he's called VVP),[10] they are scared that Russian Latvians (*russkie latviitsy*) will turn to him. (SDPH 28 May 2014)

Again, it appears that political considerations have necessitated this eth-nicisation. This highlights once more the non-static nature of Russian-speaking discourse in Latvia. Not only do discursive agents have to respond to changes in Latvian and Russian discourses, at a political level they also have to consider how Russian speakers are relating to and integrating these various discourses. In terms of discursive change this also further highlights the inability of discourses to be transformed overnight. While SDPH is keen to integrate many of its discourses into those of the Latvian state, the party still has to contend with nodal points that are not necessarily ready to be displaced.

The response of the Russian Union of Latvia has therefore been to adopt an increasingly radical tone. The name change from 'For Human Rights in a United Latvia' to 'the Russian Union of Latvia', adopted in early 2014, is indicative of this shift in discourse. Whereas SDPH have been steadily integrating into Latvian state discourses, RUL have progressively been moving towards those of the Russian Federation. This was apparent in the analysis of materials from the RUL website. The scope of interests of RUL was very narrow and focused exclusively on ethnicised issues such as the protection of Russian schools (RUL 3 March 2014), calls for protests and pickets in support of Russia's actions in Crimea (RUL 10 March 2014), diatribes against corrupt Western values (RUL 12 March 2014), celebration of Victory Day (RUL

16 March 2014), and underlining Russophobia and anti-Russian senti-ments in the Baltic states (RUL 6 May 2014). Policies outside ethnic issues were entirely ignored.

It was notable that the discourse of RUL matched almost entirely that of the compatriot discourse (see above). RUL is an active participant of the ICC. Viktors Guščins, RUL candidate for the European elections, was also Latvia's representative at the ICC's regular session in Moscow in April 2014. Guščins notes that during previous meetings he had asked Russian Foreign Minister Sergei Lavrov to pass comment on mass non-citizenship in Latvia:

> S. V. Lavrov always answered 'we are thinking how to act'. But this year the Minister's answer was completely different. He said that this is our position and we need to plainly state it: elections wherein thousands of people are prevented from participating cannot be considered democratic. I will highlight one more phrase of S. V. Lavrov . . . Raising a toast to compatriots living abroad, the Minister of Foreign Affairs said that 'Russia will no longer be weak.' (RUL 30 April 2014)

There is therefore a clear link between the intensification (and Rossiisification) of Russian discourses towards their compatriots abroad, and the discursive positions adopted by RUL. Russia is portrayed as a benevolent backer of the rights of Russian speakers in Latvia, and its policies are endorsed wholesale. For example, on the question of Russia's annexation of Crimea, RUL adopt an entirely pro-Russian position: 'the Russian army, as is natural, came to the defence of peaceful citizens and its co-citizens' (20 May 2014).

In line with Russian discourses of mobilisation that were seen in the discourses of *Ruvek*, an increasing amount of RUL's activities focused on more militant forms of action, including protests, pickets, and marches. During the monitoring period calls were made for pickets outside the Ministry of Culture against further education reforms (RUL 24 February 2014), numerous marches in support of Crimea (for example, RUL 6 March 2014), various protests in support of Russian schools (for example, RUL 7 March 2014), a picket for the resignation of Ombudsman Jānis Jansons (RUL 13 April 2014), and a picket outside the *Saeima* against censorship of Russian TV stations (RUL 11 May 2014). Tatjana Ždanoka (RUL Member of the European Parliament) talked of the 'total Latvianisation of Russian schools' and called for 'a corresponding mobilisation in the face of real threat' (RUL 26 February 2014).

Rather than integrating into Latvian discourses, the discourses of RUL present Russians as a unique nation with its own traditions and values. Mirroring the compatriot discourse, one article lists the values of the Russian nation as 'patriotism, serving the community, charity, collectivism (*sobornost'*), mutual assistance, and self-sacrifice'. These values are described in historical terms, as rooted in 'Orthodox spiritual traditions'. According to this same article, 'The traditions and culture of the Russian person define his behaviour' (RUL 19 February 2014). Just as in the compatriot discourse, RUL therefore set out predicational strategies that discursively outline appropriate values and behavioural patterns for Russians.

Paralleling the compatriot discourse once more, these predicational strategies are also based on the othering of European (and Latvian) values. Just like the *Ruvek* discourse, one article on the RUL website contrasts corrupt European and Western postmodern thinking (signified by neo-liberalism and atheism) with 'moral-spiritual values of society' (RUL 12 March 2014). Listing the evils of neo-liberalism, the author names, among other things, 'the indulgence of base instincts, and the elevation of the most unattractive things into the cult of casual sex'. Among the instruments of neo-liberalism are 'the rewriting of history, changes to world outlooks . . . the propaganda of perversion and sodomy, and bribery of important figures in government structures by Western transnational corporations'. 'Western' values are therefore depicted as contrary to the rich cultural traditions of the Russian nation. This is a strategy that serves to remove Russians and Russian speakers from association with the Latvian state and its discourses and practices which are tied to an unnatural atheism and individualism.

On the question of history, it is no surprise that RUL are keen to celebrate the achievements of the Soviet Union and, by extension, the Russian nation:

For children, native culture (*rodnaia kul'tura*) forms historical memory of their nation which is the most important condition to be able to correctly determine good from evil. This is why, for the Russian person, Victory Day will always be a celebration, and the Soviet period – a manifestation of Russian social justice. (RUL 19 February 2014)

One article notes that Victory Day is 'a bright and pure celebration of saving the world' while Latvia's Independence Day (18 November) and Lāčplēsis Day (11 November) 'are insipid celebrations, devoid of ideology, and for the amorphous masses of greyish little people' (RUL

16 March 2014). Naturally, the party categorically rejects the assertion that Latvia was occupied, noting that 'the "fact of occupation" is a crude historical falsification' (RUL 20 May 2014).

The analysis of SDPH's and RUL's discourses at the time of turmoil in Ukraine is very telling. If we accept that politics plays an inordinately important role in determining discursive strategies and group identities (see Chapter 7), then it is important to understand the trends that are currently occurring in Latvian politics. SDPH has shown signs of wanting to move away from the ethnicisation of Latvian politics, towards a model of political antagonism that is based on economic and social principles. However, the party's rhetoric also belies moments of tension when it feels forced to revert to discourses of ethnic discrimination. RUL, on the other hand, has embraced Russian discourses that portray their party as the only body that 'honestly, with dignity, and openly defends the rights and needs of the Russian population, remaining true to its ideology and values' (RUL 20 May 2014). Its discursive position increasingly mirrors that of the Russian state as it emphasises the historical, cultural, spiritual, and civilisational uniqueness of the Russian nation and its separateness from 'postmodern' Europe and 'fascistic' Latvia.

Tellingly, and to the relief of many, RUL did not achieve any notable success in the parliamentary elections of October 2014. The party garnered a rather modest 1.6 per cent of the vote, far short of the required 5 per cent barrier for entry to the *Saeima*. Harmony, for its part, performed slightly worse than the previous election but was still able to maintain its position as Latvia's most represented party, obtaining twenty-four out of 100 seats (down from thirty-one). This gives some ground to suggest that overly radicalised and mobilising Russian discourses lack resonance with the majority of Latvia's Russian speakers, at least among the politically enfranchised members of society. Of course, we may also expect that RUL discourses could have more impact among non-citizens who are traditionally more inclined towards Russia and who generally articulate less allegiance and belonging to Latvia (SKDS 2014).

CONCLUSIONS

In this chapter it has been possible to see evidence of some links between the discourses of the Russian Federation and those of Latvia's political parties. RUL, for example, show a clear link between Russia's increased discursive emphasis on spiritual, cultural, historical, and civilisational values, and the salience of such discourses in Latvia's political space. However, the official discourses from Russia, as a possible 'external homeland', have not been able to penetrate entirely into political and group consciousness in Latvia. SDPH's public discourse demonstrates that there is still plenty of political will to move beyond overt ethnicisation. The party also rejects many nodal points that anchor Russian discourses and instead generally seeks to integrate itself into many discursive positions associated with the Latvian state. At the same time, some pressures to play the ethnic card were evident even in the discourse of SDPH.

In line with Brubaker's triadic nexus, the discursive strategies adopted by both RUL and SDPH need to be contextualised within the political climate of the Latvian state. As the case studies above highlight, Russia has attempted to intensify and Rossiisify its compatriots. However, the Latvian state has also recently undertaken a number of Latvianising measures that have been aimed at renationalising the state. These developments have been put into sharper focus by the horrific events in Ukraine where protecting the rights of Russian speakers has been widely cited by the Russian state to justify its positions. Latvia's Russian speakers therefore continue to be faced with contradictory discursive messages, from both Russia and Latvia. These contradictions are not only evident within the competing Latvian and Russian mythscapes, but are also apparent within Latvia, and even between political parties that are commonly accepted as 'Russian'.

Russia has been attempting to strengthen political ties by associating cultural preferences with political ones. This strategy has been aided, paradoxically, by the renewed emphasis on the cultural aspects of Latvianness that underpin the Latvian state. Latvia's preamble, for example, now defines Latvia's political statehood in ethnic and cultural terms. This therefore opens up the discursive space for Russia to present its own political pole of attraction by tying cultural preferences to political ones (see also Cheskin 2015).

This chapter therefore draws attention to two largely contrasting discursive strategies available to Russian speakers in Latvia. SDPH and RUL certainly do not represent the whole, complex spectrum of available identities and discursive positions available to Russian speakers. Owing to the public nature of their discourses, however, these parties present important discursive frameworks. Changes in the strategies of both the Russian and Latvian states have meant that there has been a certain radicalisation of Russian identities and increased incentives for mobilisation among a certain segment of the population. At the same time, the fact that SDPH are still the largest and most successful 'Russian' party in Latvia is testament to the lack of widespread appeal of wholesale pro-Russian discourses.

Following RUL's poor electoral showing in the elections, the party's co-chairperson himself admitted that the party had overestimated the importance of 'Russian matters' for its potential electorate (Latvian Centre for Human Rights 2014). While this does not mean that Latvia's Russian speakers are immune to the discursive productions of the Russian state, it does provide evidence to suggest that Russia does not have the hypodermic influence that some political forces and commentators have previously suggested.

NOTES

1. English translation from Durham 2000.
2. Available at <http://www.ruvek.ru> (last accessed 22 June 2015).
3. Available at <http://www.mid.ru/BDOMP/ns-dgpch.nsf/min?openandStart=1> (last accessed 10 June 2015). This is a subsection of the website's 'Compatriots Abroad' page, available at <http://mid.ru/bdomp/sitemap.nsf/kartaflat/03.04>.
4. Pilkington and Flynn (1999: 173) note that, in addition to twenty-five million ethnic Russians, there were three million people who were not ethnically Russian, but whose homeland was now located in the Russian Federation, and a further eleven million individuals who were not Russian but had a strong cultural allegiance to Russia.
5. The author was also contacted by a number of media outlets who were suddenly interested in this question, including BBC World, who ran an extended piece on Russians in the Baltic states.
6. Also commonly referred to as 'Benderites' (*benderovtsi*), in reference to individuals who support the nationalist ideology of Stepan Bandera, the controversial leader of the Ukrainian Insurgent Army that was responsible for the ethnic cleansing of thousands of Poles in western Ukraine. Bandera remains one of the most controversial figures in Ukrainian history and while many see him as nothing more than a Nazi collaborator, others view him as a national hero fighting for Ukrainian independence. His personal culpability in the crimes of the Insurgent Army are, however, difficult to determine as he was held captive in Nazi Germany for a number of years. See Marples 2006 and Liebich and Myshlovska 2014 for overviews of the political controversies surrounding memorialisation of Bandera in post-Soviet Ukraine.
7. In this article six 'young compatriots in Australia' are asked for their opinions on events in Ukraine. Of these six, one respondent, originally from Kyiv, notes that he is now more likely to favour Europe following the introduction of Russian troops into Ukrainian territory. He also notes that he has never encountered any discrimination against the Russian language or Russians in western Ukraine. Another interviewee takes a neutral position, preferring Crimea to gain more autonomy from Kyiv, but opposing an armed invasion of Russian troops. The other four individuals stick closely to the official line of the Kremlin (*Ruvek* 11 March 2014).
8. SDPH website: <http://www.saskanascentrs.lv/> (last accessed 22 June 2015) and RUL website: <http://zapchel.lv/> (last accessed 22 June 2015).
9. This was the ironic name given to the armed soldiers who appeared without insignia in the Crimean peninsula before the region was incorporated into the Russian

Federation. President Putin later admitted to the presence of Russian troops operating in Crimea. Previous to this the Kremlin had maintained that these were local militias.

10. Initials for Vladimir Vladimirovich Putin.

CHAPTER 9

A Bright Future?

Ne zeme pret zemi tad karos, Bet visas kopā pret tumsu.
Not then land against land will fight, but all together against the
darkness. (Rainis, Uguns un Nakts)

This work has traced Russian-speaking discourses in Latvia from the
late Soviet period to the present. Naturally not every available discourse
has been examined. However, the broad scope of analysed materials
helps to build up a picture of how discursive strategies have developed
in Latvia over the course of the last thirty years. A key argument of this
work is that discursive and identity strategies do not develop *ex nihilo*.
Foucault (2002a: 28) argues that 'Discourse must not be referred to the
distant presence of the origin, but treated as and when it occurs.' While
it is important to treat discourse 'as and when it occurs', this research
has sought to demonstrate how Russian-speaking discourses respond
to, alter, and maintain already existing discursive understandings. The
study has therefore adopted a temporal approach to the investigation of
Russian-speaking identity in Latvia.

Because Russian-speaking discourse is best understood as a reaction to
existing discourses, the position of the Latvian state is of central importance. As the analysis has shown, from the late Soviet period onwards, a
'Latvian' hegemonic order has been created that has established a series
of sacred nodal points for Latvian statehood. These nodal points revolve
around historical interpretations of the past and are used to create and
justify a political and cultural state that privileges an imagined community of 'Latvians'. The majority of Latvia's Russian speakers, by
nature of their linguistic, cultural, and genealogical histories, do not
fit neatly within the core group of the '*latviešu nācija*' (ethnic Latvian
nation) that is now codified in the preamble to the country's constitution.

Consequently many within this group struggle to find discursive acceptance within the prevailing political order.

Previously it has been argued that Latvian nationalism and nation-building have enabled the country to transition relatively smoothly to a form of liberal democracy (Karklins 1994a; Jubulis 2001). Whether or not this is true, these nationalising measures present serious obstacles to individuals who lie outside the imagined community of ethnic Latvians, and who wish to integrate their identity within the discourses of the Latvian state. This has serious implications for possible identity strategies for non-Latvian minorities. As this research highlights, it leads to a series of complex, overlapping discursive strategies. In many respects integrational Russian-speaking discourses are used to align Russian-speaking identities with the nodal points of Latvia's state discourses. On the other hand, anti-discursive strategies are employed that seek to dismantle and delegitimise Latvian discourses. Simultaneously, discursive entrepreneurs also utilise constructive discursive strategies that seek to transform existing discourses and create new meanings for contemporary Latvia, for example trying to legitimise the notion of Latvia as a multicultural country and as a bridge between East and West.

Within all of these strategies the Russian state also has great potential to affect identity strategies of Russian speakers. Latvia's Russophone communities continue to consume Russian (*rossiiskii*) media products and are therefore continually exposed to the discursive articulations that are produced within the Russian Federation. The examination of Russia's compatriot discourse has shown how Russia has been intensifying its claims to represent and protect the interests of Russian speakers outside Russia (Rossiisification). The tragic and destabilising events in Ukraine in 2013–14 have added impetus to Russia's efforts to lay discursive claim to its Russian 'diaspora' and such developments are sure to have (at the very least, limited) consequences in Latvia.

Alongside the potential for Russia to encourage Russian speakers to adopt strategies that are more aligned to Russia than Latvia, the Latvian state has demonstrated a willingness to continue to pursue nationalising policies of its own. As evidenced in this research, over the course of Latvia's post-Soviet statehood, a number of Latvia's Russian speakers have been able to build strong discursive ties with Latvia. However, aggressively nationalising policies have the potential to weaken such ties. This is even more the case when coupled with increasingly assertive Russian discourses that highlight the 'fascistic' nature of the Latvian state, and argue that Russian speakers should be true to their historical and ancestral roots.

For many people these contexts could be rather depressing. However,

Russian speakers have shown an incredible resilience in Latvia's period of post-Soviet independence. As this research attests, many have also shown ingenuity in terms of their identity and discursive strategies. Numerous Russian-speaking discourses have been remarkably successful in creating meaningful attachments to Latvia in spite of many of the actions of the respective Latvian and Russian states. This can be seen in 2014, during the Ukrainian crises and not long after a period of heightened tensions surrounding language referendums and constitutional amendments. While these tensions produced some sharp rhetoric and political posturing, a majority of Russian speakers continue to profess loyalty to Latvia over Russia.

As the Ukrainian political crises were unfolding, the Latvian Ministry of Culture commissioned a special survey in order to take stock of the attitudes of the country's minority groups. The survey demonstrates that the majority of non-Latvians – 74.6 per cent – feel a close or very close sense of belonging to Latvia. This compares to only 22.4 per cent who feel close or very close to Russia (SKDS 2014: 10). While there are undoubtedly many Russian speakers who continue to feel alienated by the Latvian state, a majority of Latvia's Russian speakers have managed to foster and maintain some forms of discursive and material links with Latvia. These links have often been achieved in spite of state policy and in spite of Russia's efforts to act as a sponsor of their identities.

Of course, this study has not been able to survey the entire scope of Russian-speaking discourses. The analysis has focused on media representations in national newspapers, political articulations by nationally represented parties, discursive constructions sponsored by the Russian state, and the reception of these discourses by limited groups of Russian speakers in the capital city Riga. Unfortunately it has not been possible to conduct a more exhaustive examination along Latvia's regional and socio-economic axes. While the political and media landscapes within the national territory are fairly unified, the discursive reception of their associated discourses may not be. Further work is therefore needed in order to build up a more comprehensive picture of how Latvia's Russian speakers are discursively orienting themselves towards the respective Latvian and Russian media and political spaces. It is hoped, however, that this work offers a workable framework with which further research can be conducted.

The post-Soviet formation of Latvia's hegemonic order has been largely based on notions of historical grievance and ethnic division. Unfortunately, the analysis of political strategies and discourses suggest that these logics are unlikely to disappear any time soon. In fact we have seen a recent renationalisation of the Latvian state that has sought to reassert and re-emphasise the privileged position of Latvian culture and the 'Latvian (ethnic) nation'. In light of the hardening discursive positions of the respective Latvian and Russian states, Latvia's Russian speakers will continue to be faced with contradictory identity pressures. In order to negotiate these ambiguities, they may have to articulate increasingly complex discursive strategies.

Arguably, the Ukraine crisis has forced the Latvian state to reconsider the prudence of its renationalising policies. LTV, the state broadcaster, for example, has recently launched a number of daily, Russian-language news programmes that are now slotted into the main Latvian-language content. The slick graphics, modern studio, and youthful presenters perhaps hint at the start of a genuine discursive shift from the perspective of Latvia's political and cultural hegemonic order. Certainly, by articulating the notion that Russian speakers are also an important part of the Latvia nation, this would potentially make it easier for Russian speakers to employ integrational, rather than anti-discursive, strategies. If, on the other hand, we do not witness the denationalisation and de-ethnicisation of Latvia's political space, Russian-speaking elites will have to continue to search for ways to integrate their complex identities into the discourses of the Latvian state. To date, the experience of Russian speakers in post-Soviet Latvia suggests that, against the odds, there is still considerable scope for this to occur.

Materials presented to focus group participants for discussion

1: EXCERPT FROM *CHAS* 20 SEPTEMBER 2010

The presence of the Russian language is a peculiarity which we in Latvia need to utilise.

Latvia, who best understands the peculiarities of Russia, should make the most of these advantages and become a mediator in business contacts and in forming relations between western countries and Russia.

2: EXCERPT FROM *CHAS* 6 OCTOBER 2010

For Russian-speakers the so called ethnic problems – language, education in ones native language, voting rights for non-citizens etc., are no longer so heated, and it seems simply not relevant. Of course they are annoyances; they bring discomfort into our lives. But they are no longer so defining. In Latvia social and economic problems have worsened, which have moved FHRUL's hobby horse – the rights of national minorities – into the background.

3: EXCERPT FROM *CHAS* 26 FEBRUARY 2009

It is a paradox: the government is toughening up its requirements for knowledge of the state language while consecutively reducing the budget of the organisation which is responsible for the issuing of the vital 'apliecības.'[1] Here one does not need to be a political scientist to understand that they are artificially creating impediments and obstacles for Russian-speakers who wish to acquire the required [language] category for their profession. What follows is simple: no language, no job; no job, no income. That means poverty which means the street.

Who does this benefit? It benefits those who don't need to sit an exam and who have, in the mean time, managed to secure a plush position in the state bureaucracy and local government.

4: EXCERPT FROM *CHAS* 11 DECEMBER 2008

The European Russian forum 'The EU and Russia: New challenges' was held in Brussels... One of the participants of the forum was the chairman of the State Duma Committee on Foreign Relations, and vice president of PACE Konstantin Kosachev. 'Chas' put a number of questions to him.

What role does the Russian diaspora have in various countries in the estranged relations between Russia and the EU?

I hope the subject of the Russian world will have all the more meaning in Europe. But here it's important to stress that Russia would make a serious mistake if it tried to use the Russian diaspora in a primitive way as a 'fifth column'. It is not like that!

... But another thing which is very important. We should not restrict our campaigning for the Russian world simply to its cultural and historical aspects. It is all good and well if people love Russia, speak Russian, and play Russian folk instruments. But this is not enough.

Does not every diaspora lobby for the interests of its fatherland from the country of its residence?

Do not disrespect your homeland. Work so that, as for any other country, attitudes towards it are fair. This is the natural and feasible task for the Russian world.

---

[1]   In the original text the author uses the Latvian word 'apliecības' (certificates), written in Cyrillic. This refers to the graded language tests in Latvian which are required in order to find employment in most professions.

5 : EXCERPT FROM *CHAS* 6 SEPTEMBER 2010

I like to walk round Riga and catch the sounds of today

'Viņam ir baigi тупой-s image!'[2] – I hear this on the table next to me on Līvu Square, next to the Russian theatre . . . Next to me a husband ingratiatingly asks his wife, who is looking at some garish umbrellas: 'Maybe we could have a beer?'[3] . . . Telephone conversations are like songs! 'Viņš, типа, grib ar mani uz кинчику . . . Ну, okay. Labi. Давай!'[4]

6 : EXCERPT FROM HARMONY CENTRE WEBSITE

Attachment to the Memorandum on 'Harmony Centre'
Project
http://www.saskanascentrs.lv/ru/o-nas/ [last accessed 14.07.11]
Attachment to the Memorandum on 'Harmony Centre'
Project
Declaration of the Saeima of the Latvian Republic on interethnic trust
The Saeima of the Latvian Republic considers that an earnest expression of respect for the interests, values, and historical experience of various ethnic groups is an essential condition for improving interethnic trust. In particular:

• Acknowledgement of the fact that Latvia is the only place on earth where Latvians can expect to receive state guarantees for the preservation and development of their language and culture;

• The recognition by all Latvians, irrespective of their ethnic roots, of their responsibility to preserve the Latvian language, and the acknowledgement for the Latvian language of the status of the sole state language of the Latvian Republic;

• An expression of gratitude for the huge sacrifices which have been borne by preceding generations of Latvia's inhabitants during the World Wars in the fight against tyranny and injustice, so that freedom, democracy, and human rights triumphed in Europe;

• Compassion towards the victims of the Hitlerite and Stalinist

---

[2] Latvian, English, and Russian are all mixed into this sentence. The Russian Word тупой is Latvianised by adding an -s at the end. A literal translation of the resulting sentence is, 'He has a really stupid image!'. The original 'Russian' reads: 'Виням ир байги тупойс имиджс!'

[3] Here the Latvian 'aliņa' (diminutive of 'alus' – beer) is Russianised to 'алыне'.

[4] 'He wants to go to the cinema with me. Well, okay. Good. Let's go!'

regimes which took away thousands of lives, decided the fate
of the people, and split the country in two – the consequences
of which we are living with to this day;

- Acknowledgement that all inhabitants of Latvia, irrespective of
  ethnic belonging, who were born here, or who resettled here in
  Soviet times, belong to Latvia and are of value to Latvia;
- Acknowledgement that the Russian language, alongside Latvian,
  is an important language for interethnic communication for the
  inhabitants of Latvia which is spoken in a majority of families
  within the country.

Full results of 9 May survey

1. The main reason that I came here today is to pay my respects to those who fought in the Second World War

	Agree	Disagree	Partly agree	Difficult to say	Valid answers
18–25	50 (91%)	0 (0%)	5 (9%)	0 (0%)	55
26–30	28 (93%)	0 (0%)	2 (7%)	0 (0%)	30
31–40	27 (90%)	0 (0%)	3 (10%)	0 (0%)	30
41–50	41 (100%)	0 (0%)	0 (0%)	0 (0%)	41
51+	42 (93%)	0 (0%)	3 (7%)	0 (0%)	45
Total	188 (94%)	0 (0%)	13 (6%)	0 (0%)	201

2. 9 May should become an official holiday in Latvia

	Agree	Disagree	Partly agree	Difficult to say	Valid answers
18–25	48 (87%)	1 (2%)	6 (11%)	0 (0%)	55
26–30	24 (80%)	4 (13%)	0 (0%)	2 (7%)	30
31–40	21 (70%)	5 (17%)	2 (7%)	2 (7%)	30
41–50	35 (88%)	1 (3%)	3 (8%)	1 (3%)	40
51+	43 (93%)	2 (4%)	0 (0%)	1 (2%)	46
Total	171 (85%)	13 (6%)	11 (5%)	6 (3%)	201

3. I can understand why some people do not like to see 9 May being celebrated in Latvia

	Agree	Disagree	Partly agree	Difficult to say	Valid answers
18–25	11 (20%)	11 (20%)	30 (55%)	3 (5%)	55
26–30	6 (20%)	14 (47%)	10 (33%)	0 (0%)	30
31–40	10 (33%)	8 (27%)	11 (37%)	1 (3%)	30
41–50	13 (32%)	16 (39%)	12 (29%)	0 (0%)	41
51+	11 (24%)	21 (47%)	13 (29%)	0 (0%)	45
Total	51 (25%)	70 (35%)	76 (38%)	4 (2%)	201

4. We should show compassion towards the victims of the Hitlerite and Stalinist regimes which took away thousands of lives, decided the fate of the people, and split the country in two – the consequences of which we are living with to this day

	Agree	Disagree	Partly agree	Difficult to say	Valid answers
18–25	48 (87%)	1 (2%)	6 (11%)	0 (0%)	55
26–30	26 (87%)	0 (0%)	4 (13%)	0 (0%)	30
31–40	26 (87%)	1 (3%)	2 (7%)	1 (3%)	30
41–50	28 (72%)	4 (10%)	7 (18%)	0 (0%)	39
51+	35 (76%)	2 (4%)	8 (17%)	1 (2%)	46
Total	163 (82%)	8 (4%)	27 (14%)	2 (1%)	200

5. In 1944 Latvia was liberated by Soviet troops

	Agree	Disagree	Partly agree	Difficult to say	Valid answers
18–25	39 (71%)	4 (7%)	11 (20%)	1 (2%)	55
26–30	25 (8%)	1 (3%)	4 (13%)	0 (0%)	30
31–40	24 (80%)	0 (0%)	5 (17%)	1 (3%)	30
41–50	36 (90%)	0 (0%)	3 (8%)	1 (3%)	40
51+	40 (91%)	0 (0%)	4 (10%)	0 (0%)	44
Total	164 (82%)	5 (3%)	27 (14%)	3 (2%)	199

6. 9 May is a symbolic day when non-Latvians can voice their dissatisfaction with the unfairness of the state

	Agree	Disagree	Partly agree	Difficult to say	Valid answers
18–25	0 (0%)	38 (70%)	16 (29%)	1 (2%)	55
26–30	1 (3%)	23 (77%)	6 (20%)	0 (0%)	30
31–40	7 (23%)	12 (40%)	7 (23%)	4 (13%)	30
41–50	18 (44%)	14 (34%)	5 (12%)	4 (10%)	41
51+	29 (64%)	10 (22%)	5 (11%)	1 (2%)	45
Total	55 (27%)	97 (48%)	39 (19%)	10 (5%)	201

7. It is not right to talk of Soviet 'occupation'. There was no Soviet occupation

	Agree	Disagree	Partly agree	Difficult to say	Valid answers
18–25	20 (36%)	7 (13%)	27 (49%)	1 (2%)	55
26–30	15 (50%)	4 (13%)	10 (33%)	1 (3%)	30
31–40	17 (57%)	4 (13%)	8 (27%)	1 (3%)	30
41–50	31 (76%)	4 (10%)	6 (15%)	0 (0%)	41
51+	40 (87%)	4 (9%)	2 (4%)	0 (0%)	46
Total	123 (61%)	23 (11%)	53 (26%)	3 (15%)	202

8. History is never straightforward. For this reason I can come to terms with the fact that different people have different interpretations of the Second World War and its consequences

	Agree	Disagree	Partly agree	Difficult to say	Valid answers
18–25	48 (87%)	2 (4%)	5 (9%)	0 (0%)	55
26–30	21 (70%)	3 (10%)	6 (20%)	0 (0%)	30
31–40	17 (57%)	4 (13%)	8 (27%)	1 (3%)	30
41–50	17 (41%)	14 (34%)	10 (24%)	0 (0%)	41
51+	21 (47%)	13 (29%)	11 (24%)	0 (0%)	45
Total	124 (62%)	36 (18%)	40 (20%)	1 (0%)	201

9. When celebrating Victory Day we should also take into account the fact that the incursion of Soviet troops into Latvia in 1944 had many terrible consequences for the country and its inhabitants

	Agree	Disagree	Partly agree	Difficult to say	Valid answers
18–25	13 (24%)	25 (45%)	15 (27%)	2 (4%)	55
26–30	5 (17%)	12 (40%)	11 (37%)	2 (7%)	30
31–40	6 (20%)	10 (33%)	7 (23%)	7 (23%)	30
41–50	6 (15%)	22 (54%)	12 (29%)	1 (2%)	41
51+	8 (18%)	25 (56%)	11 (24%)	1 (2%)	45
Total	38 (19%)	94 (47%)	56 (28%)	13 (6%)	201

10. The parades of the Latvian legionnaires cover Latvia in shame

	Agree	Disagree	Partly agree	Difficult to say	Valid answers
18–25	43 (78%)	2 (4%)	6 (11%)	4 (7%)	55
26–30	18 (60%)	3 (10%)	6 (20%)	3 (10%)	30
31–40	26 (87%)	1 (3%)	2 (7%)	1 (3%)	30
41–50	37 (90%)	0 (0%)	4 (10%)	0 (0%)	41
51+	42 (91%)	2 (4%)	2 (4%)	0 (0%)	46
Total	166 (82%)	8 (4%)	20 (10%)	8 (4%)	202

11. It would be better if more Latvians participated in the 9 May celebrations

	Agree	Disagree	Partly agree	Difficult to say	Valid answers
18–25	45 (82%)	0 (0%)	9 (16%)	1 (2%)	55
26–30	20 (67%)	1 (3%)	3 (10%)	6 (20%)	30
31–40	21 (70%)	1 (3%)	7 (23%)	1 (3%)	30
41–50	37 (90%)	1 (2%)	3 (7%)	0 (0%)	41
51+	43 (93%)	0 (0%)	2 (4%)	1 (2%)	46
Total	166 (82%)	3 (1%)	24 (12%)	9 (4%)	202

12. Irrespective of the fact that 9 May marks a great victory over fascism, for Latvia it also marks the loss of its state freedom

	Agree	Disagree	Partly agree	Difficult to say	Valid answers
18–25	14 (25%)	26 (47%)	12 (22%)	3 (5%)	55
26–30	4 (13%)	16 (53%)	8 (27%)	2 (7%)	30
31–40	1 (3%)	9 (30%)	11 (37%)	9 (30%)	30
41–50	9 (22%)	20 (49%)	6 (15%)	6 (15%)	41
51+	8 (17%)	26 (57%)	6 (13%)	6 (13%)	46
Total	36 (18%)	97 (48%)	43 (21%)	26 (13%)	202

13. We should not condemn too harshly those who served in the 'Waffen SS' legions

	Agree	Disagree	Partly agree	Difficult to say	Valid answers
18–25	10 (18%)	21 (38%)	17 (31%)	7 (13%)	55
26–30	12 (40%)	12 (40%)	6 (20%)	0 (0%)	30
31–40	5 (17%)	14 (47%)	10 (33%)	1 (3%)	30
41–50	6 (15%)	19 (46%)	12 (29%)	4 (10%)	41
51+	19 (42%)	16 (36%)	9 (20%)	1 (2%)	45
Total	52 (26%)	82 (41%)	54 (27%)	13 (6%)	201

14. I do not like the big fuss that surrounds the 9 May celebrations. It would be better to concentrate on the memory of the fallen

	Agree	Disagree	Partly agree	Difficult to say	Valid answers
18–25	14 (25%)	26 (47%)	14 (25%)	1 (2%)	55
26–30	9 (30%)	14 (47%)	7 (23%)	0 (0%)	30
31–40	7 (23%)	18 (60%)	3 (10%)	2 (7%)	30
41–50	16 (40%)	17 (43%)	5 (13%)	2 (5%)	40
51+	12 (28%)	24 (56%)	5 (12%)	2 (5%)	43
Total	58 (29%)	99 (50%)	34 (17%)	7 (35%)	198

15. Latvia was forcefully annexed by the Soviet Army against the will of the majority of its inhabitants

	Agree	Disagree	Partly agree	Difficult to say	Valid answers
18–25	15 (27%)	12 (22%)	21 (38%)	7 (13%)	55
26–30	2 (7%)	16 (53%)	11 (37%)	1 (3%)	30
31–40	2 (7%)	16 (53%)	8 (27%)	4 (13%)	30
41–50	0 (0%)	38 (93%)	3 (7%)	0 (0%)	41
51+	1 (2%)	40 (89%)	2 (4%)	2 (4%)	45
Total	20 (10%)	122 (61%)	45 (22%)	14 (7%)	201

Preamble to the Latvian Constitution (Satversme)

The State of Latvia, proclaimed on 18 November 1918, has been established by uniting historical Latvian lands and on the basis of the unwavering will of the Latvian nation to have its own State and its inalienable right of self-determination in order to guarantee the existence and development of the Latvian nation, its language and culture throughout the centuries, to ensure freedom and promote welfare of the people of Latvia and each individual.

The people of Latvia won their State in the War of Liberation. They consolidated the system of government and adopted the Constitution in a freely elected Constitutional Assembly.

The people of Latvia did not recognise the occupation regimes, resisted them and regained their freedom by restoring national independence on 4 May 1990 on the basis of continuity of the State. They honour their freedom fighters, commemorate victims of foreign powers, condemn the Communist and Nazi totalitarian regimes and their crimes.

Latvia as democratic, socially responsible and national state is based on the rule of law and on respect for human dignity and freedom; it recognises and protects fundamental human rights and respects ethnic minorities. The people of Latvia protect their sovereignty, national independence, territory, territorial integrity and democratic system of government of the State of Latvia.

Since ancient times, the identity of Latvia in the European cultural space has been shaped by Latvian and Liv traditions, Latvian folk wisdom, the Latvian language, universal human and Christian values. Loyalty to Latvia, the Latvian language as the only official language, freedom, equality, solidarity, justice, honesty, work ethic and family are the foundations of a cohesive society. Each individual takes care of oneself, one's relatives and the common good of society by acting responsibly toward other people, future generations, the environment and nature.

While acknowledging its equal status in the international community, Latvia protects its national interests and promotes sustainable and democratic development of a united Europe and the world.

God, bless Latvia!

Bibliography

9may.lv (2011), *О нас* [About us], available at <http://9may.lv/ru/about/o-proekte/> (last accessed 17 July 2013).

Aasland, A. (1994), 'The Russian population in Latvia: An integrated minority?', *Journal of Communist Studies and Transition Politics* 10(2): 233–60.

Aasland, A. (2002), 'Citizenship status and social exclusion in Estonia and Latvia', *Journal of Baltic Studies* 3(1): 57–77.

Aasland, A. and Flotten, T. (2001), 'Ethnicity and social exclusion in Estonia and Latvia', *Europe-Asia Studies* 53(7): 1023–49.

Agarin, T. (2010), *A Cat's Lick: Democratisation and Minority Communities in the Post-Soviet Baltic*, Amsterdam: Rodopi.

Aidarov, A. and Drechsler, W. (2013), 'Estonian Russification of ethnic minorities in Estonia? A policy analysis', *Trames* 17(2): 103–28.

Althusser, L. (2008), *On Ideology*, London: Verso.

Anderson, B. (2006), *Imagined Communities: Reflections on the Origin and Spread of Nationalism*, Rev. edn, London: Verso.

Anderson, P. (1976), 'The antimonies of Antonio Gramsci', *New Left Review* I(100): 5–78.

Antane, A. and Tsilevich, B. (1999), 'Nation-building and ethnic integration In Latvia', In P. Kolstø (Ed.), *Nation-Building and Ethnic Integration in Post-Soviet Societies: An Investigation of Latvia and Kazakhstan*, Boulder, CO: Westview Press, 63–152.

Arendt, H. (1951), *The Origins of Totalitarianism*, New York: Harcourt Brace and Co.

Arklina, I. (2001), 'Artistic controversy erupts around president's memory', *Baltic Times*, 1 November 2001, <http://www.baltictimes.com/news/articles/5663/> (last accessed 7 March 2013).

Assmann, A. (2004), 'Four formats of memory: From individual to collective constructions of the past' in C. Christian and D. Midgely (eds), *Cultural Memory and Historical Consciousness in the German-Speaking World since 1500*, Oxford: Peter Lang, 19–38.

Assmann, J. (1995), 'Collective memory and cultural identity', *New German Critique* 65: 125–33. Translated by J. Czaplicka.

Auers, D. (2012), 'An electoral tactic? Citizens' initiatives in post-Soviet Latvia', in M. Setälä and T. Schiller (eds), *Citizens' initiatives in Europe: Procedures and Consequences of Agenda-Setting by Citizens*, Basingstoke: Palgrave Macmillan, 53–65.

BBC (2014), 'Crimea crisis sharpens Latvia ethnic tensions' 26 March 2014, <http://www.bbc.co.uk/news/world-africa-26720549> (last accessed 8 August 2014).

Bell, D. (2003), 'Mythscapes: Memory, mythology, and national identity', *British Journal of Sociology* 54(1): 63–81.

Berg, E. and Ehin, P. (eds) (2009), *Identity and Foreign Policy: Baltic-Russian Relations and European Integration*, Farnham: Ashgate.

Berry, J. W. (1997), 'Immigration, acculturation, and adaptation', *Applied Psychology: An International Review* 46(1): 5–68

Blackledge, A. (2002), 'The discursive construction of national identity in multilingual Britain', *Journal of Language, Identity and Education* 1(1): 67–87.

Boeck, B. J. (1993), 'Legacy of a shattered system: The Russian-speaking population in Latvia', *Demokratizatsiya* 1(2): 70–85.

Brown, A. (1996), *The Gorbachev Factor*, Oxford: Oxford University Press.

Brown, R. H. and Davis-Brown B. (1998), 'The making of memory: The politics of archives, libraries and museums in the construction of national consciousness', *History of the Human Sciences* 11(4): 17–32.

Brubaker, R. (1992), 'Citizenship struggles in Soviet successor states', *International Migration Review* 26(2): 269–91.

Brubaker, R. (1996), *Nationalism Reframed: Nationhood and the National Question in the New Europe*, Cambridge: Cambridge University Press.

Brüggemann, K. and Kasekamp, A. (2008), 'The politics of history and the "war of monuments" in Estonia', *Nationalities Papers* 36(3): 425–48.

Budryte, D. (2005), *Taming Nationalism?: Political Community Building in the Post-Soviet Baltic States*, Aldershot: Ashgate.

Bulgakov, M. (2004a) Мастер и Маргарита [*The Master and Margarita*]. Moscow: Olma-Press, p. 268.

Bulgakov, M. (2004b) *The Master and Margarita*. Translated by Michael Glenny. London: Vintage, p. 329.

Burch, S. and Smith, D. J. (2007), 'Empty spaces and the value of symbols: Estonia's "war of monuments" from another angle', *Europe-Asia Studies*, 59(6): 913–36.

Cabinet of Ministers of the Republic of Latvia (2013) *Cooperation agreement*, available at <http://www.mk.gov.lv/en/mk/darbibu-reglamentejosie-dokumenti/cooperation-agreement/> (last accessed 13 August 2014).

Castles, S. and Davidson, A. (2000), *Citizenship and Migration: Globalization and the Politics of Belonging*, London: MacMillan.

Central Statistical Bureau of Latvia (2011), *Population census*, available at <http://www.csb.gov.lv/en/statistikas-temas/population-census-30761.html> (last accessed 18 July 2013).

Chernov, V. and Shlyakhtunov, A. (2004), *Прибалтийские Waffen-SS. Герои или палачи. . .?* [*The Baltic Waffen SS. Heroes or Executioners?*], Moscow: Lin-Inter.

Cheskin, A. (2010a), 'The discursive construction of "Russian-speakers": The Russian-language media and demarcated political identities in Latvia', in M. Golubeva and R. Gould (eds), *Shrinking Citizenship: Discursive Practices That Limit Democratic Participation in Latvian Politics*, Amsterdam: Rodopi.

Cheskin, A. (2010b), 'The successes and failures of Russian foreign policy towards the "Russian diaspora": Soft power and the Baltic states', conference paper, University of Bath, available at <https://www.academia.edu/4095150/The_successes_and_fail ures_of_Russian_foreign_policy_towards_the_Russian_diaspora_Soft_power_and_ the_Baltic_states> (last accessed 7 August 2014).

Cheskin, A. (2012a), 'History, conflicting collective memory, and national identities: How Latvia's Russian-speakers are learning to remember', *Nationalities Papers* 40(4): 561–84.

Cheskin, A. (2012b), 'Synthesis and conflict: Russian-speakers' discursive response to Latvia's nationalising state', *Europe-Asia Studies* 64(2): 325–47.

Cheskin, A. (2013), 'Exploring Russian-speaking identity from below: The case of Latvia', *Journal of Baltic Studies* 44(3): 287–311.

Cheskin, A. (2015), 'Identity and integration of Russian speakers in the Baltic States: A framework for analysis', *Ethnopolitics* 14(1): 72–93.

Chinn, J. and Truex, L. (1996), 'The question of citizenship in the Baltics', *Journal of Democracy* 7(1): 133–47.

Cianetti, L. (2014), 'Representing minorities in the city. Education policies and minority incorporation in the capital cities of Estonia and Latvia', *Nationalities Papers* 42(6): 981–1001.

Čigāne, L. (2007), *2006. gada Saeimas vēlēšanas medijos: partiju reprezentācija* [The 2006 Saeima elections in the media: Party representation], Riga: PROVIDUS, available at <http://politika.lv/temas/mediju_kritika/12875/> (last accessed 22 October 2009).

Conlin Casilla, E. and Fowler, C. (eds) (2005), *The Archaeology of Plural and Changing Identities*, New York: Kluwer.

Constitutional Protection Bureau of the Latvian Republic (2013), *2013.gada darbības pārskats* [An overview of SAB activities in 2013], available at <http://www.sab.gov.lv/downloads/2013_parskats.pdf> (last accessed 20 August 2014).

Council of Europe (1995), *Framework convention for the protection of national minorities and explanatory report*, available at <http://www.coe.int/t/dghl/monitoring/minorities/1_AtGlance/PDF_H(1995)010_FCNM_ExplanReport_en.pdf> (last accessed 12 December 2009).

Craib, I. (1998), *Experiencing Identity*, London: Sage.

Crawford, K. and Foster, S. (2007), *War, Nation, Memory: International Perspectives on World War II Ii School History Textbooks*, Charlotte: IAP.

Cropley, A. (2006), *Bearslayer: A free translation from the unrhymed Latvian into English heroic verse*. Project Gutenburg eBook, available at <http://www.gutenberg.org/files/17445/17445-8.txt> (last accessed 26 August 2014).

Croucher, S. (2004), *Globalization And Belonging: The Politics of Identity in a Changing World*, Lanham: Rowman and Littlefield.

Culture Ministry of the Republic of Latvia (2011) *Nacionālās identitātes, pilsoniskās sabiedrības un integrācijas poiltikas pamatnostādnes (2012–2018)* [*Guidelines for national identity, civil society and integration politics (2012–2018)*], available at <http://www.km.gov.lv/lv/ministrija/integracijas_pamatnostadnes.html> (last accessed 9 February 2012).

De Cilia, R., Reisigl, M. and Wodak, R. (1999), 'The discursive construction of national identities', *Discourse and Society* 10(4): 149–73.

Denis, S. (2008), 'The story with history', in N. Muižnieks (ed.), *Manufacturing Enemy Images: Russian Media Portrayal of Latvia*, Riga: Academic Press of the University of Latvia, 79–108.

Diuk, N. (2012), *The Next Generation in Russia, Ukraine, and Azerbaijan: Youth, Politics, Identity, and Change*, Plymouth: Rowman and Littlefield.

Doroņenkova, K. (2008), 'Latvia's culture in Russia's media', in N. Muižnieks (ed.), *Manufacturing Enemy Images: Russian Media Portrayal of Latvia*, Riga: Academic Press of the University of Latvia, 109–26.

Durham, F. J. (2000), *The complete poems of Tyutchev in an English translation (Nature love and politics)*, available at <http://www.tyutchev.ru/Works/poems/Jude399.html> (last accessed online 21 August 2014).

Eglitis, D. (2002), *Imagining the Nation History, Modernity, and Revolution in Latvia*, University Park: Pennsylvania State University Press.

Ehala, M. (2009), 'The Bronze Soldier: Identity threat and maintenance in Estonia', *Journal of Baltic Studies* 40(1): 139–58.

Epstein, S. (1992), 'Gay politics, ethnic identity: The limits of social construction', in E. Stein (ed.), *Forms of Desire: Sexual Orientation and the Social Constructionist Controversy*, New York: Routledge, 239–94.

Ernstsone, V. and Mežs, I. (2008), 'Language proficiency of the Latvian population', in R. Apinis et al. (eds), *Break-Out of Latvian: A Sociolinguistic Study*, Riga: Zinātne, 187–95.

Fairclough, N. (2003), *Analysing Discourse: Textual Analysis for Social Research*, London: Routledge.

Fawn, R. (2009), 'Bashing about rights'? Russia and the "new" EU states on human rights and democracy promotion', *Europe-Asia Studies* 61(10): 1777–803.

Fein, L. (2005), 'Symbolic boundaries and national borders: The construction of an Estonian Russian identity', *Nationalities Papers* 33(3): 333–44.

Felder, B. (2009), *Lettland im Zweiten Weltkrieg. Zwischen sowjetischen und deutschen Besatzern 1940–1946* [*Latvia in World War II. Between Soviet and German occupiers 1940–1946*], Paderborn: Ferdinand Schoningh.

Foreign Policy Concept of the Russian Federation (2013) available at <http://www.mid.ru/brp_4.nsf/0/76389FEC168189ED44257B2E0039B16D> (last accessed 11 July 2013).

Forest, B. and Johnson, J. (2002), 'Unravelling the threads of history: Soviet-era monuments and post-Soviet national identity in Moscow', *Annals of the Association of American Geographers* 92(3): 524–47.

Foucault, M. (2002a), *The Archaeology of Knowledge*, Abingdon: Routledge.

Foucault, M. (2002b), 'Truth and power', in D. Faubion (ed.), *Michel Foucault: Power: Essential Works of Foucault 1954–1984. Volume 3*, London: Penguin, 111–33.

Fowkes, B. (1997), *The Disintegration of the Soviet Union: The Triumph of Nationalism*, London: Macmillan.

Friedrich, B. and Brzezinski, Z. (1966), *Totalitarian Dictatorship and Autocracy*, New York: Praeger.

Galbreath, D. (2005), *Nation-Building and Minority Politics in Post-Socialist States Interests, Influence and Identities in Estonia and Latvia*, Stuttgart: Ibidem-Verl.

Galbreath, D. (2006a), 'European integration through democratic conditionality: Latvia in the context of minority rights', *Journal of Contemporary European Studies* 14(1): 69–87.

Galbreath, D. (2006b), 'From nationalism to nation-building: Latvian politics and minority policy', *Nationalities Papers* 34(4): 383–406.

Galbreath, D. and Galvin, M. (2005), 'The titularization of Latvian secondary schools: The historical legacy of Soviet policy implementation', *Journal of Baltic Studies* 36(4): 449–66.

Gay, C. and Tate, K. (1998), 'Doubly bound: The impact of gender and race on the politics of black women', *Political Psychology* 19(1): 169–84.

Geras, N. (1987), 'Post-Marxism?', *New Left Review* I(163), available at <http://www.newleftreview.org/?page=artivleandview=509> (last accessed 15 June 2010).

Gerbner, G. (1985), 'Mass media discourse: Message system analysis as a component of cultural indicators', in T. van Dijk (ed.), *Discourse and Communication: New Approaches to the Analysis of Mass Media Discourse and Communication*, Berlin: W. de Gruyter, 13–25.

Golubeva, M. (2010), 'Multicuturalism as imperialism: Condemnation of social diversity within a discourse of threat and blame', in M. Golubeva and R. Gould (eds), *Shrinking Citizenship: Discursive Practices That Limit Democratic Participation in Latvian Politics*, Amsterdam: Rodopi, 322–5.

Golubeva, M. (2011), 'Different history, different citizenship? Competing narratives and diverging civil enculturation in majority and minority schools in Estonia and Latvia', *Journal of Baltic Studies* 41(3): 315–29.

Golubeva, M. and Kažoka, I. (2010), 'Moral superiority and the Soviet stigma: Parliamentary speech and attribution of blame in political discourse' in M. Golubeva and R. Gould (eds), *Shrinking Citizenship: Discursive Practices That Limit Democratic Participation in Latvian Politics*, Amsterdam: Rodopi, 171–94.

Golubeva, M., Rožukalne, A. and Kažoka, I. (2007), *Izaicinājums pilsoniskajai līdzdalībai: Analītiskais ziņojums par Saeimas un mediju monitoringu* [A call for civil participation: Analytical report on parliamentary and media monitoring], Riga: Sabiedriskās politikas centrs Providus.

Gorbachev, M. (1991), Resignation speech, New York Times, 26 December, available at <http://www.nytimes.com/1991/12/26/world/end-of-the-soviet-union-text-of-gorbachev-s-farewell-address.html> (last accessed 19 June 2015).

Gramsci, A. (1971), *Selections from the Prison Notebooks*, London: Lawrence and Wishart.

Hackmann, J. and Lehti, M. (2008), 'Introduction: Contested and shared places of memory. History and politics in North Eastern Europe', *Journal of Baltic Studies* 39(4): 377–9.

Halbwachs, M. [1952] (1992), 'Social frameworks of memory', in L. Coser (ed.), *On Collective Memory*, Chicago: University of Chicago Press, 37–167.

Hall, S. (1980), 'Encoding/decoding', in S. Hall, D. Hobson, A. Lowe and P. Willis (eds.), *Culture, Media, Language: Working Papers in Cultural Studies, 1972–79*, London: Hutchinson, 128–38.

Harmony Centre (2005), *Декларация учредительной конференции «Центра Согласия»* [Declaration from the founding conference of 'Harmony Centre'], available at <http://www.saskanascentrs.lv/ru/declaration/> (last accessed 19 December 2009).

Harmony Centre (2011), *Борис Цилевич: оккупация стала идеологическим кодом* [Boriss Čilevičs: Occupation has become an ideological code], available at <http://www.saskanascentrs.lv/ru/prjamaja-rech/boris-cilevich-okkupacija-stala-ideologicheskim-kodom102/> (last accessed 1 May 2012).

Harmony Centre (2012), *Меморандум о политическом объединении «Центр Согласия»* [Memorandum on the political union 'Harmony Centre'], available at <http://www.saskanascentrs.lv/ru/o-nas/> (last accessed 4 April 2012).

Haas, A. (1996), 'Non-violence in ethnic relations in Estonia', *Journal of Baltic Studies* 27(1): 47–76.

Haukkala, H. (2009), 'A close encounter of the worst kind? The logic of situated actors and the statue crisis between Estonia and Russia', *Journal of Baltic Studies* 40(2): 201–13.

Hewstone, M., Cairns, E., Voci, A., Hamberger, J. and Niens, U. (2006), 'Intergroup contact, forgiveness, and experience of "the troubles" in Northern Ireland', *Journal of Social Issues* 62(1): 99–120.

Hiden, J. and Salmon, P. (1994), 'Soviet winter', in J. Hiden (ed.), *The Baltic Nations and Europe: Estonia, Latvia and Lithuania in the 20th Century*, Rev. edn, London: Longman, 126–44.

Hobsbawm, E. (1992), 'Mass-producing traditions', in E. Hobsbawm and T. Ranger (eds), *The Invention of Tradition*, Cambridge: Cambridge University Press, 263–307.

Hogan-Brun, G. (2006), 'At the interface of language ideology and practice: The public discourse surrounding the 2004 education reform in Latvia', *Language Policy* 5: 313–33.

Hopkins, M. (1970), *Mass Media in the Soviet Union*, New York: Pegasus.

Howarth, D. and Stavrakakis, Y. (2000), 'Introducing discourse theory and political analysis', in D. Howarth, A. Norval and Y. Stavrakakis (eds), *Discourse Theory and Political Analysis*, Manchester: Manchester University Press, 1–23.

Jaeger, Ø. (2000), 'Securitizing Russia: Discursive practices of the Baltic States', *Peace and Conflict Studies* 7(2): 17–36.

Jenkins, R. (1996), *Social Identity*, London: Routledge.

Jubulis, M. (2001), *Nationalism and Democratic Transition: The Politics of Citizenship and Language in Post-Soviet Latvia*, Oxford: University Press of America.

Kaiser, R. (1997), 'Nationalism and identity', in M. Bradshaw (ed.), *Geography and Transition in the Post-Soviet Republics*, Chichester: John Wiley & Sons, 9–30.

Karahassan, H. and Zembylas, M. (2006), 'The politics of memory and forgetting in history textbooks: Towards a pedagogy of reconciliation and peace in divided Cyprus', in A. Ross (ed.), *Citizenship Education: Europe and the World*, London: CiCe, 701–12.

Karklins, R. (1994a), *Ethonopolitics and Transition to Democracy: The Collapse of the USSR and Latvia*, London: Johns Hopkins University Press.

Karklins, R. (1994b), 'Explaining regime change in the Soviet Union', *Europe-Asia Studies* 46(1): 29–46.

Kattago, S. (2010), 'Memory, pluralism and the agony of politics', *Journal of Baltic Studies* 41(3): 383–94.

Katz, E. and Lazarsfeld, P. (1955), *Personal Influence: The Part Played By People in the Flow of Mass Communications*, Glencoe, IL: Free Press.

Kažoka, I. (2010) 'Latvian political party system and the discourse on parties', in M. Golubeva and R. Gould (eds), *Shrinking Citizenship: Discursive Practices That Limit Democratic Participation in Latvian Politics*, Amsterdam: Rodopi, 67–80.

Kelley, J. (2004), *Ethnic Politics in Europe: The Power of Norms and Incentives*, Princeton: Princeton University Press.

Ķencis, T. and Kuutma, K. (2011), 'National museums in Latvia', in P. Aronsson and G. Elgenius (eds), *Building national museums in Europe 1750–2010: Conference proceedings from EuNaMus, European national museums: Identity politics, the uses of the past and the European citizen, Bologna 28–30 April 2011*. Linköping, Sweden: Linköping University Electronic Press, 497–520, available at <http://www.ep.liu.se/ecp/064/ecp064.pdf#page=501> (last accessed 7 June 2013).

Khanov, D. (2002), *Роль русской прессы в создании русской идентичности в современной Латвии – утраченная идентичность* [The role of the Russian press in the creation of Russian identity in contemporary Latvia – a lost identity], conference paper, available at <http://politika.lv/temas/mediju_kritika/6860/> (last accessed 5 September 2009).

Kirch, A. (1992), 'Russians as a minority in contemporary Baltic States', *Security Dialogue* 23(2), 205–12.

Kolstø, P. (1999), 'Territorializing diasporas. The case of the Russians in the former Soviet republics', *Millennium: Journal or International Studies* 28(3): 607–31.

Kosmarskaya, N. (2011), 'Russia and post-Soviet "Russian diaspora": Contrasting visions, conflicting projects', *Nationalism and Ethnic Politics* 17(1): 54–74.

Kronenfeld, D. (2005), 'The effects of interethnic contact on ethnic identity: Evidence from Latvia', *Post-Soviet Affairs* 21(3), 247–77.

Kruk, S. (2009), 'Wars of statues: *Ius imaginum* and *Damnatio memoriae* in the 20th century Latvia', conference paper, Conference on the Historical Use of Images Vrije Universiteit Brussel, 10–11 March 2009, available at <http://www.vub.ac.be/C–HIM/attachments/papers/Vladimir_Kruk.pdf> (last accessed 7 June 2013).

Kruks, S. and Šulmane, I. (2002), *Pilsoniskās sabiedrības attīstība un sabiedrības integrācija: 8. Saeimas priekšvēlēšanu kampaņas preses un politiķu diskurss* [The development of civil society and social integration: The press and political discourse of the pre-election campaign for the 8th *Saeima*], Riga: Komunikācijas studiju nodaļa.

Laclau, E. (1995), 'Subject of politics, politics of the subject', *Differences* 7(1): 146–65.

Laclau, E. (2005), 'Democracy and the question of power', in J. Hillier and E. Rooksby (eds), *Habitus: A Sense of Place (2nd Edition)*, Aldershot: Ashgate, 53–66.

Laclau, E. and Mouffe, C. (1985), *Hegemony and Socialist Strategy: Towards a Radical Democratic Politics*, London: Verso.

Laclau, E. and Mouffe, C. (1987), 'Post-Marxism without apologies', *New Left Review* 166: 79–106.

Laitin, D. (1995), 'Identity in formation: The Russian-speaking nationality in the post-Soviet diaspora', *European Journal of Sociology* 36(2): 281–316.

Laitin, D. (1998), *Identity in Formation: The Russian-Speaking Populations in the Near Abroad*, London: Cornell University Press.

Laitin, D. (2003), 'Three models of integration and the Estonian/Russian reality', *Journal of Baltic Studies* 34(2): 197–222.

Lapsa, L., Metuzāls, S. and Jančevska, K. (2007), *Mūsu vēsture, 1985–2005* [*Our History, 1985–2005*], Rīga: Atēna.

Latvian Centre for Human Rights (2014), Integration Monitor October 16 2014, available at <http://cilvektiesibas.org.lv/en/monitoring/search/?date_from=2014.10.16&date_to=2014.10.16&query> (last accessed 17 October 2014).

Latvian Citizenship Law (1998), Unofficial English translation, available at <http://unpan1.un.org/intradoc/groups/public/documents/untc/unpan018407.pdf> (last accessed 12 April 2011).

Latvian National Security Concept (1995), Available (in Latvian) at <http://www.mod.gov.lv/lv/Par_aizsardzibas_nozari/Politikas_planosana/Koncepcijas/~/media/AM/Plani,%20koncepcijas/1995_nd.ashx> (last accessed 31 May 2011).

Latvian National Security Concept (2008), Available (in Latvian) at <http://www.mfa.gov.lv/lv/dp/Pamatdokumenti/Drosibas-koncepcija/> (last accessed 1 June 2011).

Latvian SSR Supreme Soviet (1989), 'Declaration of the Latvian SSR Supreme Soviet on the national sovereignty of Latvia', in C. Furtado and A. Chandler (eds), *Perestroika Documents in the Soviet Republics: Documents on the National Question*, Oxford: Westview Press, 133–4.

Latvijas Republikas Saeima (2014), The Constitution of the Republic of Latvia, available at <http://www.saeima.lv/en/legislation/constitution/> (last accessed 15 August 2014).

Lavinski, K. (2013), 'Non-governmental organizations in Russia: Legal aspects', *Voprosy rossiiskogo i mezhdunarodnogo prava* 1: 10–34.

Lazda, M. (2009), 'Reconsidering nationalism: The Baltic case of Latvia in 1989', *International Journal of Culture and Society* 22: 517–36.

Lenin, V. (1972), 'The right of nations to self-determination', in *Collected Works* vol. 20, Moscow: Progress Publishers, 393–454.

Lerhis, A., Kudors A. and Indāns, I. (2007), *Outside influence on the integration process in Latvia*, Riga: Centre for East European Political Studies, available at <http://lsif.lv/files/pics/angliski_08.pdf> (last accessed 26 May 2011).

Levits, E. (2013), *Izvērstas Satversmes preambulas Iespējamā teksta piedāvājums un komentārs* [Possible textual addition and commentary for an extended preamble to the Constitution], *Jurista Vārds* 39(790): 14–46.

Liebich, A. and Myshlovska, O. (2014), 'Bandera: Memorialization and commemoration', *Nationalities Papers*. DOI: 10.1080/00905992.2014.916666

Linz, J. J. and Stepan, A. (1996), *Problems of Democratic Transition and Consolidation: Southern Europe, South America, and Post-Communist Europe*, London: Johns Hopkins University Press.

Lublin, D. (2012), 'The 2012 Latvia language referendum', *Electoral Studies* 32: 370–87.

Makarov, V. (2002), *Latvian political culture: Democratic or authoritarian bias? An interpretation attempt based on a survey study*, Riga: Baltic Forum, available at <http://www.balticforum.org/files_uploads/files/vm_survey2002-1.pdf> (last accessed 18 October 2011).

Makarov, V. and Boldāne, I. (2008*), 20. gadsimta vēstures pretrunīgo jautājumu pasniegšana Latvijas skolās un muzejos* [The teaching of conflicting questions of 20th century history in Latvian schools and museums], Riga: Sorosa Fonds Latvija, available at <http://www.politika.lv/index> (last accessed 2 June 2011).

Mälksoo, L. (2011), '*Kononov v. Latvia*', *The American Journal of International Law* 105(1): 101–8.

Mälksoo, M. (2009), 'Liminality and contested Europeanness: Conflicting memory politics in the Baltic space', in E. Berg and P. Ehin (eds), *Identity and Foreign Policy: Baltic-Russian Relations and European Integration*, Farnham: Ashgate, 65–83.

Martin, T. (2001), *The Affirmative Action Empire*, London: Cornell University Press.

Marples, D. (2006), 'Stepan Bandera: The resurrection of a Ukrainian national hero', *Europe-Asia Studies* 58(4): 555–66.

Melvin, N. (1995), *Russians beyond Russia: The Politics of National Identity*, London: The Royal Institute of International Affairs.

Mikkel, E. and Pridham G. (2005), 'Clinching the "return to Europe": The refurendums on EU accession in Latvia and Estonia', in A. Szczerbiak and P. Taggart (eds), *EU Enlargement and Referendums*, Abingdon: Routledge, 160–92.

Ministry of Foreign Affairs of the Republic of Latvia (2010), *Inhabitants of Latvia – ethnicity and citizenship*, available at <http://www.mfa.gov.lv/en/policy/4641/4642/4659/> (last accessed 18 July 2013).

Ministry of Foreign Affairs of the Russian Federation (2010a), *Федеральный закон о государственной политике Российской Федерации в отношении соотечественников за рубежом* [On the State Policy of the Russian Federation in relation to Compatriots Abroad], available at <http://www.mid.ru/bdomp/ns-dgpch.nsf/1a268548523257ccc325726f00357db3/8440d36903c217a4c3257776003a73f5!OpenDocument> (last accessed 22 June 2015).

Ministry of Foreign Affairs of the Russian Federation (2010b), 'Statement by the Russian

Foreign Ministry following the pronouncement on May 17, 2010, of the ruling of the Grand Chamber of the European Court of Human Rights in the case of Vasily Kononov', available at <http://www.mid.ru/Brp_4.nsf/arh/898C56838D6A6BAA C325772700420E6B?OpenDocument> (last accessed 31 May 2011).

Ministry of Foreign Affairs of the Russian Federation (2013a), *Выступление Министра иностранных дел Российской Федерации С.В.Лаврова на заседании Попечительского совета Фонда поддержки и защиты прав соотечественников, проживающих за рубежом, Москва, 13 мая 2013 года* [Speech of the Minister of Foreign Affairs of the Russian Federation S. V. Lavrov at the Board of Trustees' meeting for the Fund for the Support and Protection of the Rights of Compatriots Living Abroad, Moscow, 13 March 2013], available at <http://mid.ru/bdomp/ns-dgpch.nsf/bab3c4309e31451cc325710e004812c0/44257b100055de8444257b6a004d7 8bd!OpenDocument> (last accessed 4 March 2015).

Ministry of Foreign Affairs of the Russian Federation (2013b), *Интервью директора Департамента по работе с соотечественниками МИД России А.А.Макарова радиостанции «Голос России», 5 августа 2013 года* [Interview with A. A. Makarov, Director of the Compatriot department of the MFA of Russia, for the radio station 'Voice of Russia', 5 August 2013], available at <http://mid.ru/bdomp/ns-dgpch. nsf/bab3c4309e31451cc325710e004812c0/c4445d504044c32c44257bc90040852e!Op enDocument> (last accessed 4 March 2015).

Ministry of Foreign Affairs of the Russian Federation (2013c), *Интервью директора Департамента по работе с соотечественниками за рубежом МИД России А.А.Макарова информпорталу «Русский век», 26 декабря 2013 года* [Interview with A. A. Makarov, Director of the Compatriot department of the MFA of Russia, for the information portal 'Russian Century', 26 December 2013], available at <http:// mid.ru/bdomp/ns-dgpch.nsf/bab3c4309e31451cc325710e004812c0/2f2bcfd68a007a 0844257c5100332955!OpenDocument> (last accessed 4 March 2015).

Mole, R. (2007), 'Discursive identities/identity discourses and political power', in R. Mole (ed.) *Discursive Constructions of Identity in European Politics*, Basingstoke: Palgrave Macmillan, 1–24.

Morozov, V. (2004), 'Russia in the Baltic Sea region: Desecuritization or deregionalization?', *Security and Conflict* 39: 317–31.

Morris, H. M. (2003), 'EU enlargement and Latvian citizenship policy', *Journal on Ethnopolitics and Minority Issues in Europe* 1: 1–37.

Mouffe, C. (1995), 'Politics, democratic action, and solidarity', *Inquiry* 38(1 and 2): 99–108.

Muižnieks, N. (ed.) (2010), *How Integrated is Latvian Society? An Audit of Achievements, Failures and Challenges*, Riga: University of Latvia Press.

Muižnieks, N. (2011a), 'Latvian-Russian memory battles at the European Court of Human Rights', in N. Muižnieks (ed.), *The Geopolitics of History in Latvian-Russian Relations*, Riga: Academic Press of the University of Latvia, 219–38.

Muižnieks, N. (2011b), *Latvian-Russian Relations: Dynamics since Latvia's Accession to the EU and NATO*, Riga: University of Latvia Press.

Muižnieks, N. and Zelče, V. (eds) (2012), *Karojošā piemiņa: 16. marts un 9. maijs* [*Antagonistic Memory: 16 March and 9 May*], Riga: Zinātne.

Mums pa ceļam (2011) *Кто мы?* [Who are we?], Available at <http://www.young.lv/ about.html> (last accessed 31 August 2011).

National Alliance (2014), *Latvieši ir Latvijas valstnācija* [Ethnic Latvians are Latvia's nation state]. Official website of the National Alliance, available at <http://www.

nacionalaapvieniba.lv/aktualitate/latviesi-ir-latvijas-valstsnacija/> (last accessed 15 August 2014).

Neidhardt, F. (1993), 'The public as a communication system', *Public Understanding of Science* 2: 339–50.

Nimmerfeldt, G., Schilze, J. and Taru, M. (2011), 'The relationship between integration dimensions among second generation Russians in Estonia', *Studies of Transition States and Societies* 3(1): 76–91.

Nozhenko, M. (2006), 'Motherland is calling you: Motives behind and prospects for the new Russian policy on compatriots abroad', *Lithuanian Foreign Policy Review* 18, available at <http://www.lfpr.lt/index.php?id=104> (last accessed 5 May 2011).

Olick, J. and Robbins, J. (1998), 'Social memory studies: From "collective memory" to the historical sociology of mnemonic practices', *Annual Review of Sociology* 24: 105–40.

Onken, E. (2007), 'The Baltic States and Moscow's 9 May commemoration: Analysing memory politics in Europe', *Europe-Asia Studies* 59(1): 23–46.

Onken, E. (2010), 'Memory and democratic pluralism in the Baltic States - Rethinking the relationship', *Journal of Baltic Studies* 41(3): 277–94.

Oxford Dictionary (2013), *Identify*, Oxford: Oxford University Press, available at <http://oxforddictionaries.com/definition/english/identify> (last accessed 11 June 2013).

Peschel, K. (1998), 'Perspectives of regional development around the Baltic Sea', *The Annuls of Regional Science* 32: 299–320.

Petrenko, D. (2008), 'How does the Russian community live in Latvia?', in N. Muižnieks (ed.), *Manufacturing Enemy Images? Russian Media Portrayal of Latvia*, Riga: University of Latvia Press, 45–78.

Pettai, V. (2006), 'Explaining ethnic politics in the Baltic states: Reviewing the triadic nexus model', *Journal of Baltic Studies* 37(1): 124–36.

Pettigrew, T. and Tropp, L. (2006), 'A meta-analytic test of intergroup contact theory', *Journal of Personality and Social Psychology* 90(5): 751–83

Pilkington, H. and Flynn, M. (1999), 'From "refugee" to "repatriate": Russian repatriation discourse in the making', in R. Black and E. Koser (eds), *The End of the Refugee Cycle? Refugee Repatriation and Reconstruction*, Oxford: Berghahn, 171–97.

Pisarenko, O. (2006), 'The acculturation modes of Russian speaking adolescents in Latvia: Perceived discrimination and knowledge of the Latvian language', *Europe-Asia Studies* 58(5): 571–3.

Popescu, N. (2006), 'Russia's soft power ambitions', *CEPS Policy Brief* 115: 1–4, available at <http://aei.pitt.edu/11715/1/1388.pdf> (last accessed 16 February 2012).

Poppe, E. and Hagendoorn, L. (2001), 'Types of identification among Russians in the "near abroad"', *Europe-Asia Studies* 53(1): 57–71.

President.lv (2012), *Konstitucionālo tiesību komisija: Par Latvijas valsts konstitucionālajiem pamatiem un neaizskaramo Satversmes kodolu* [Commission of Constitutional Rights: On the constitutional foundations of the Latvian state and the inviolable core of the Constitution], available at <http://www.president.lv/images/modules/items/PDF/17092012_Viedoklis_2.pdf> (last accessed 21 August 2014).

President of Russia (2014), Address by President of the Russian Federation, official presidential website of the Russian Federation, available at <http://eng.kremlin.ru/transcripts/6889> (last accessed 8 August 2014).

Priedīte, A. (2005), 'Surveying language attitudes and practices in Latvia', *Journal of Multilingual and Multicultural Development* 26(5): 409–24.

PROVIDUS (2007a), *2006. gada Saeimas vēlēšanas medijos: iespējamā slēptā reklāma* [The

2006 *Saeima* elections in the media: Possible hidden advertising], available at <http://www.politika.lv/index.php?f=1088> (last accessed 23 November 2009).

PROVIDUS (2007b), *2006. gada Saeimas vēlēšanas medijos: partiju reprezentācija* [The 2006 *Saeima* elections in the media: Party representation], available at <http://www.politika.lv/index.php?f=1082> (last accessed 23 November 2009).

PROVIDUS (2008), *Izaicinājums pilsoniskajai līdzdalībai 2008. gada gala ziņojums* [A call for civil participation: 2008 year-end report], available at <http://www.politika.lv/temas/politikas_kvalitate/17057/> (last accessed 15 October 2009).

Purvis, T. and Hunt, A. (1993), 'Ideology, discourse, ideology, discourse, ideology. . .', *The British Journal of Sociology* 44(3): 473–99.

Reisigl, M. and Wodak, R. (2001), *Discourse and Discrimination: Rhetorics of Racism and Anti-Semitism*, London: Routledge.

Rislakki, J. (2009), *The Case for Latvia: Disinformation Campaigns Against a Small Nation*, Amsterdam: Rodopi.

Rodins, M. (2005), 'National identity and democratic integration in Latvia in the middle of the 90s', *Latvijas Universitātes Raksti* 686: 40–63.

Rose, R. (1995), 'New Baltic barometer II: A survey study', *Studies in Public Policy* 251.

Rose, R. (1997), 'New Baltic barometer III: A survey study', *Studies in Public Policy* 284.

Rose, R. (2000), 'New Baltic barometer IV: A survey study', *Studies in Public Policy* 338.

Rose, R. (2002), 'New Baltic barometer V: A pre-enlargement survey', *Studies in Public Policy* 368.

Rose, R. (2005), 'New Baltic barometer VI: A post-enlargement survey', *Studies in Public Policy* 401.

Rose, R. and Maley, W. (1994), 'Nationalities in the Baltic States: A survey study', *Studies in Public Policy* 222.

Rožukalne, A. (2010), 'Latvian print media as opinion leaders', in M. Golubeva and R. Gould (eds), *Shrinking Citizenship: Discursive Practices That Limit Democratic Participation in Latvian Politics*, Amsterdam: Rodopi, 67–80.

Ruvek.ru (2014), *О проекте* [About the project], available at <http://www.ruvek.ru/?module=pagesandaction=viewandid=13> (last accessed 7 August 2014).

Sam, D. and Berry, R. (2010), 'Acculturation: When individuals and groups of different cultural backgrounds meet', *Perspectives on Psychological Science* 5(4): 472–81.

Saussure, F. [1916] (1966), 'Nature of the linguistics sign', in C. Bally and A. Sechehaya (eds), *Cours de linguistique générale*, New York: McGraw Hill Education.

Schleifman, N. (2001), 'Moscow's Victory Park: A monumental change', *History and Memory* 13(2): 5–34

Schuman, H. and Scott, J. (1989), 'Generations and collective memories', *American Sociological Review* 54(3): 359–81.

Schwartz, K. Z. S. (2007), 'The occupation of beauty: Imagining nature and nation in Latvia', *East European Politics and Societies* 21(2): 259–93.

Shlapentokh, V. (2001), *A Normal Totalitarian Society: How the Soviet Union Functioned and How It Collapsed*, New York: M. E. Sharpe.

SKDS (2014), *Piederības sajūta Latvijai: Mazākumtautību Latvijas iedzīvotāju aptauja* [Feeling of belonging to Latvia: A survey of Latvia's inhabitants], available at <http://www.mk.gov.lv/sites/default/files/editor/atskaite_piederiba_08_2014.pdf> (last accessed 12 September 2014).

Smith, D. J. (2002), 'Framing the national question in Central and Eastern Europe: A quadratic nexus?', *Ethnopolitics* 2:1, 3–16.

Smith, D. J. (2008), '"Woe from stones": Commemoration, identity politics and Estonia's "war of monuments" from another angle', *Journal of Baltic Studies* 39(4): 419–30.

Smith, G. (1999a), *The Post-Soviet States: Mapping the Politics of Transition*, London: Arnold.

Smith, G. (1999b), 'Transnational politics and the politics of the Russian diaspora', *Ethnic and Racial Studies* 22(3): 500–23.

Smith, G. and Wilson, A. (1997), 'Rethinking Russia's post-Soviet diaspora: The potential for political mobilisation in eastern Ukraine and north-east Estonia', *Europe-Asia Studies* 49(5): 845–64.

Smith, G., Law, V., Wilson, A., Bohr, A. and Allworth, E. (1998), *Nation-Building in the Post-Soviet Borderlands: The Politics of National Identities*, Cambridge: Cambridge University Press.

Society for Openness 'Delna' (2002) *Analysis of possible occurrences of hidden advertisements in the media before the 8th Saeima elections*, available at <http://politika.lv/temas/mediju_kritika/6769> (last accessed 14 September 2009).

Solska, M. (2011), 'Citizenship, collective identity and the international impact on integration policy in Estonia, Latvia and Lithuania', *Europe-Asia Studies* 63(6): 1089–108.

Sparks, G. G. (2013), *Media Effects Research: A Basic Overview (Fourth Edition)*, Boston: Wadsworth.

State Language Commission (2008), *Break-Out of Latvian: A Sociolinguistic Study of Situation, Attitudes, Processes, and Tendencies*, Riga: Zinatne.

Šulmane, I. and Kruks, S. (2001), *Stereotipi Latvijas presē: Latvijas mediju analīze* [Stereotypes in the Latvian press: Latvian media analysis], Riga: Daudzveidība III, 11–50.

Suny, R. (2001), 'Russia's identity crisis', in A. Brown (ed.), *Contemporary Russian Politics: A Reader*, Oxford: Oxford University Press, 363–8.

Šupule, I. (2007), '*Etniskās attiecības un akulturācijas procesi Latvijā: Iedzīvotāju attieksmes pret dažādām akulturācijas stratēģijām*' [Ethnic attitudes and acculturation processes in Latvia: Resident attitudes towards various acculturation strategies], *Latvijas Universaitātes Raksti* 714: 31–43.

Šupule, I. (2011), 'The construction of national and ethnic identity in online discussions on referenda initiatives in Latvia', *Baltic Journal of European Studies* 2(1): 119–37.

Tabuns, A. (1999), *Changing national, state and regime identities in Latvia*, Open Society Institute, available at: <http://rss.archives.ceu.hu/archive/00001156/01/168.pdf> (last accessed 13 December 2011).

Tabuns, A. (ed.) (2006), *Kultūras. Jaunieši. Mediji* [Cultures. Youth. Media], Riga: Latvijas Universitāte, Sociālo zinātņu fakultāte.

Tabuns, A. (2010), 'Identity, ethnic relations, language and culture', in, N. Muižnieks (ed.), *How integrated is Latvian society? An audit of achievements, failures and challenges*, Riga: University of Latvia Press.

The Constitution of the Republic of Latvia (2014), Official English translation, available at <http://www.saeima.lv/en/legislation/constitution> (last accessed 22 June 2015)

The Spectator (2014), 'Today Crimea, tomorrow Estonia?' 8 March 2014, <http://www.spectator.co.uk/features/9153391/estonias-angst/> (last accessed 8 August 2014).

Till, B. (2011), 'Mikhail Gorbachev: The West Could Have Saved the Russian Economy', *The Atlantic*, 26 June 2011, <http://www.theatlantic.com/international/archive/2011/06/mikhail-gorbachev-the-west-could-have-saved-the-russian-economy/240466/> (last accessed 19 June 2015).

Tisenkopfs, T. (2002), *Latvijas politikas mazā intelektuālā vēsture* [A short, intellectual history of Latvian politics], available at <http://www.politika.lv/index. php?id=102286andlang=lv> (last accessed 18 October 2011).

Tolz, V. (1995), 'The impact of *glasnost*' in V. Tolz and I. Elliot (eds), *The Demise of the USSR: From Communism to Independence*, Basingstoke: Macmillan, 94–106.

Tumarkin, N. (1987), 'Myth and memory in Soviet society', *Culture and Society* 24(6): 69–72.

Tuminez, A. (2003), 'Nationalism, ethnic pressures, and the breakup of the Soviet Union', *Journal of Cold War Studies* 5(4): 81–136.

van Dick, R., Wagner, U., Pettigrew, T. F., Christ, O., Wolf, C., Petzel, T., Castro, V. S. and Jackson, J. S. (2004), 'The role of perceived importance in intergroup contact', *Journal of Personality and Social Psychology* 87(2): 211–27.

van Dijk, T. (1989), 'Mediating racism: The role of the media in the reproduction of racism', in R. Wodak (ed.), *Language, Power and Ideology*, Amsterdam: J. Benjamins, 199–226.

van Dijk, T. (2001), 'Critical discourse analysis', in D. Tannen, D. Schiffrin and H. Hamilton (eds), *The Handbook of Discourse Analysis*, Oxford: Blackwell, 352–71.

Velmet, A. (2011), 'Occupied identities: National narratives in Baltic museums of occupations', *Journal of Baltic Studies* 42(2): 189–211.

Vihalemm, T. and Masso, A. (2003), 'Identity dynamics of Russian-speakers of Estonia in the transition period', *Journal of Baltic Studies* 34(1): 92–116.

Volkmer, I. (ed.) (2006), *News in Public Memory: An International Study of Media Generations Across Generations*, Oxford: Peter Lang.

Vysotskaya, A. (2005), 'The "Alliance For Human Rights in a United Latvia" in the European Parliament: Europeanisation of a Soviet legacy?', Leuven, available at <http://soc.kuleuven.be/iieb/ibl/docs_ibl/WP28-Vysotskaya.pdf> (last accessed 15 August 2010).

Wallander, C. (2003), 'Western policy and the demise of the Soviet Union', *Journal of Cold War Studies* 5(4): 137–77.

Wawrzonek, M. (2014), 'Ukraine in the "gray zone": Between the "Russkiy mir" and Europe', *East European Politics and Societies and Cultures* 28(4): 758–80.

Weiner, A. (1996), 'The making of a dominant myth: The Second World War and the construction of political identities within the Soviet polity', *Russian Review* 55(4): 638–60.

Wertsch, J. (2008), 'Collective memory and narrative templates', *Social Research* 75(1): 133–56.

Wilkinson, C. (2012), 'Putting traditional values into practice: Russia's anti-gay laws', *Russian Analytical Digest* 138: 5–7.

Wohlforth, W. (1994), 'Realism and the end of the Cold War', *International Security* 19(3): 91–129.

Zelče, V. (2009), 'History – responsibility – memory: Latvia's case', in J. Rozenvalds and I. Ivars (eds), *Latvia: Human Development Report 2008/2009*, Riga: Advanced Social and Political Research Institute.

Zelče, V. and Brikše I. (2008), 'The Latvian media in the new millennium: Trends in development, content and usage and the emergence of a community of media users', *Informacijos mokslai* 47: 87–111.

Zepa, B. (2006), *The Changing Discourse of Minority Identities: Latvia*, Riga: Baltic Institute for Social Sciences.

Zepa, B. (2011) *Nacionālās identitātes dimensijas: iedzīvotāju attieksmju izpēte* [Dimensions of national identity: Research into residents' attitudes], in B. Zepa and E. Kļava (eds), *Latvija. Pārskats par tautas attīstību: Nacionālā identitāte, mobilitāte un rīcībspēja [Latvia. An Overview of the Nation's Development: National Identity, Mobility and Potential]*, Riga: LU SPPI, available at <http://www.biss.soc.lv/downloads/resources/tap/latvija_tap_2011.pdf> (last accessed 3 March 2015).

Zepa, B., Šūpule, I., Peņķe, I., Kļave, E. and Krišāne, J. (2001), *Cela uz pilsonisko sabiedribu: Latvijas iedzivotaju aptauja* [On the path to civil society: A survey of Latvia's inhabitants], Riga: The Baltic Institute of Social Science, available at <http://www.politika.lv/index.php?id=3968> (last accessed 3 December 2009).

Zepa, B., Šūpule, I., Kļave, E., Krastiņa, L., Krišāne, J. and Tomsone, I. (2005a), *Etnopolitiskā spriedze Latvijā: Konflikta risinājuma meklējumi* [Ethnopolitical tension: The search for conflict resolution], Riga: Baltic Institute for Social Sciences, available at <http://www.bszi.lv/downloads/resources/Etnopol_krize/Atskaite_LV.pdf> (last accessed 16 June 11).

Zepa, B., Šūpule, I., Kļave, E., Krastiņa, I., Krišāne, J. and Tomsone, I. (2005b), *Ethnopolitical tensions in Latvia: Looking for the conflict solution*, Riga: Baltic Institute for Social Sciences, available at <http://pdc.ceu.hu/archive/00003174/01/ethnopolitical_tension_in_latvia.pdf> (last accessed 3 March 15).

Zepa, B., Šūpule, I., Krastiņa, L., Ķešāne, I., Grīviņš, M., Bebriša, I. and Ieviņa, I. (2006), 'Integration practice and perspectives', Baltic Institute of Social Sciences, available at <http://www.bszi.lv/download/resources/integracijas_prakse/brosura_EN.pdf> (last accessed 13 December 2011).

Zepa, B., Kļave, E., Žabko, O., Krastiņa, L., Bebriša, I., Jansone, Z., Vaivode, L. and Beriņa, L. (2008a), *We. Celebrations. The state: A sociological study of how national holidays are celebrated*, Riga: Baltic Institute of Social Sciences.

Zepa, B., Žabko, O. and Vaivode, L. (2008b), *Language: Report*, Riga: Baltic Institute of Social Sciences.

Index